GW00838387

NINU

Grandmothers' Law

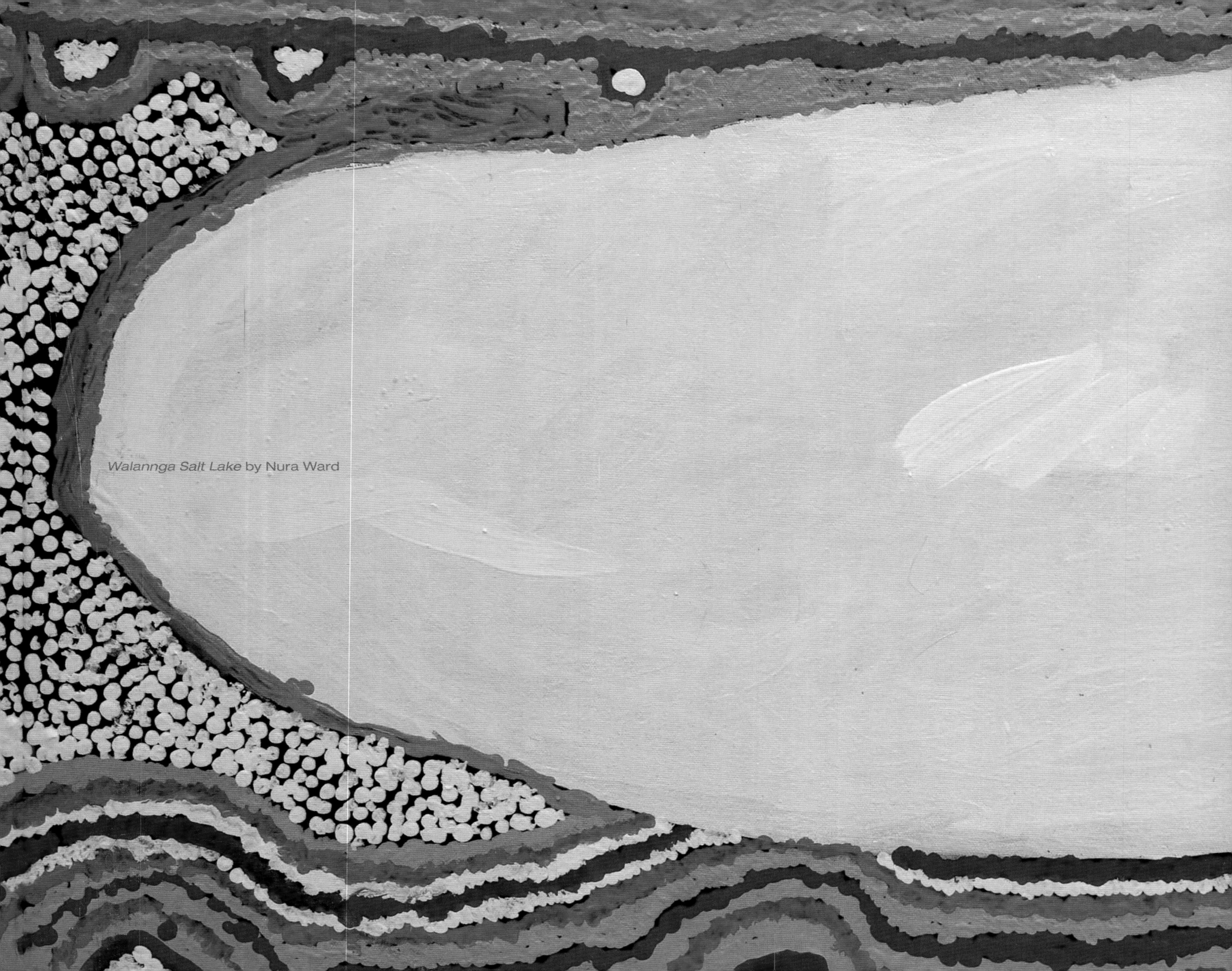

Walannga Salt Lake by Nura Ward

NINU

GRANDMOTHERS' LAW

The autobiography of Nura Nungalka Ward

Readers are advised that this book contains images and the names of people who have passed away.

Foreword

My auntie Nura grew me up. She used to take me all around the bush, teaching me things. She would take me fencing with her husband. She used to sit me down at a safe distance, and I would watch the two of them building fences at Black Hill. That was their work. Anne and Ampita were much older than me, and played with the bigger girls. Nura taught me inma when I was just a little girl. I first went with her to Law and Culture at Fregon. I danced inma from Atila. It was about two Wanampi. Two children were stamping on the ground and caved in the Wanampi underground home. I danced that when I was around ten years old. I started from there, and I still love my Law and Culture. Usually Nura and I go to Law and Culture together. She is my auntie, and I normally go with her. Every time we are together there. Back then when the women were sitting getting ready and painting up and I was waiting Nura would say 'no, you are dancing now' and she showed me how and I practised and she encouraged me. So I was very sad at Kiwirrkurra Law and Culture because Nura wasn't there. I saw someone who was the same size as her and I was reminded of her, they had that same short stature. Straight away I wanted to ring Nura up, because of my feelings for her. She is my close auntie. That's why.

MELISSA THOMPSON

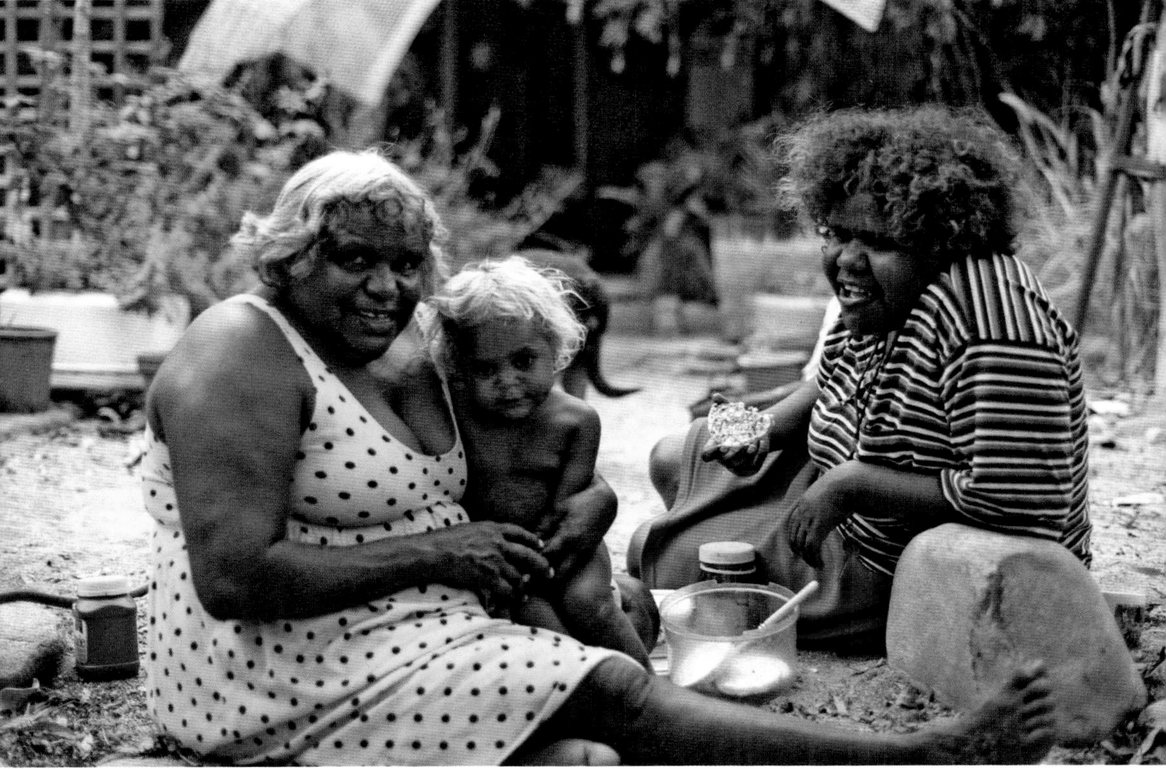

Nura with her granddaughter Jasmine, and niece Melissa Thompson. (Photo: Suzanne Bryce / Ara Irititja 124059)

Foreword

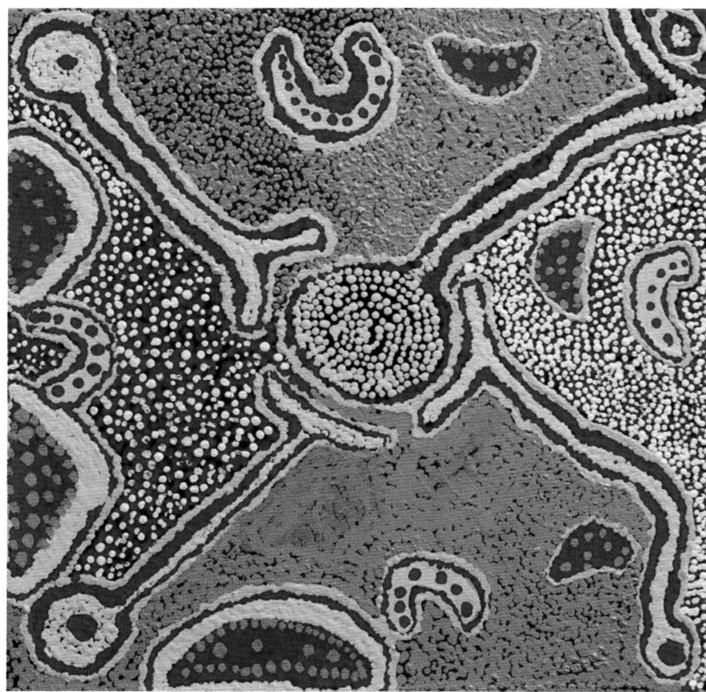

Mai putitja (bush foods), Nura Ward, 2012, acrylic on canvas, 510 x 510 mm. The painting depicts women collecting seeds to make damper.

It is a delight to read Nura's book because as I read, I can hear the sound of her voice. I can hear her good-humoured bossiness as she kept whitefellas like me in line and I can hear her enjoyment in teaching me and others about bushtucker and families and the right and wrong ways to do things. Most of all, I can hear the sound of her laugh.

My experience of Nura was in the mid 1980s, when she was working in health with mothers and babies, introducing new staff to community and culture. I had first come to Pukatja late in 1983 because I was married to Paul Torzillo, who became one of the first doctors employed by Nganampa Health Council. I had the luxury of not working in a formal job for six months, spending time learning language from wonderful teachers like Nura, Anmanari, Yuminia, Muwitja, Purki, Nyingulta, Fairy, Imuna and the many great women in the communities then called Ernabella, Kenmore Park, Fregon and Number 15. I drove our Toyota to wherever Nura and the others wanted – I was able to spend time with them as they gathered bush tucker, as they told the first stories filmed for EVTV or as they practised inma, the dancing that brought the stories of history, land and culture to life. I was able to be the driver for Nura and others to Women's Council meetings, to far away places like Uluṟu and Pipalyatjara. They were wonderful days and nights camping out, watching and learning, and being watched over all the time by Nura! She was never far away with an order for me to do one thing or another – make tea! fetch wood! – all followed by her peals of laughter.

Later on I was asked to work for the Pitjantjatjara Council, to use my trade of historical research for the Aṉangu case for the Maralinga Royal Commission. I learned a different side of Nura then, understanding better what a thoughtful and incisive researcher she was, how committed a community advocate and how tireless a communicator, as she went from person to person explaining, interpreting, listening.

Nura has filled this wonderful book with so much memory work! She tells stories with great care about the detail of healing methods and medicinal uses for the plant and animal parts of the many species she had grown up with. She is just as meticulous about the detail in the habits and anatomy and use of the new animals in the environment, like feral cats and rabbits.

And she tells us, with the same attention to detail, about her childhood – taking time and pleasure in her explanations and openness as she reveals to us the very different world in which she grew up. All the while she is teaching us through this book, Nura is generously acknowledging those who taught her. She gives us warm accounts of the women, like Anmanari, who so patiently nurtured Nura as they taught her from their deep knowledge and skills.

But Nura was not a woman of the past alone, despite admitting she feels sad at times because her childhood was so happy and she feels it is much harder and bleaker for young people today. Instead, during all her energetic working life, she was building wellbeing – teaching and thinking hard about how to address the new problems that young people face, especially young mothers and girls. She worked with many organisations with key roles in building resilience and strength within the communities – Nganampa Health, the Pitjantjatjara Land Council, the Women's Council, UPK, Mai Wiru – and dancing!

Nura was tireless in teaching inma. While she felt the other dimensions of wellbeing were all very important, inma was for Nura the way to teach law and history – Tjukurpa – to young women and to the whole community. This was Grandmothers' Law – Kamiku Tjukurpa – and for her it was central to the way to build the future.

There is a rich archive of photographs to accompany Nura's book of memories, many of them drawn from Aṟa Irititja, the building archive of pictures and stories. These do a great deal to show us the world that Nura is talking about. There has been wonderful insight and enormous skills shown by the interpreters and researchers – all of them Nura's close friends over many years – who worked with Nura to create this book. As a historian myself who works with memory and oral history, I know how easy it is to stifle storytellers with the limited understanding we bring to our research. Instead, Linda, Suzanne and Julia have enriched and nurtured Nura's storytelling.

So this makes it especially enjoyable to read these pages and *hear* Nura – to hear her interests and her priorities, her focal themes, her turns of speech, her voice – and to hear her laughing!

HEATHER GOODALL
Professor Emerita, History
University of Technology Sydney

Contents

Nura Ward dancing with the Bangarra Dance Theatre, Sydney 1999. (Photo: Branco Garcia, courtesy Bangarra Dance Theatre)

I am really proud of my own history book. I have good knowledge, old knowledge. My story is filled with this knowledge, which I am revealing. I have stories about my early life, when I was a child: how we travelled, what our lives were like and how we lived, what we did on our old traditional campsites, and how my mother and father taught me so many things.

I am very happy about my book. I thank you three women — Suzanne Bryce, Linda Rive and Julia Burke — for helping me to make my book. I am lucky to have such good friends to help me make my book.

NURA WARD, PUKATJA, 2012

Nura, and her dog Mutjaru at Black Hill, 1999. (Photo: Heidrun Lohr)

Ninu

Nura Nungalka Ward dances the intricate steps of the Ninu Ceremony, Ernabella, 1999. The dots and designs on her body represent the culture and country associated with Ninu. (Photo: NPY Women's Council / Ar̲a Irititja 35368)

Ngayulu Minyma Ninu. Ngayulu pakal̲pai Inma Minyma Ninu. Ngayuku ngunytjuku nguratja tjukurpa. Ilturta itingka, palu ini miil̲miil̲pa, ngayulu put̲u wangkapai. Mal̲u, Ninu, Mingkiri ankunytja, Coffin Hillta ngur̲u Mintupaila kutu. Minyma Ninu ankunytja. Minymaku tjitji tjunkunytja. Watiku minymaku kutju kulintjaku. Palur̲u kanyiningi tjitji mankurpa: kutjara tjan̲angka munu kutju ampungka. Munu kutju tjuningka. Palumpa kuri anu Mintupaiku, inmaku, ka Minyma Ninu tjitji mankurpa tjara anu, kuri nyakunytjaku, Mintupaila. Palumpa kuri pitjangu, kuri pitjangu munu nyangu palumpa wife, munu palur̲u pukul̲aringu.

I am Minyma Ninu — a Rabbit-eared Bandicoot Woman. I dance Inma Minyma Ninu. This dance is my mother's tjukurpa, and comes from my mother's country near Iltur (Coffin Hill). I cannot speak the name of the place because it is too sacred to utter aloud. The place is connected to the journeys of Mal̲u, Ninu and Mingkiri. They travel from near Iltur all the way over to Mintabie. Minyma Ninu herself makes this journey in order to give birth to her babies there. She walks there to be reunited with her husband. The details of this story are for senior men and women only. Minyma Ninu has two children with her: one she carries on her back and one she carries in her arms. One more is not yet born. This baby was born south of Walalkara. Her husband has gone to Mintabie for ceremonies, so Minyma Ninu travels there to be with him. When her husband comes out of the ceremonies to greet his wife, he is filled with joy and happiness.

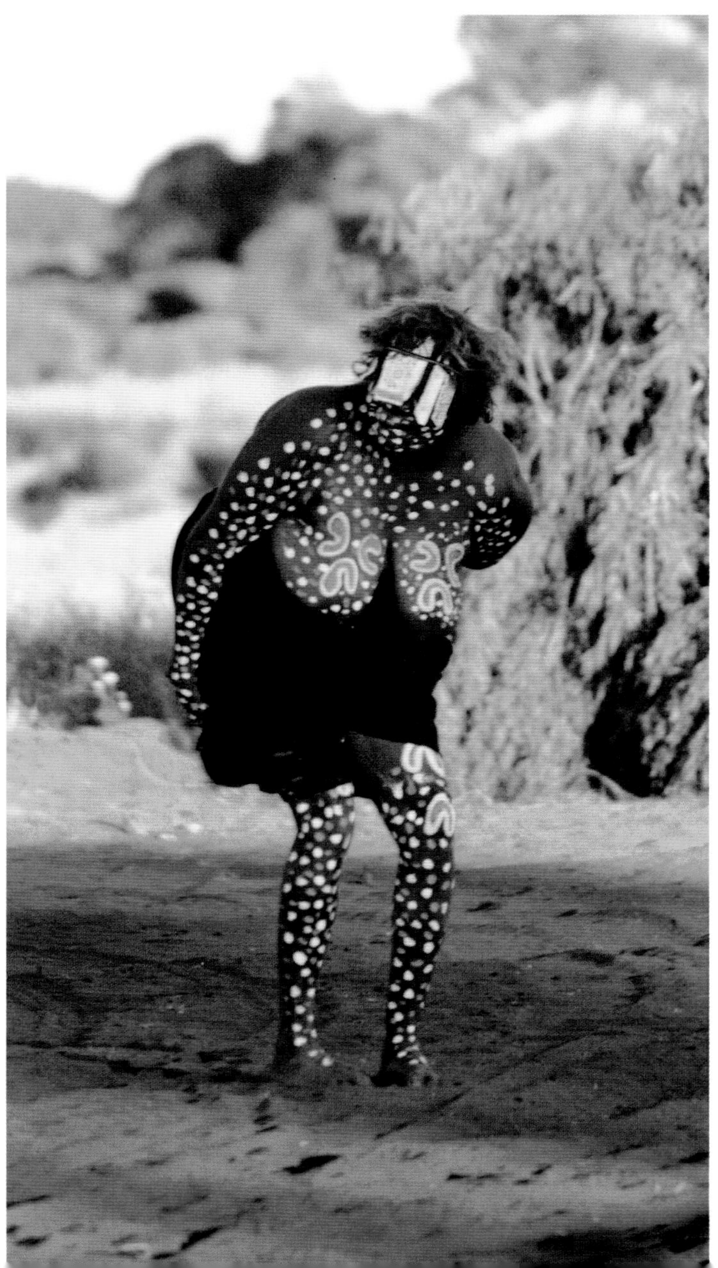

Why I am recording my story

Ngayuku tjukurpa irititja, ngayunya nyinantja, ngayulu kulintja, ngayulu pulkaringkunytja tjakultjunanyi, munula tjunanyi Ara Irititjangka, nyakunytjaku panya tjitji tjuta pitjapai, Anangu winki, tjinguru nyanga paluru panya photograph nganana apu inkantjanya, nganana malanypa tjuta helpamilantjanya, palunytjanala tjunkuntjaku. Ka tjana nyakula readamilara kutjupa wangka kulinma, 'Munta uwa! Nyanga ara alatji alatji tjana iriti palyaningi munuya wirura pukulpa uwankara nyinangi. Wiru alatjitu. Munu tjungungku ngapartji ngapartjiku nintiningi tjilpi tjuta nguru kami tjuta nguru tjamu tjuta nguru ngunytju nguru mama nguru kulypalpa nguru kuntili nguru munu palula nguru tjitji tjuta wirura kanyiningi ka ngananaanya wirura kanyinytja wangkapai atunymankunytjaku tjitji tjuta. Wiruraya atunymananma lirungku patjalku. Kana tjukurpa palatja tjuta tjunanyi, nyura readamilara nyakunytjaku, kulintjaku, nganampa photograph nyakunytja, nyinantja, munu photograph palangka, tjukurpa nyangatja nganana tjitji tjuta wirura nyinantja munu nganana makuku ankunytja munu tamaltjara ankunytja munu kulypurpaku ankunytja. Tjitji winkingku kulypurpa ngalkupai. Mai kulypurpa nyura ninti wiya, palu paluru apungka ngaranyi.

This is my history. I am talking about the early days of my life to put on to Ara Irititja, for all the younger generations to read and hear. I want them to be able to look at the photographs of us, and for them to read the stories about how their predecessors lived. It is a little bit of their history. I want them to know how we all used to live and play as children, how we used to climb mountains, how we lived our lives, and how good it was.

Everyone has grandmothers and grandfathers, uncles and aunts, mothers and fathers, and each of those people have a story to tell. We were all raised up beautifully and we had good lives. I want everyone to know that. We all want our stories to be told and remembered. We were well looked after as children; we grew up in a safe environment and we were always guarded from snake bite. We want our stories put down for the future generations to read.

We want you to look at the photographs of us doing things like digging maku (witchetty grubs), gathering tawaltawalpa

Nura and family look at photos, Pukatja, 2013. Until the very end of her life Nura and family enjoyed her photo collection and seeing new drafts of her book. (Photo: Suzanne Bryce / Ara Irititja 157824)

(wild tomatoes) and kulypurpa (wild gooseberries). When we were children we were always eating kulypurpa. You've probably never heard of kulypurpa, but they grow in rocky places.

We would forage for tawaḻtawaḻpa on the flat ground. They would be easy to find for us children. Those bush foods are very nutritious; we grew up healthy and strong from eating them. We would go hunting and gathering every day. We'd be told by the white mission staff, 'Don't hang around the houses or school! Go off and play!' So we'd cross to the other side of the creek and go out into the bush away from the mission, and we'd go a long way out, until we'd come to where the goats were. We'd always go to the goats because we would take their milk!

We were such healthy children. We never had scabies or boils, skin infections or sicknesses. We never saw a doctor, never had to have needles. We were just very healthy active children. We used to play together so well; we were happy and co-operative with each other and this will be clearly evident in the photographs.

If we needed it, we'd use bush medicines from plants and bushes. We'd be taught by the women how to prepare these medicines. They were always very effective medicines, especially the plants called irmangka-irmangka (native fuchsia) and papawitilpa (creeper vine). These plant medicines would be made into ointments and we needed nothing else. I do love that special bush medicine that we make with oil and beeswax and we put it into empty bottles. It is very good indeed.

Things are different today though, because we all use different modern medicines and go to hospitals. There are clinics in every community nowadays, and we go there for treatment for scabies or fevers, and we have needles and bandages and creams for everything.

Back then it was unheard of for children to sniff petrol or to steal anything and we never did; we were good children. I feel so sorry for children of today. They are so deprived compared to us. I think things started to go bad for children, and everything else, at around 1985 or 1986. Since then our lives, and the lives of children growing up have been impoverished and deprived. But if the younger generations can read about our earlier lives, perhaps it may help them to turn things around. That's the idea, anyway.

It has given me great joy to see some young people growing up and doing well for themselves, but I do worry that they still need to learn more about our culture and bush medicine. I want to teach them more even now, but they still don't know enough. I have so much knowledge I am carrying, but I can only hobble around now, so it isn't easy. The knowledge I am carrying was taught to me by all the older women, the minyma pampa tjuṯa and I still carry all that knowledge with me today. I teach what I can and I want to support the old women by continuing to teach the old laws, so I do what I can, but I want the children to learn more about bush medicines, because there is an abundance of bush medicine everywhere. Someone has already collected some today, and will heat it up and make some rubbing medicine. I wish I could do more, but I'm just not well enough today. Well, not sick, but my knees are weak, and my hips are bad and I'm just no good.

The first copies of my history book were made in 2009 and everyone went crazy for it! All the white people, the teachers, the sisters, the policemen, everyone went mad for it! People from the Stolen Generation want to read my history book. They are asking for my good knowledge. I want my book to be in every clinic across the APY Lands.

My family

I want to talk about our family. I want all our future generations to know about our family. It is important to me that children in the future know who their forebears are. My children and my little brother, Kawaki's children are all very knowledgeable about their family, but it is the children of the future that I am more concerned with. Our children's own grandchildren and great grandchildren are the ones who will benefit most from my history. They will derive great joy in knowing their family's roots. They will be happy to see our genealogies written down. I carry all that information and knowledge in my head, but they are going to need to have it written down for them.

Nura revisits one of her old campsites in the blue saltbush on Victory Downs, 1999. The crossbar once held up the roof of her and her husband's traditional shade shelter, known as a wiltja. (Photo: Heidrun Lohr / Aṟa Irititja 128931)

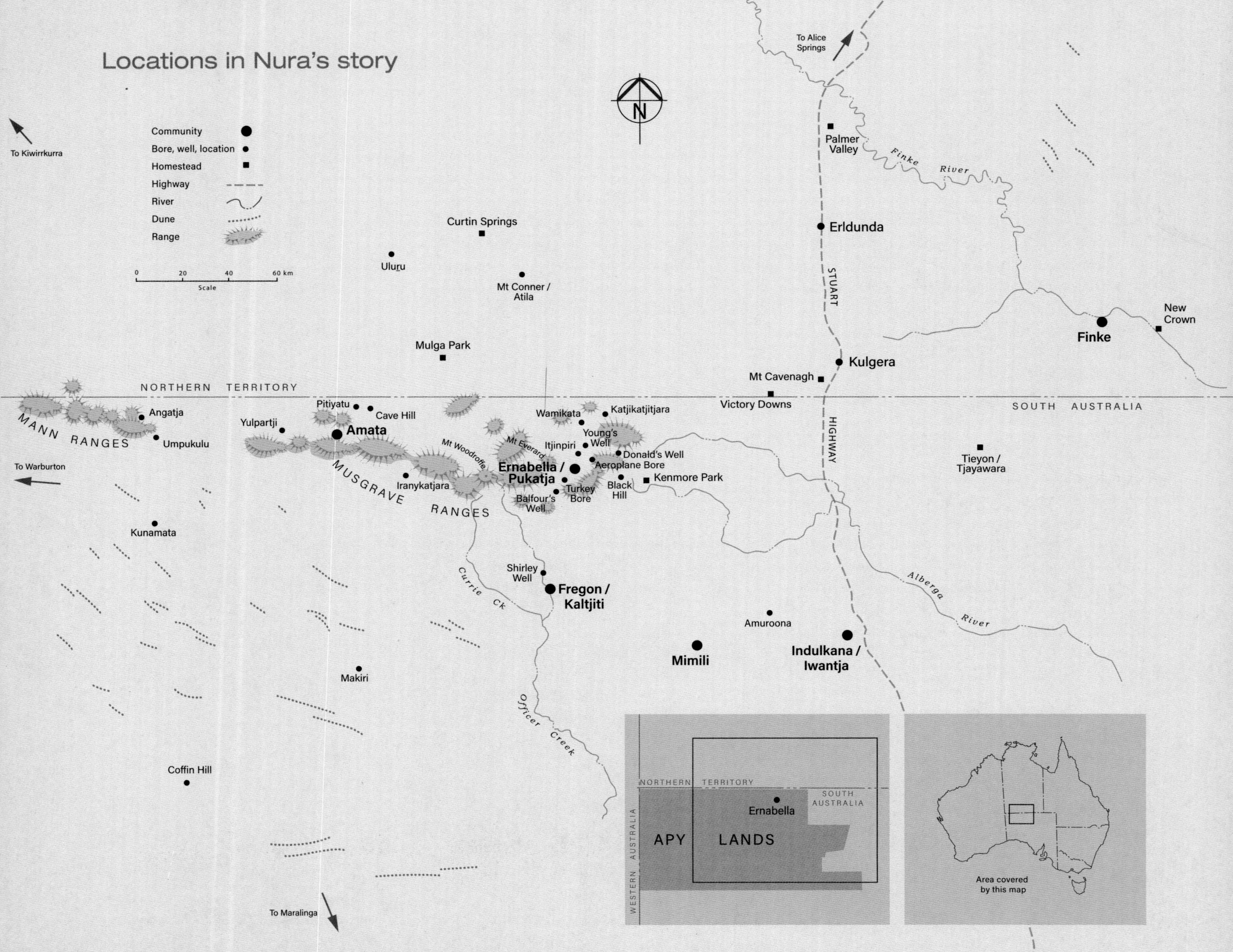

Locations in Nura's story
Community
Bore, well, location
Homestead
Highway
River
Dune
Range
0
20
40
60 km
Scale
To Kiwirrkurra
To Alice Springs
Palmer Valley
Finke River
Curtin Springs
Uluru
Mt Conner / Atila
Erldunda
STUART
HIGHWAY
Finke
New Crown
Mulga Park
Kulgera
Mt Cavenagh
Victory Downs
NORTHERN TERRITORY
SOUTH AUSTRALIA
MANN RANGES
Angatja
Umpukulu
Yulpartji
Pitiyatu
Cave Hill
Amata
Wamikata
Katjikatjitjara
Young's Well
Itjinpiri
Mt Everard
Mt Woodroffe
Donald's Well
Aeroplane Bore
Ernabella / Pukatja
Kenmore Park
Black Hill
Turkey Bore
Balfour's Well
Iranykatjara
MUSGRAVE RANGES
Tieyon / Tjayawara
To Warburton
Kunamata
Shirley Well
Fregon / Kaltjiti
Currie Ck
Alberga River
Amuroona
Mimili
Indulkana / Iwantja
Makiri
Officer Creek
Coffin Hill
To Maralinga
NORTHERN TERRITORY
SOUTH AUSTRALIA
WESTERN AUSTRALIA
Ernabella
APY LANDS
Area covered by this map

1. My father and mother

Once upon a time my mother and father were a kungkawara and a youngfella. My father lived at Angatja, Atal and Irurpa. He went, with a lot of other men, down to a sacred site at Makiri and while there, he met a young woman. His future brother-in-law took him there as part of a large group of young men. The father of that young woman was a man from Coffin Hill, more properly known as Iltur, from a place named Anmangu. The young girl was from there. They met during his visit to Makiri. Everyone, however, was on their best behaviour, because they were at a sacred site. At a sacred site – ngura miilmiilpa – nobody disrespects it by playing around. No way would anybody flirt or play around while at a place like that. That young woman was not the main promised wife for him, and he was not really arranged to be her husband; the main promised one didn't like him but the one who did like him wasn't his first promised partner! The one who wasn't promised to him thought he looked like a fine northern man. He was a handsome northern man who spoke Tjaa Wirtjantjatjara. She liked him, but he spoke only a little bit of Pitjantjatjara and he would say things like wirtja-wirtjantja and kutitjakantja.

A large family of sisters-in-law, husbands and children return to camp after a day of hunting and gathering, Musgrave Ranges, c. 1920s. (Photo: University of Sydney collection / Ara Irititja 30451)

I don't speak the way my father did. I don't use his language. He only started talking like we do now, when he and my mother moved to Ernabella for the first time, and learnt to speak like we do. Anyway the girl really liked him, this Wati Wirtjantjatjara, one reason being that he was a highly successful hunter and he would always bring home the meat. He always speared his prey and he would bring back the meat and hand it out to anyone that asked. She liked him for that.

Wanngilpai is a word referring to the way a man falls in love and follows a woman around. Other men will tell him if she's around, and he'll come rushing back to see her. He'll brush against her hand, or he'll grab her by the arm. He'll touch her by the right arm and brush against her breast at the same time! Little bit sexy way! That's the way it is done, in fact, it is traditional Law to do it that way. This is called wanngintja, and it signals his intention to marry her. What he will do is build a special camp in order to provide for the two of them, and to get her for his wife. The girl, in the meantime, will either stay in his camp at night or she'll go home. If she doesn't stay, he will follow her again the next day.

If you were a young man and you wanted to marry a young woman, that young woman's father will become the young man's waputju, the father-in-law. That man becomes a waputju to the young suitor as soon as he makes his interest in the young woman publicly known. That's our Law. If he agrees, the waputju will give his daughter to the young man immediately – only a daughter of marriageable age, with fully developed breasts. Also, the young man's brothers – not close brothers, but brothers a bit further apart – will then give one of their sisters, either younger or older, to one of her brothers, in exchange. These sisters become nyarumpa. Nyarumpa refers to the person's sister or brother or cousin, but from the opposite sex. This girl could come from kuntili, or auntie's side of the family. She could be the daughter of his auntie, from that man's auntie's side. His auntie's daughter could be given to the other side in exchange. The girl could be the young man's ukari – or

Two sisters nap on soft ashes in the afternoon sun, digging sticks close by, Musgrave Ranges, c. 1929. (Photo: AA42/1/12, Brumby Collection, South Australian Museum)

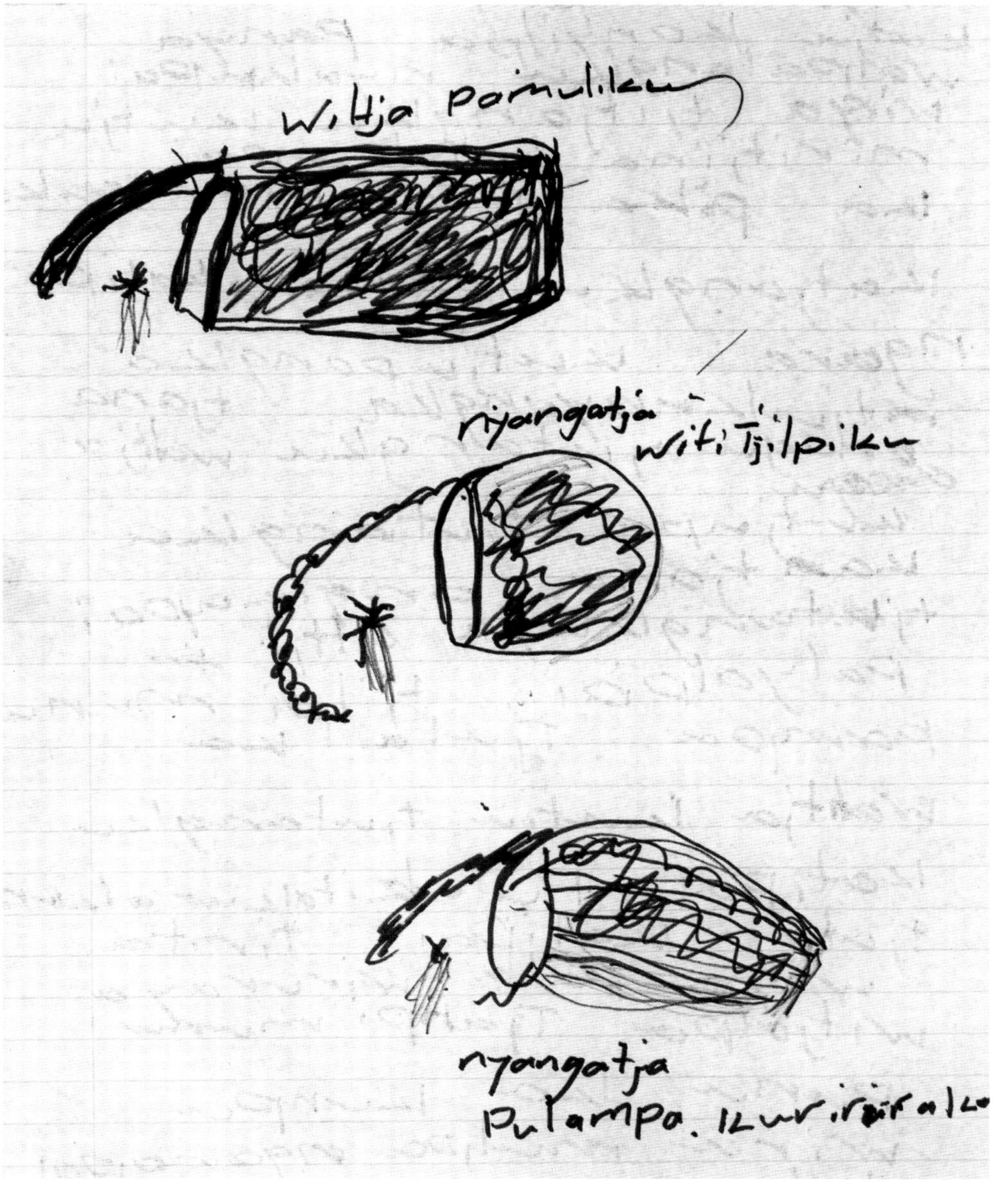

Nura's words and drawings of various types of dwellings, 2006. Top to bottom: a family's wiltja; an old man's shelter; a married couple's wiltja.

the child of his sister – what you would call his cousin. This is our Law and this is our culture. This culture comes from ancient times; it is the way we do things.

Let's say, for example, you were to be married to a nyarumpa but you were furious about it. You'd be told, 'Don't worry! He's from the family! He is from our family! Why are you in this state? When you see him you will love him, or when he sees you he will love you. It will happen quickly. Everyone approves of the match. You can go to him as soon as you want, in full view of everyone. Everyone is happy for you. He is now your kuri pikatja – your promised husband. That man will soon become our waputju because we now have a marital arrangement with him and will have to avoid him soon'. Again, this is our Law. The person being given is of the nyarumpa group and the grandmothers or grandfathers can give this girl in marriage. 'If you live alone you could easily be bitten by a snake'. This is what might be said. 'Your prospective husband is kukaputju, which means he's a skilled and prolific hunter. He spears kangaroos successfully. He's your kuri pikatja now. Your father has been checking him out. Don't make your father sad. Your father would be sad if you didn't accept'. This is our Law.

Women walk while holding their dogs against their backs for warmth, Kunapanti area, c. 1921. (Photo: Herbert Basedow Collection, National Museum of Australia)

Nobody gets married in the middle of the day when the sun is high in the sky. No. Marriage occurs at night. The couple will be called over. 'Come on you two! Go over there! You fellow! Go over to your marutju and show your face!' A marutju is a man's brother-in-law. His marutju will be very proud, and delighted to see him, and he will say, 'This is the man that everyone has promised shall have my sister. He is my relative now, and I will call him marutju!' Addressing someone by a relationship term is called walkuni, and he becomes that from now on.

If there is a refusal, if one of the prospective couple refuses to go ahead with the marriage, then big trouble will ensue. If one of them refuses, it causes a great deal of shame and embarrassment. There is a big fight, spears and punches are thrown. The man, in particular, is greatly shamed, and he will leave the area and his potential father-in-law and mother-in-law are greatly saddened. 'Why has my child refused this offer of marriage? Is there somebody else? Why else would you cause such trouble?' The prospective husband would also suspect this and wonder whom it could be, that she preferred over him. She obviously prefers to get married to somebody else. The prospective husband will leave the area, running away secretly, not allowing himself to be seen.

A man who is accepted will go about his arrangements openly. However, his prospective wife's older brothers will not lead her by the hand to his camp and sit down with them and chat. No! Nothing is said. The man will quietly go about his arrangements himself and will take a firestick and make a fire a little bit away from everyone else. He won't say anything. He'll then lie down next to his fire. The young woman will not follow

A family rests on a bed of freshly dug earth after a day's hunting and foraging while on the move through the Musgrave Ranges, 1928. (Photo: AA42/1/9, Brumby Collection, South Australian Museum)

Husbands, wives and children on the move with hunting equipment, Musgrave Ranges, c. 1928. (Photo: University of Sydney collection / Ara Irititja 30455)

him, at this point. She'll continue to sleep in her own camp. Again, this is our Law, or at least it was our strong Law.

Unfortunately, today people are in and out of each other's blankets without any regard for etiquette or tradition. But in the days before blankets, social arrangements were carried out respectfully and considerately. These were good laws, for everybody's good.

The following day the prospective man and wife will not walk around together. The young woman will go hunting with her grandmother while the man will go hunting. He'll spear the meat he is after and bring it back to his own mother and father. The young woman will come over for her portion, and everyone will see this and be really happy for them. Everyone will be excited and thrilled. Another way a man tells a girl he is interested is to take her some meat. He'll think, 'Hmm, I think I'll take her some meat'. He'll take her a kangaroo thigh or some ribs. The girl will either take the meat from him, or she won't. If she doesn't, then he'll think, 'Hmm, I don't think she likes me after all. Perhaps she isn't interested. She must like somebody else. But if she does accept the meat, then he knows he's got hope. If she takes it and eats the meat, everyone will be happy. So after that, he'll call for her formally to become his wife.

But if that girl really wants somebody else, yet still goes and eats his meat, this will make everybody wild. Especially that man! He will be furious! He'll say, 'She is my pikatja! She was promised to me! She is mine, not yours!' The two opponents will then fight and spear each other. They'll not hesitate to run each other through with a spear, and then they'll hit the girl. They'll hit her hard and there will be blood everywhere from the hitting and spearing. One man will spear the other and then he will say, 'Come on then, spear me too! Come on! Let's spear each other and then we can both limp around for the rest of our lives! Look at all the others all hobbling around from their spear wounds! Let's do the same!' The prospective waputju will become involved and then he'll be speared too. The young woman's father will be speared next. But people will be shouting out, 'How come this has all gone wrong? Why can't you two be friends? How come there has been a refusal? I am sorry my

Nura's mother, Topsy Anawari Thompson, carrying a huge bundle of prized mingkulpa (bush tobacco) back to camp for drying and preparation, Mimili, 1975. (Photo: Noel and Phyl Wallace / A<u>r</u>a Iritija 47897)

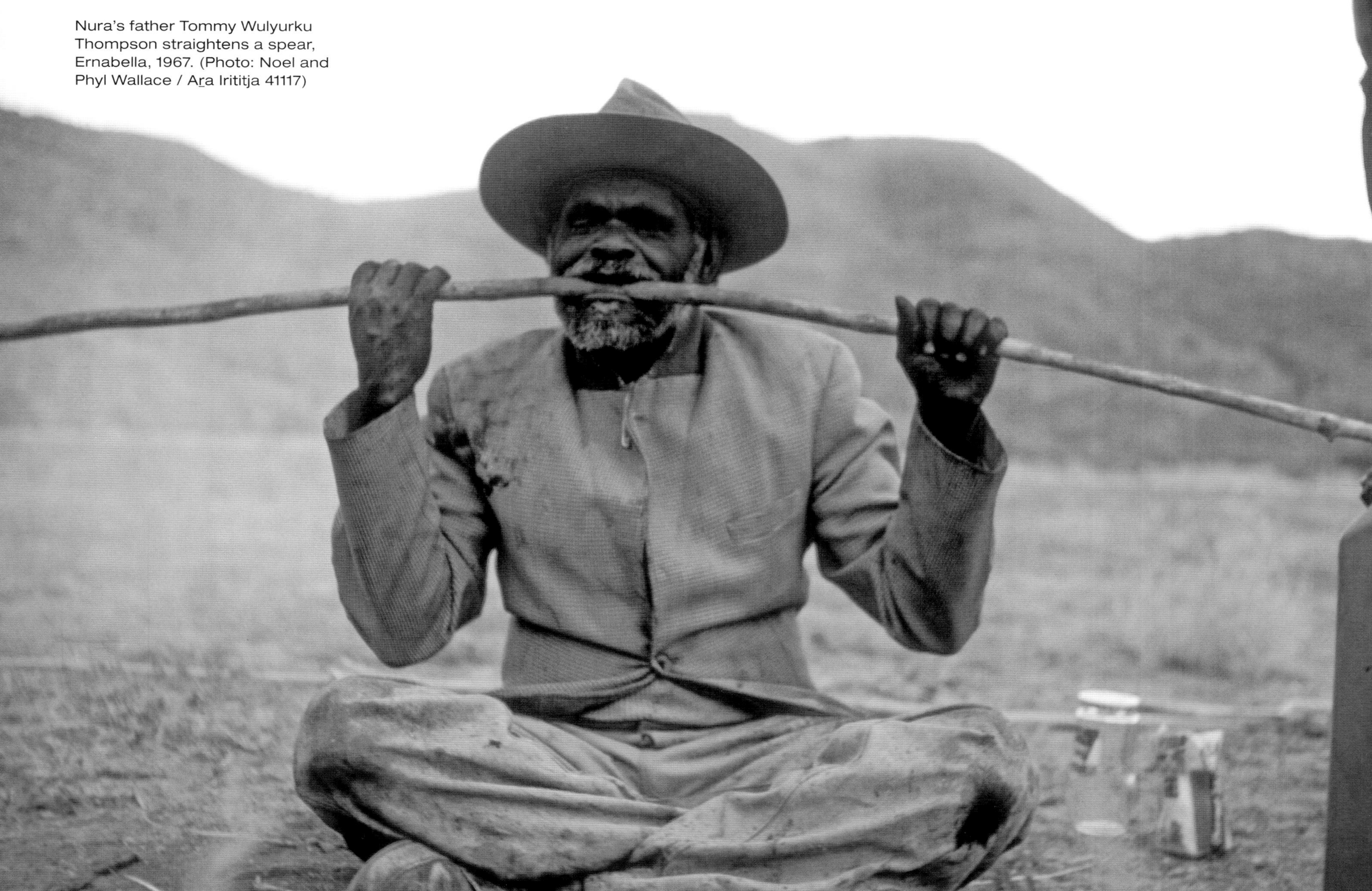

Nura's father Tommy Wulyurku Thompson straightens a spear, Ernabella, 1967. (Photo: Noel and Phyl Wallace / A̲ra Irititja 41117)

child has caused this trouble'. The young girl's prospective mingkayi or mother-in-law will become involved. 'Why does this girl cause so much trouble for my son? You should have gone along with the arrangements!' This is how things will go. It is our Law and our culture – it was their Law and culture. It is from so long ago that it goes right back to the Tjukurpa or to creation times. This Law is Tjukuritja or from the days of our ancient ancestors.

The Law allowed for a couple to be promised to each other from the nyarumpa group from the opposite side, and for that couple to come together as man and wife, and for them to live together happily. The girl could be taken by the hand, and led over to the man's camp, and there she will stay. The couple will live a happily married life and travel together and have good relations with each other's families. On another occasion, the prospective brother-in-law might say, 'Go on sister, go and follow your prospective husband,' and she will. Of course occasionally, there would be illicit affairs carried out, and someone will take someone by the hand and lead them away for illicit relations. This is called wa<u>n</u>ngitjara, which is a very sensitive word, to be used with care. Only girls with fully developed breasts will indulge in illicit sex or get married. They will become married women only when they are big enough. Young girls will be too scared to marry if they are too young and will be frightened of being sworn at, so a lot of care is taken to make arrangements at the correct time. When the time is right though, the young woman will go willingly to her partner and may even love him by the time she is married. So the married couple live a happy life together, show each other care and respect, and supply each other with food.

These newly married couples may wait for a while before they have children. They may live together, hunt together and supply meat and food to each other for a long time before

Women and children move through grasslands carrying wooden vessels, billycans and tarpaulins, Ernabella area, 1937. (Photo: Image courtesy of the State Library of South Australia, PRG 214/45/D8, J.B. Love)

they finally lie together. They will wait until they are alone together in a new and distant camp before they lie together intimately. They show this restraint because they love and respect each other, and also to show love and respect to their family members. Again, this is traditional Law. These are good laws, good for both parties and for the families.

The old ways of matchmaking, relationships and marriages were carried out with the full co-operation and participation of the entire community. It was all out in the open. The old way was carried out with love and respect, and the parents of the newly married couple were always as proud as could be for their children. They were proud and they showed it. This is how I was married. I was followed like that. Yet my husband was an older man already.

And so this is what happened to my mother and father. They got married like that. Nevertheless, they had a strong attraction to one another. They fell in love. When my mother and father were married, they did not get married at Makiri. They didn't dare because the men would kill them if they did. Nobody got married at Makiri on pain of death. They knew if they got together there, they would be killed so they did not get married there and kept their relationship totally hidden. They had a secret relationship in another place, further away, where they were married in secret. This is because it is against the Law to get married at Makiri, just as it is against the Law to get married at Wawi. Everyone is too frightened to, in such important sacred miiḻmiiḻpa sites. People are scared to put a foot wrong in important sacred sites. My mother was a bit more confident because she was from around there. You see, there are a number of important sacred sites — Kunamaṯa, Apaṟatjara, Iltur, Makiri and Wawi — and young women that come from these special places are very fortunate in that they do not need

Family group, Musgrave Ranges c. 1930. (Photo: AA338/41/420, Tindale Collection, South Australian Museum)

A man relaxes with his children in a windbreak, Pukatja, 1930. His tools lie against the windbreak. (Photo: H.H. Finlayson, Duguid Family / Aṟa Irititja)

to try too hard to find a husband; they are lucky. Young men that go to these places are often too nervous to ask for their hand in marriage. And yet, my father went there and simply walked away with his wife! My mother.

From there they went to Shirley Well, near Fregon, and lived there for a while. My grandfather — my mother's father — was coming up from Iltur, and he couldn't find his daughter anywhere. He was asking around, 'Where is my child?' The others told him, 'Your child has married'. He asked, 'Married which man? Which man did she marry?' My grandfather was rather angry about this, but not too seriously. He got angry for a while but then he settled down. The others told him, 'Look, your wife has died, you are a widow now. You have a son and two daughters. You should be happy and just support them in their marriage. Leave them be'. He was still rankled, and said, 'Well, I'm not going to accept any meat from him'. And so he decided he would follow them and see where his waputju was from.

The man turned up and my grandfather became very angry with him, his young waputju. The waputju man got angry with his waputju and he wanted to fight him, in fact, my grandfather did hit him but he didn't spear him. He didn't spear him, deciding instead to speak to his daughter separately. So he left it, and he spoke to his daughter, at her camp in the bush.

The newly married couple departed for Angatja, for Ernabella and Angatja. They were living at Angatja then along with Kutjukuru, Nganyinytja's father. Her family were all

A senior man carves a spear-thrower with an adze, Puka, 1933. Repairing and making weapons was a daily activity. (Photo: AA122/1/1-p44/1, Hackett Collection, South Australian Museum)

A child brings smiles to the faces of a family group, Musgrave Ranges, c. 1929. (Photo: AA42/1/13, Brumby Collection, South Australian Museum)

Strict laws of behaviour are enforced at sacred sites like this one at Wawi waterhole near Iltur, including access to the waters, 1891. (Photo: AA85/1/1/12, Elder Collection, South Australian Museum)

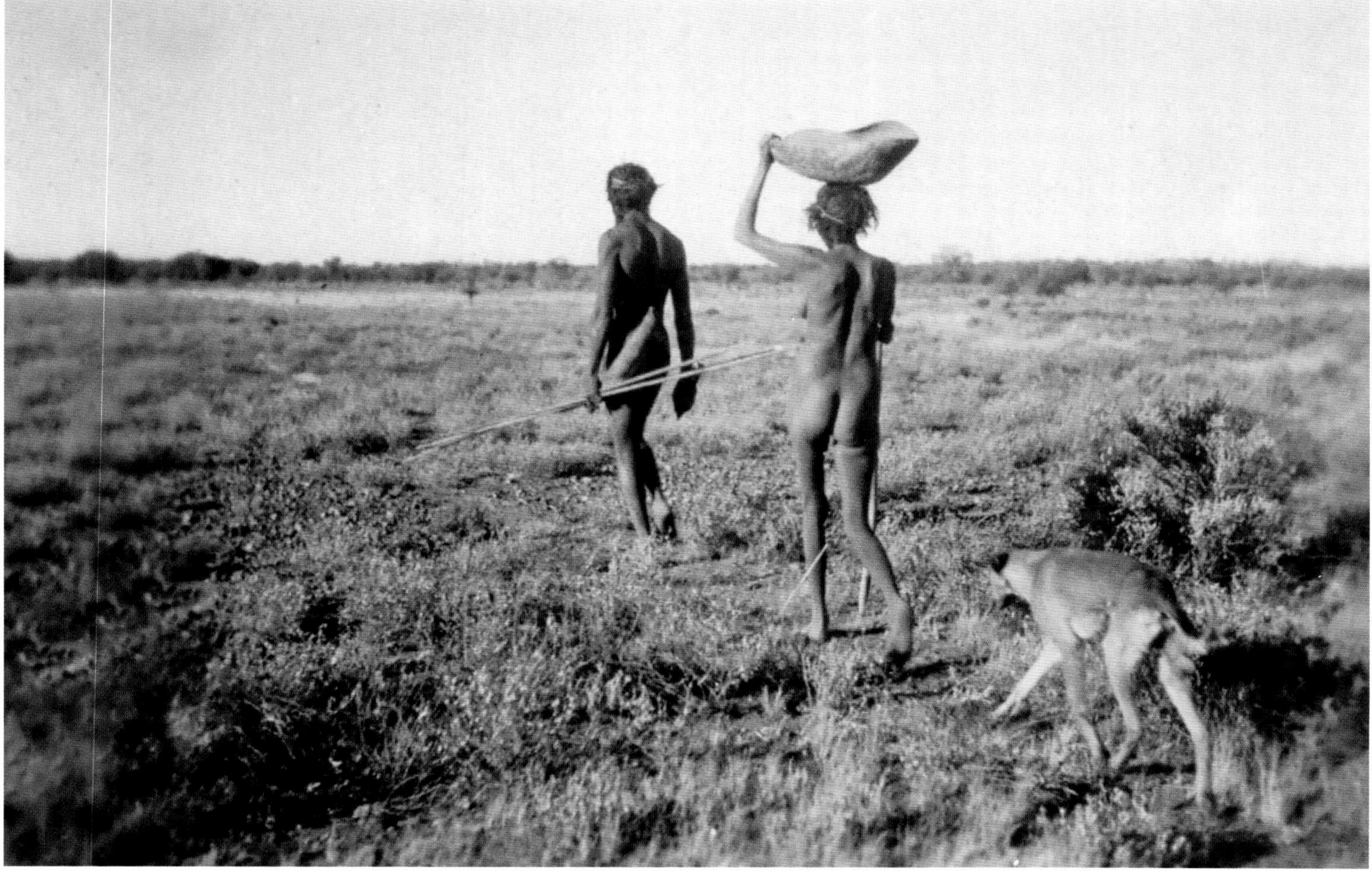

Newly married, Nura's mother and father set out for a day's hunting and foraging in the Atila (Mount Conner) area, 1940. (Image courtesy of the State Library of South Australia, PRG 1218/34/1302B, C.P. Mountford)

living together there, on their own traditional country. They lived there with them and then they travelled again to Pirurpa Kaalarinytja. They lived around the Pirurpa Kaalarinytja area for a while.

My father was a working man and he wanted to go back to work. My father told my mother, 'Come on, let's go to Watita'. He started work at Mulga Park where the whitefellas were running bullocks, while my mother stayed there in camp. While they were living there, she became pregnant with me. My father had a job to look after bullocks, and he learnt how to ride a horse, so he could round up the bullocks. He also taught my mother how to ride a horse, and so the two of them would ride horses together. She would ride quiet horses, until she began expecting me. After a while they returned to Ernabella, with a group of men, in order for my father to be with all the men. When the men had grouped, everyone went to Katjikatjitjara and lived there for a while, living around that area. The men had gone to Katjikatji, and the women had gone too, including my mother. This is tjaka, what we always do, the men and the women had gone to the men's sacred site there and this is near where I was born.

2. My birth

I was born in 1939 or 1941, but I am not sure about the exact date. I was born near Katjikatji. My pulyi umbilical cord came off, pulyi punkanu, at Katjikatji, right at Katjikatji. Just east of Katjikatji. After that my mother took me to a woman's sacred site, to a Two Women place, a Minyma Kutjara place, and I was put through the smoke. My mother was put through the smoke, her body and breasts were put through the smoke, and I was smoked also. To dry the cord out. They do it to dry the cord out, because they worry about flies infecting the umbilical area and laying their eggs in it, and so the smoke dries it out to keep it clean.

After I was born my family went back to Ernabella. I was taken to the buildings in Ernabella and that is where my first very early days were and we stayed around Ernabella for a long while. I always used to wonder where I was born and where I spent my earliest life, and so I asked and I was told, 'You spent your early life in Ernabella! That's where you grew up!' I replied, 'Ah, I see, so that is where!' Ernabella was like our proper home, but of course we were from the bush and I was born in the bush not in a hospital.

We moved between Kenmore and Ernabella, wherever my parents had work. They'd go to Kenmore for work and then they'd return to Ernabella, or they'd go to Mulga Park. There were bullocks everywhere because there had been big rains. My mother and father took me on a bullock-mustering trip, when I was a tiny infant. I was still breastfeeding, still a tiny baby. I was taken wherever they went! There was a terrific amount of rain one time, and we had to stop to make a shelter, a wiltja, out of grass, tjanpi, long tjanpi, and go inside for shelter to get out of the rain. While we were sheltering, many of the bullocks were swept away by the floods. Mulga Park can flow with floods sometimes you know! The water was powerful, pouring everywhere in fast, deep floods, and everywhere looked like an inland sea. I've never seen such floods! There were floods on Mount Cavenagh and Shirley Well where some white people

Aerial view of Nura's birthplace, Katjikatji, 1975. (Photo: Noel and Phyl Wallace / Ara Irititja 47709)

Children play in Ernabella Creek after a downpour on Christmas Day, 1957. (Photo: Bruce Edenborough / Ara Irititja 4402)

were killed by the floods. Their house caved in from the floods, and this killed both the husband and the wife. I remember hearing about that. Men were drowned on Lambina as well, in the floods. I remember hearing about an old man who was swept away in those floods. People searched and searched for him everywhere, and he was finally found, dead and drowned. They had heard him calling and had followed him as best they could, but he drowned. Some people may find it hard to believe, but we have had some dangerous floods in times gone past, in the early days before there were houses on our lands, when we were living only in a wiltja, in the bush.

Then we lived in Ernabella, and then we went to Amata, and after that we went to Apara, and so it went, travelling around and around. After that, we kept living at Atila. White people call this place Mount Conner. My father was working there, but he was never paid. All he ever received for his work was rations. We lived only on rations: flour, sugar, tea leaf, milk and something sweet, not jam and not treacle, like treacle but a dark colour, like molasses. Nobody was paid in money back then. There was no money. They were just paid in blankets and tents. After a while we went back to Mulga Park and lived there for a while, because my father had work there. We returned to Atila with some other people, and we continued to live there, living on rations, while my father kept working and working.

Our family lived for some time at Atila. A big rain had come, a very big rain, and this was the time when we went to Mount Conner. There was my auntie Ada, my father's mother, my father, my mother, and me. I was still only a little girl. My mother was pregnant at the time. We were all working at the house, at the homestead there. The white people, Paddy and Phyllis de Conlay, were living there in that old homestead at Atila, Mount Conner, and the tall white man called Victor Dumas was staying there

Tjilpi Rama herds goats in the hills around Ernabella Mission, 1952. At this time, shepherds and workers received rations as payment. (Photo: Hamilton Aikin / Aṟa Irititja 5380)

Nura's Uncle Hector (left) and relatives visit Ernabella, 1935. They were now station employees and wearing clothes for the first time. (Photo: H.H. Finlayson / Aṟa Irititja 5380)

Atila (Mount Conner), the birthpace of Nura's brother, is a significant sacred place. (Photo: Ian and Anne Congdon / Ara Irititja 8269)

too. The men had dug this hole, right under the sandhill, right into the limestone at Aniri. It is like a tube and it goes right into the sandhill. They dug it out, they'd made it. It is still there today, like a kind of dugout house, the kind they have in Coober Pedy.

They were making a garden and had camels pulling a plough to dig the earth for the garden. The camels were also used to pull up water for the bullocks. When I was a tall young girl, my mother used to work with the camels, digging out earth with a scoop, in order to make a dam for the water. The camels would pull the scoop along, and my mother would dig it out. It looked as though they were making a garden, but it was really for collecting water. The water was for the bullocks, eventually. It was hard work and my mother worked continually, without stopping. Later on, an engine was put there and a pumpjack, and the water was pumped up that way.

I don't think my mother and father were ever paid in money back in those first early days of working. They were paid in food, mai, for their work. They'd get mai ratjina, that's rations: flour, sugar, milk. Flour, sugar and milk. Not tinned milk but a different kind of milk. They'd get flour by the bagful, large bags of white flour, or small bags. I remember seeing those bags of flour. We used to eat it.

Anyway we had been working with Victor up at the homestead and mum had been working with the camels, when I looked over and saw my mother had disappeared. 'Where's mum?' I asked, 'There's two camels standing there, but I can't see mum. Where's mum gone?' 'You'll soon see,' I was told.

My mum was ready to have her baby. She stopped working the camels, and my father's mother had helped her into the dugout tunnel. They'd disappeared into the tunnel. Then the baby came. Mrs de Conlay came out later and told us, 'There's a brand new baby boy!'

Before I went in, my father's mother played a trick on me and said to me, 'Go in and see! But be careful, because there might be a Wati Tjangara in there!' I was frightened, because Wati Tjangara are man-eating ogres, but I went in anyway. When I was inside the tunnel, I saw my mum and I asked her, 'Where's the Tjangara?' There was no Tjangara though, just a baby boy lying in the warm soft ashes, as warm as toast! A new baby boy, just born! My little baby brother Kawaki!

Frank Malparin guides a camel and plough to create one of the first vegetable gardens in Ernabella, 1943. (Image courtesy of the State Library of South Australia, PRG 214/45/C13, J. R. B. Love)

Mr Victor Dumas was married also, and they had a baby the same time as my baby brother was born, so that baby and Kawaki are the same age. That baby was born at Victor's place. We enjoyed ourselves living there, and my brother and I were healthy children. We'd both been put through the smoke, we were both given this traditional baby care, so we were both strong and healthy and neither of us ever needed to go to hospital. I'm referring to the first hospital that was there at Ernabella. It was there, but we never went when we were growing up. After another long stay, we returned again to Ernabella.

We used to go travelling and hunting at the end of winter at piriyakutu time, when the west winds bring the hot weather, hunting for papa miri or dingo scalps, from the dingo pups we hunted out of their lairs, when they were big enough. We would skin them carefully and prepare the skins. Men and women carried the dingo skins, which they would be able to sell or trade. It enabled us to buy flour, sugar, tea leaf, milk and all sorts of things.

We'd go up to Kenmore, camp at Kenmore, keep going, go to Victory Downs, which is really called Wapirka. We'd go on a hunting trip all together, travelling along the boundary fence. My mother was paku at the time. Paku means she was expecting a baby. After that trip, we went to Kulgera or rather to Watju, which is Mount Cavenagh. We went from Mount Cavenagh to Kulgera, where we all gathered together for a week, and then we travelled on camels heading towards Erldunda from Kulgera. We were walking, and we walked a long way, so we camped half way at Kungka Kutjara, the Two Sisters, a place where the Kungka Kutjara lay down. The next day we kept going, until we got to Erldunda. We arrived at Erldunda in the evening, and rested there. At Erldunda my mother knew that her baby wouldn't be long in coming, so she moved away from the camp and made a separate bush camp. Her camp was not too far, but far enough away from the main camp to be safe for her. The next morning I went along to see her and to my surprise, there was a new baby! She was lucky we had arrived at Erldunda because she had people to help.

It was a good camp with plenty of bush onions, tjanmaṯa. We'd all been gathering tjanmaṯa and had a good feed. We'd roasted them and eaten them. The new baby was getting bigger and stronger each day and his skin was darkening up nicely. He was put through the smoke in her camp, and after he had gone through the smoke, he was well and strong and he was taken to the main camp. In the main camp the baby thrived and grew bigger. He was my youngest baby brother, Tony Thompson. Kawaki's younger brother. Tony had two children of his own,

Wilton Foster's father Nyatanytju Nyukapinakunu shelters in his wiltja on a wet Christmas Day, Ernabella, 1957. (Photo: Bruce Edenborough / Ara Irititja 4405)

who I raised. I raised them because he died in a car accident. His son is now a wati, an adult.

My first baby brother Kawaki Thompson was born at Atila (1947), and my second baby brother Tony Thompson was born at Erldunda (1954). And I (the oldest) was born at Katjikatji. The first brother was Kuniya Tjukurpa and Wanampi Tjukurpa and this second brother was Kuniya Tjukurpa, whereas I was Malu Tjukurpa because Katjikatji is such an important place. Atila is also a very important place.

We based ourselves for a very long time at Erldunda, until my father decided to go by himself up to Palmer Valley to do some work for a white man. He really wanted to go to Palmer Valley, to go and see the place, so off he went. When he arrived, he wasn't the man who was expected to arrive, but all the same he was asked, 'Hey? Can you ride a horse?' He replied, 'Yes, I can ride a horse'. So he was accepted for the job.

Meanwhile my mother and I stayed back in the camp at Erldunda, for a very long time, living there, until we decided to go travelling again. We set off, travelling with two camels — no, three camels, it was. We walked along and we arrived at Palmer Valley! And there we stayed. My father still had his job and he was still working there, but mother stayed at home with the children. The whitefella came by and saw us three children and said that we ought to be in school. Frank Young was with us, and so we were four children, with some of us ready for school, and so we went to school at Palmer Valley! We went to school every morning and we loved it! We'd come home at lunchtime, in just the same way that we did in Ernabella. It was good fun and we enjoyed it. We had a lovely time living there, and never felt that we wanted to be anywhere else. It was like our own real home.

My mother and father worked at Palmer Valley for quite some time. Palmer Valley was a proper station. They worked with the horses and the bullocks. We lived there for one year, and then we returned back to our country. From Palmer Valley we used to visit Henbury frequently, travelling in the company of my old father, Nura Rupert's uncle. That old man would go there and he'd take all us children along with him. While he was there we used to play with all the Henbury kids. We always used to play together. Sometimes my mother and father would take us too, and we used to camp there and play there with the Henbury kids. We stayed at Henbury for quite some time also. I learnt Pertame from all the women that were there. They all used to speak the Pertame language and we used to listen. Children readily pick up languages, and I was the same. I learnt that language by listening to people speaking, but I could never reply, because I could never speak it, but I understood it. I quickly learnt that language, but over the years I have forgotten it all again! I knew Pertame Arrernte. But I've forgotten it all now. Can't remember any of it!

A family traverses Henbury Station with camels and equipment, 1965. (Photo: Jack Hanney / Ara Irititja 10351)

* * *

My father worked hard at Palmer Valley for the rest of the year, until Christmas. One day, in the late afternoon, mungartji-mungartji, we heard a loud explosion. We heard about it on the ABC Radio, that a bomb exploded at Maralinga. The British had tested a bomb there. That was when the Maralinga smoke came

The Ernabella stockyard, c. 1950. (Photo: Annis Bennett / Ara Irititja 18948)

through, the red smoke, the puyu. The smoke came through at the same time as the measles and it got all mixed up. Each sickness masked the other sickness. The bomb smoke was red, the dust was red, and the whole sky looked like it does when the sun goes down, and the glow shines out from it. Everyone was worried about it and were asking, 'What is going on?' The old people who are now all deceased were saying, 'It is mamu. It is a dangerous malignant force'. They were saying that the men were out killing all the mamu. That is what they said then. That's their Law. That's their Law. All I remember is the puyu, which was really red. A bomb exploded earlier without notifying us; we were quite unaware of it. The first bombs we did not hear, but I certainly heard the last bomb. I heard the 'taa' detonation sound. Three times we heard that noise: Dooff. Dooff. Dooff. When the wind came, it was just like smoke or dust coming in to all the communities.

My mother wept with grief over worry for her country. She was homesick for her country, but more than that, she was grief-stricken with worry over the state of her traditional estates, and worried that they had been destroyed by the bomb. Luckily, we did not experience any sickness, at first, even though a puyu pulka, a massive cloud of dusty smoke arrived and enveloped everything. We were living in the bush at the time, amongst the bushes and beside a small hill. Not a large one, but a small one; we were inside a small house, in the shelter of this small hill. The smoke came down to the ground and landed on everything, but we didn't allow it to land on us; we flapped it away from us, and that gave us a clear way through. We stayed on there, living on hunted meat, which was cooked by the men in the traditional way. The men would go hunting kangaroo on donkeys and then bring the kangaroo meat back on the donkeys or camels. They'd cook the kangaroos where they were killed, and brought back to us already roasted.

Back near Ernabella, there is a big pass through the mountains around Ernabella, where the Umuwa road is now, and where that big creek runs down the bottom. The bomb smoke and the dust drifted down through there. Some people made a break for it to get away and went up along the Kenmore road, taking fire sticks and using it to burn into coals to make warm beds with. They'd use the coals to warm the soft soils to make warm beds to sleep in beside a hot fire, inside a solid wind-break. They did not go up into any of the mountains, preferring to stay inside the safety of thick scrub. In the scrub they could get big kangaroos, and then they'd drink the fresh kangaroo blood, and the women would dig honey ants as well. That's what they did.

We, meanwhile, were staying at Palmer Valley all through Christmas, and we had our Christmas dinner there. One day my mother said, 'Come on, let's go! I am getting homesick!' Poor thing; she had been thinking about her own father, who was still alive then and she wanted to see him. She was beside herself, worrying that he may have been killed by the bomb explosion. Luckily he had walked into Mimili, and that' s where he was. So, after Christmas, we left that place and walked back to Erldunda. The weather was cooling off by then. We went on further and walked to Kulgera. About this time, some of the older women were starting to become ill from the effects of the bomb. I was confused, because I didn't really understand what that big cloud of smoke was, or why people were getting sick.

We reached Kulgera and camped there, and I remember seeing the big blue Ernabella truck come through on the way to Finke. We asked for a lift, and on we hopped. We were on our way back to Ernabella and it was then that I got the sickness. I was one of the last to fall sick, when we were near Kulgera, on our way towards Ernabella. I got the last bomb measles sickness and I was so ill I nearly died. I had awful nosebleeds and bleeding from the mouth.

Perhaps it was as a result of the bomb? I'll never know for sure. I was lucky; I was still young, and I survived because I was treated by our excellent bush medicines, which were prepared for me by Kukika. Kukika is Mr Fraser's grandmother. She looked after me so well with the bush medicine, even though I did wonder, 'Why isn't she trying to get any whitefella medicine for me?' But she didn't. She rubbed me all over with pounded medicine plant. I had an awful dry mouth, glaring eyes, and I was skin and bone — but lucky — I was given kangaroo meat. A white man had shot a number of kangaroos and had given them to us, and the men had cooked them, and I had been given a lot of kangaroo meat to eat, which had an instant effect on me. The next morning they cooked more kangaroo and I was given kangaroo juice to drink. This made me much stronger, without any need for medicines, and, although some of the elderly ladies and men had died at Kulgera and continued to die, I survived. That old lady Kukika showed my mother, Topsy, what to do; Kukika taught her and she used it all her life. Topsy looked after me and made me better. I was very ill for a while with a lot of symptoms, dry skin and vomiting; but I was healed with bush medicines.

I became strong enough to keep travelling and so we moved on. My youngest brother was crawling around then. We walked to Mount Cavenagh and camped there. It was there in that camp that I had a dream about a great big fire that was burning

Tjipukuta Young cooks a kangaroo in the traditional way, Mann Ranges, 1972. (Photo: Noel and Phyl Wallace / Ara Irititja 45556)

Papawitilpa was highly regard as a 'number one medicine'. (Photo: Noel and Phyl Wallace / A<u>r</u>a Irititja 46457)

Honey ants are sweet and can be lifesaving. (Photo: Sometimes and Freedman / A<u>r</u>a Irititja 39254)

towards me, and which I had to put out by putting earth over it. That night I nearly died for the second time.

It was because of that very hot fire that I got really sick. I got too hot. Ka<u>l</u>i, my grandfather was cooking kangaroo tail. There was a very big hot fire to cook kangaroo in. My grandfather was cooking kangaroo tail to give to the older sisters. He'd cooked and cut up a kangaroo and had handed out all the portions. He looked at me and he could see I was getting sick. I nearly died from the heat. However, the others had brought more bush medicine along with them, and I was treated with papawitilpa, the medicinal creeper vine. Papawitilpa was used on me, as well as pounded aratja, the hill fuschia, all over my head.

Papawitilpa is a number one medicine! Number one! It is similar to penicillin. Whenever I think back to that time, I always think that I was saved from death by papawitilpa. Papawitilpa is not drunk, it is always rubbed onto the body. What you do is pound up the plant and rub it all over the body and the head. You might pound it up with a little drop of water, but not very much, because the plant already has enough moisture; it can easily be pounded into a paste. It pounds up easily; a drop of additional water may be added if you need it. So this is what I was treated with.

I was in the front group travelling, and we were travelling along and I nearly died again. My grandparents were following behind us, so that if or when I died, they would be coming up behind to take my body and bury me. My auntie Nyu<u>n</u>iwa, my uncle Pompey, and my parents, the four of them were coming up behind us. They had a camel. Nyu<u>n</u>iwa's husband went off and speared a kangaroo. He didn't go far. He got a kangaroo fairly close by and brought it back. He didn't have a rifle back then. He brought the kangaroo back and he began gutting it. I was made to drink the fresh blood. I drank the fresh blood. He then cooked the meat and I was given fresh kangaroo meat to eat. My father was an excellent healer, ngangka<u>r</u>i, and he looked after me really well, rubbing me all over with kangaroo muturka, which is the prized fat found in the innards and tail, and he gave me fresh kangaroo blood to drink. The sickness disappeared and I was well again – all from kangaroo blood. What great medicine! To drink it either fresh and alive or hot, cooked and gelled is marvellously rejuvenating, and that is what healed me. I always think about that, how kangaroo can get someone on the mend after a serious infection. It is marvellous medicine.

We were in the bush, in thick honey ant country. Luckily, auntie Nyu<u>n</u>iwa said, 'Look here! There's lots of tjala here, let's get some!' So they made camp, looked around and began digging for those honey ants. A great dish of honey ants was dug up, and a full dish was brought back to camp. I was given many honey ants to eat, and I felt an instantaneous wellness. My spirit, kurunpa, was revived and my lungs breathed more easily, and everything about me felt more alive. My head, my skin, all my membranes and all of me felt better from that beautiful honey. I jumped up and began to laugh and play again, and the fever left me.

With these wonderful fresh foods my strength returned and I began to regain my health. I felt so much better after eating that food. It brought me out in a sweat and I felt much better. I sweated and felt better. You see, if you get overheated, you cannot sweat and you become ill. But when the sweat comes out you are better. So they saw me sweating and they said, 'I think this child is going to be all right after all'. Poor thing!

After that I was fed witchetty grubs, maku, both gently cooked and raw. I was given cooked and raw maku and fed foods like that. I've wondered since, 'What was it that nearly killed me? I nearly died, and yet I was saved by plant medicines; not white man's medicine, but plant medicine collected from the environment!' Do you realise I was so ill, that a man and his wife arrived to dig my grave? My grandfather and grandmother arrived to dig my grave and place me in it. They'd been following up behind us to see what happened to me, expecting to find me dead, and instead they were told, 'She's alive!' I was saved!

In that time when we were living in the bush with our grandfather, kangaroo meat and blood were the most important things we could eat. I do not know his name. We just called him Tjilpi, I don't know what his name was, but he was my mother's father. He was a very strong man. He was a great hunter of pussycat. He would hunt wild pussycat, by hurling a stick at them, killing them. He'd then take the cat, gut it, open the stomach out and stomach contents and throw it away. Then he'd take the liver out, and then he would apply the liver all over his body, rubbing it in well. He would call this his medicine and he said it made him very strong. That was his medicine. He would do exactly the same with echidna liver. He said it was good medicine. He taught me, and my beautiful teacher, Anmanari, Fairy's mother. She was my bush medicine teacher.

All of these symptoms – vomiting, diarrhoea, phlegm, coughing and a headache – respond well to papawitilpa and the native

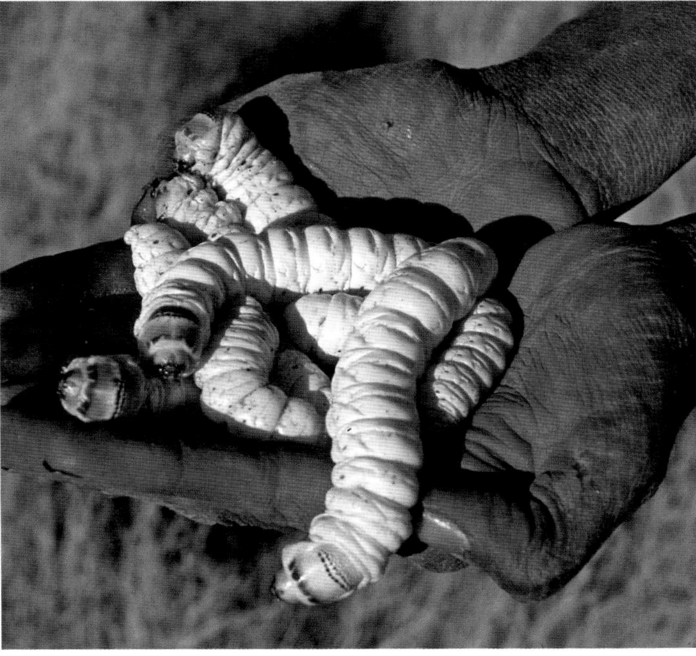

Maku (witchetty grubs) are a favourite of all A<u>n</u>angu. (Photo: Stewart Roper / A<u>r</u>a Irititja 75142)

fuschia, irmangka-irmangka. So they carried papawitilpa all the time, as well as aratja, and all of these medicines, plus healing foods like kangaroo meat and juices and blood and honey ants were tried on me in order to combat my illness. These liquids are fresh and alive and bring new life. The extreme sweetness of the honey ants brings one out in a sweat. The sweating is good for you, and this is what happened to my body.

I was fully alive by the time we arrived back at Wamitjara. We came back to Wamitjara and camped nearby, and we went to the Kungka Kutjara water there, those Two Sisters, and had a drink of water, and after that we went to Uranyanpatja and camped there. The red bomb dust was still around and it had the appearance of the kind of ash that comes out of a fire, if you splash water into the flames and ash. We were told, 'You children, stay away from that red bomb dust! Don't go anywhere near it! If you don't heed our words you'll touch it and you will get very sick! So remember what we are saying!' The dust was lying across the surface of the water. We kept our collection

of bush medicines and continued to use them even after I was better, just to make sure.

Not long afterwards, my little baby brother began to suffer from a dry mouth also. His mouth became dry and he was unable to suck breast milk. Kukika had to repeat all the treatments she'd given me, on the baby. She used the same medicines and the same treatments. She treated the baby's mouth first of all with the black powder from witjinti (corkwood trees), as well as rubbing it onto my mother's breasts and nipples, so that when the baby sucked it would take more in. The baby was dribbling a lot and this helped him.

So anyway, we arrived back at Kenmore, and everyone was cheering, 'Oh look at the new baby! A new baby has arrived!' My little baby brother was already sitting up. On arrival at Kenmore we were given food and meat, and everyone heard how ill I had been and how Mr Fraser's grandmother, Kukika, had saved my life. They were able to see with their own eyes that here I was returning safe and sound – and alive – after such a long journey. We had been eating such good meat and food while we'd been away, foods of the bush and meats of the bush, which are the best in the world.

We lived at Kenmore for a long while and many hunting groups congregated there in order to trade their dingo scalps. We then decided to return to Ernabella so I could go to school. We heard about the poor people in Ernabella, who had been so very ill, and how the hospital had been overcrowded, and how many poor people had died. When we arrived back there, we saw the evidence of all the deaths caused by the bomb; graves were everywhere, and around the hospital area. There were many sick old men lying in their camps, and we would take food to them to help them along. I was fully recovered by then and feeling well and strong, and I was happy to go and help the old men and the old women, who were still sick. Some of the old men continued to die, and the old ladies as well, because they

Nura's younger brother Kawaki is held by his mother, while his father and Nyukana Daisy Baker look on, 1948. (Photo: Source Museum Victoria, Richard Seeger, RS ER 1948/91A)

were still in the grip of the sickness, while some rallied around and survived. The poison fallout was severe, and everyone had been badly affected. The white people were shooting kangaroos and bringing them back so that people could eat fresh, strong meat. The men would take the blue truck out hunting and they would bring back the cooked kangaroos and get the sick people to drink the life-giving juices. Some people would survive, but many others died. Poor things! Uwa.

The Maralinga incident occurred on my grandfather's country at Coffin Hill, which is a very sacred place. One white man was patrolling around there, his name was Mr MacDougall; he arrived there and he saw my uncle. He spoke to him, and he said, 'Wati wiru, nyuntu ankuku? Fregonta kutu?' (Good man, will you go? To Fregon?) And my uncle replied, 'Nyaaku?' (What for?) 'How about I take you to your family members? You need to know that they are about to explode an atomic bomb. Panya nyangangka Maralingala bomb waninyi. (The effects from the atomic bomb at Maralinga will reach this far.) I am supposed to be picking you up to take you away from here. If I take you away from here, you are not to go back to Coffin Hill again, okay? You mob have got to stay in Ernabella now.' So he picked up my mother's older brother, as well as their father, and brought them all up to Mimili, where they had family. They stayed with family for a while, but then they just went back home again. Meanwhile, Mr MacDougall was picking up other people and taking them as far afield as Ooldea Tank, right down near Yalata. Other people he brought here, to Ernabella. My mother was there already when my grandfather arrived. My grandmother — my mother's mother — arrived from Makiri, and then we all lived together in Ernabella.

The measles epidemic arrived on top of the effects of the smoke, which helped to bring the measles in; and in fact the smoke and fallout made the measles worse. It was terrible. People were so ill, with terrible fevers, high temperatures, and nosebleeds and bleeding from the mouth. Old men and old women died in droves. Mamu kunpu putingka nyinantja. There was an unseen malevolent poisonous force right throughout the bush.

During the time of the fatal measles outbreak, there was also a terrible influenza outbreak (Asian flu epidemic, 1957). It happened around the same time as they dropped the bomb, and there were some terribly sick people, old ladies, old men, young girls, and young men — all sick and many of them dying. Many died and were buried in those days, when I was a big girl.

Living in Ernabella we were suffering, with everyone terribly ill with measles, dying from measles, and the effects of the fallout from the bomb blast. Everybody was extremely ill, and the hospital was filled to capacity, until people were forced to lie outside. There were sick camps everywhere, with people lying around their fires; so many people outside, while the dying were inside. My father's two fathers were both alive, Harry, and Brett who was mara-mara (he crawled around).

We did not have a plane in those days, so nobody could be evacuated. The blue truck took some people out to Finke, and they departed on the train. It was terrible, absolutely terrible. We were strong little children and we were doing all right, and those that could, helped out. I remember helping out John Bennett, Bill Edwards and Ron Trudinger. I helped those three white men as best I could. We also had Sister Donna and Sister Dugan, and we helped them also, especially Purki Edwards, who worked with them. We did what we could, helping out, being as obedient and as kindly as we could, doling out hot porridge and stew or cooked meat. We gave out the food to help keep people's strength up.

Around that time, I remember our family were way out west hunting for dingo scalps and young dingoes. A bad accident occurred on that journey. My auntie's dress caught on fire during a big wind and burnt her entire back, the poor thing. Her whole dress caught on fire during a very windy night. She was badly injured from the burns on her back and the next day she was crying out in great pain. Because of that, some of the senior ladies went and gathered some mingkulpa. Mingkulpa is wild tobacco. They broke the mingkulpa leaves off and they chopped the leaves up, and then they applied the liquid from the leaves onto her back and rubbed it in. It stung terribly, but then it began to cool down her back. I was watching the proceedings

Walter Pukutiwara (left) and a relative catch two feral cats in the Mann Ranges, 1968. (Photo: Noel and Phyl Wallace / Ara Irititja 41882)

and I asked, "What are you doing to her?" But of course, this was how things were done. It was a traditional medicine. It is probably a very good medicine too.

After that, after a period of time, they looked for a wan̲kaku man̲ngu, which is an itchy-grub or processionary caterpillar's nest, which they got. They scraped out all the dead caterpillars and their droppings from the inside and made it all clean. They took the cleaned nest, or rather, the cleaned *skin* of the nest, and then sprinkled water all over it. They washed all the raw and burnt skin on her back, and then laid the skin of the wan̲ka nest onto her back. They put some on the upper and some on the lower part of her back. After that, the poor lady had to wait until the next day. The next day, all her pain had been numbed. She had no feeling of pain anymore.

The next stage of treatment was rapita kumpu. Rapita kumpu is rabbit urine. The other women had dug out the rabbit, opened the guts and removed the bladder. They'd taken out the bladder, opened it and squeezed the kumpu onto the open wounds.

The next stage of the treatment was the pussycat, what we called ngaya, or feral cat. The cat was hunted, killed, gutted and the liver removed. The liver, or alu, was chopped, creamed into a paste and then applied to the burns. It is a very good treatment. Of course the cat meat was cooked and eaten as well! It is a delicious meat, cooked and eaten hot and fresh. The liver, though, is removed first, and prepared uncooked. The cat liver cream was smoothed onto the burns on the back, while the cat meat was eaten in order to give the body spiritual strength. In this way it acts as more than just meat, it brings life to the spirit and breath to the lungs.

After these treatments, that lady recovered enough to be able to ride on a donkey and be taken home to Ernabella. By the time she got back to Ernabella, she had vastly improved and many of her open wounds were healed, though she had many more wan̲ka nest skins applied to her burns where the skin was burnt open. I'm referring to the skin of the nest here, not the skin of the caterpillar itself. Surely you've seen one of these nests yourself? Well, they will bring skin surfaces back together. They are very healing and effective. I've seen this with

Wangunu grass seed ready for harvesting, Pipalyatjara, 1986. The seed is ground to a flour and the outer roots are roasted to charcoal then pounded to powder and used for babies' teething problems. (Photo: Suzanne Bryce / Ar̲a Irititja 27242)

The silky outer bag of itchy grub's nest was used as a burns sheet. Great care must be exercised when handling these bags: children are not allowed near, and all preparation must take place upwind. (Photo: Stewart Roper / Ar̲a Irititja 18770)

my own eyes so I know it works. Considering we had no doctors, or they were always too far away, because we were always great distances away ourselves, we had to use what we could get from the bush, which of course included bush medicines. If we were to survive whatever befell us, and return home safe and sound, we would need to know how to utilise what was around us in the bush. We had to use our survival skills. So we'd use what we had around us, to deal with problems. I'm always impressed by our innovative medical practices. They are so effective that I want everyone to know how good they are, which is why I am explaining the processes.

Our people had a huge array of different bush remedies, which were taught to us and the knowledge handed down. Too many people have forgotten it now, or never knew in the first place, or they might have seen it but never have used it, or are ignorant of its use. I too haven't necessarily prepared every single one of these bush medicines, but I have learnt about them during my life and I have made it my business to collect all the stories about them. Many of these stories I have heard while camping, when the people call out across the camps in public addresses, telling stories and giving instructions, a practice we call alpiri. The elder men would be instructing: 'Do this or that, don't forget and don't abandon the practice. Help our people. Give them assistance in these special ways. Make sure nobody gets seriously ill.'

These medicines are Ananguku – they are our medicines. Anmanari, who is Fairy's mother and Donald's grandmother, was my bush medicine teacher. She taught my mother all she knew about bush medicine. She showed me how to pound up bush medicine and apply it to the body. Anmanari and I walked the country together, around Ernabella and around Kenmore. We would go around together looking and learning, with Wawiriya. We would discuss pus in ears, which could be so bad they'd have maggots in them, and what to do about that. We worked with irmangka-irmangka and with papawitilpa. They are the most important medicines of all. So even today with the clinic, bush medicine is still good. It is wonderful. The clinic is good, and bush medicine is good.

Papawitilpa is a powerful bush medicine, which is like a kind of bean plant. It grows on a creeper vine, which wraps itself around the branches of a tree. We collect the green leaf and we grind it up. Papawitilpa is very similar to penicillin. A gentle kind of penicillin, used when someone has a fever. That is the plant that was ground up and rubbed all over me, which healed me so quickly.

Irmangka-irmangka, known as the native fuchsia, is one of the leading medicinal plants. If someone was very ill indeed, they would be treated with irmangka-irmangka. It was, and still is, a crucially important medicine. The leaves are pulled off the plant and set aside to dry. They are then broken up into small pieces, and ground into a paste and rubbed on to the body. We use the dry leaf for the tea, when it goes white and dry. We don't make tea out of the green leaf. We grind the dry leaf up and make tea from that. The broken leaf pieces can also be placed in a tin with some water and heated gently for a long time until a good medicinal brew is obtained, which is drunk hot. 'Here, drink this!' Anmanari and I would go to where the plants were growing and we cut the plant, prepared it and put it into a bottle. We would make full bottles of irmangka-irmangka medicine, and we handed it around for people to drink. White people too. The sick person will drink it, and will feel really good quite soon. It tastes like peppermint tea, which is drunk without sugar. Peppermint tea and irmangka-irmangka tea is good for bronchitis and breathing. It opens out the lungs and gives the sufferer more room to breathe and get life-giving breath into the lungs. It was the main medicine back in the days when our grandmothers were young and there were no modern medicines around. People would drink it back then and it could be used for many different ailments.

Another highly effective medical aid is wakalpuka wata or wakalpuka iwiri. Wakalpuka is dead finish. Wata is the trunk, iwiri is the root and piilyuru refers to papery bark or skin of a tree or root. If someone has fractured their arm or their thigh bone then it is a serious problem, and wakalpuka iwiri can be very useful because the pliable bark can be used to wrap tightly around the arm as a splint to help set the break. Around the

outside of the bark is placed a special mud, made by urinating into soft clay soil, and plastering the resultant mud onto the bark bandage. This has been used for centuries on men and women, on arms and legs. I have seen it used on one occasion, when an elderly lady once fell and broke her arm during a fight. She broke a bone, and had to be carried. Her arm was swollen and painful and it was wrapped in cold damp mud and the insides of a baby rabbit was also applied, which worked really well. If someone had been speared in the lower leg, or shin, and were suffering and the flesh and skin were not able to heal properly, then piilyuru was used. The piilyuru of the rhizomatous root of a wakalpuka bush would be peeled off and wrapped around the open wound and left for a while. Eventually the wound would become tiiringanyi – or begin to dry out – and start healing. The healing process is helped along by wrapping up the wound in a wanka nest, a processionary caterpillar nest. The nest would first be cut down and turned upside down and all the droppings tipped out. The skin of the nest would be thoroughly cleaned while it was upside down, and this cleaned skin would be placed onto the wound until the scar tissue – or palkunpa – formed, and the skin began to join up again. This would be a fairly rapid process.

These great ideas come from old knowledge, which is handed down to us. We retain the knowledge, use it ourselves, and hand it down too. I'm an expert on bush medicines. I do a lot of healing using bush medicines, and I work primarily on children. I've given many children treatments with my bush medicines. I don't use needles or medications. I only use plants from the bush. Bush medicines, irmangka-irmangka, for instance, and papawitilpa. Those are the two I use most, because of their active constituents, which are similar to penicillin. Our bush medicines are as good as penicillin and antibiotics. This is the truth. I'm not making it up. I was taught about our own medicines when I was quite young, and have been increasing my knowledge ever since. Those older women did a beautiful job of teaching me everything they knew. I remember everything they said. So when any child becomes sick, I remember our old bush treatments, for instance, breast milk on the mouth and in the ears, if say, flies have laid eggs and infected the eyes and ears, breast milk is a great way to clear them out. The maggots can be floated out with breast milk and then flicked out with a stick. That's an ancient treatment I always teach. Topsy and Kukika taught me and I want to teach others. It is simple and effective.

Another treatment is malu milkali – kangaroo blood. Kangaroo blood is drunk by the sick person, followed by the sweet honey nectar found inside tjala honey ants. Anangu always go for tjala honey ants, because they are good for keeping the lungs clear of fluid. Not really bronchitis, but before one gets bronchitis or flu, and is coughing a lot, honey ants will help a lot. Hot, freshly cooked kangaroo blood and body fluids are very good for keeping people healthy. Children are called over when the kangaroo is cut open, 'Children! Come here and drink this tjulku – this fluid!' We'd call the children over and they'd all get a drink. They drink it and they relish it. Everyone did this. I did. We weren't scared of it. People do not do it today. It's another practice that has ceased. Our mob don't do it now, the newest generations. But see, nowadays, our mob can't look after themselves either and anyway, they are all in hospital already. They just go straight to the hospital or the doctor for an X-ray, or a needle, or an operation straight away, while our own ngangkari healers are only infrequently consulted and our own bush medicines ignored. My own life was saved by kangaroo blood followed by honey ants. Kangaroo blood, honey ants and irmangka-irmangka can save a person's life, as can papawitilpa. These ancient treatments certainly saved my life.

For tooth problems, swollen gums or toothache, we'd use wangunu alta, which is a charcoaled naked-woollybutt outer root, or butt. If I had such bad pain that I cannot sleep, then, a twig will be cut, sharpened, heated and pushed into the gap between the teeth. I'd go back to sleep, and after a while the heat from the swelling will rise back up again, brought on by the applied heat. I would wake up and be told to bite onto to it again, 'Bite onto this with your teeth!' So I'd bite onto it hard, and very soon all the pain would be numbed and I wouldn't feel a thing. 'Still painful?' 'No, I can't feel a thing. The pain's gone!' Alternatively, we would use alkarka, which is the meat ant, or

Zebra finch droppings are pounded and added to water to make a white paste, which is used to clear up sore eyes or headaches. (Photo: Uluṟu – Kata Tjuṯa National Park / Aṟa Irititja 0114499)

The fruit of the bush fig is both food and medicine. Strict rules guide plant usage: branches must not be broken. (Photo: Noel and Phyl Wallace / Aṟa Irititja)

large black ant. After using alkarka we would have a drink of water and be better soon after.

If any of the children got unhealthy, for instance, if their mouths got dry and crusty, then they would be treated also with alkarka. It would be pounded up along with kaḻtukaḻtu rhizomatous roots and mixed with a little water, and the resultant cream would be placed onto the sore, dry mouth. A little of the liquid could be drunk too, and this treatment would have an immediate healing effect on the sore mouth. The mouth would be good very quickly. Alkarka ants are a surprisingly good medicine.

What's another treatment we use? Okay, if someone has very sore red eyes, with conjunctivitis that has been there for days and is burning the eyes, then consider that small bird, the zebra finch, or nyii-nyii. Zebra finches drop many small droppings, called nyii-nyii kuna. These fine white droppings would be collected and ground up into smooth paste with a few drops of water, using stones to do the grinding, and then stirred and stirred until it was perfect. The paste can be applied gently into the eyelids where all the pus is. Just place a small amount into the eyes. This will fix you up quickly. It can also be plastered on all about the head as treatment for serious headache.

We do indeed have a big list of bush medicines that can be turned to in time of need, such as iḻi, which we would use for a child's diarrhoea. Iḻi are figs. We would forage for the dry figs under the tree, gather them and pound them up. After pounding them up we'd add a little water to make them moist and then we'd give them to the sick child. The child would eat the iḻi and be cured of the diarrhoea. If a child has diarrhoea, the first thing Aṉangu think of is iḻi. Iḻi is the number one treatment for diarrhoea. If it looks like diarrhoea is developing, we eat iḻi straight away to ward it off. I am also convinced at the effectiveness of the wanguṉu treatment for the treatment of dry and scabby sores and skin infections like chicken pox.

For headache, bad headaches, we use papawitilpa or aratja. Aratja, or hill fuchsia, is very good. We pound up aratja and rub it onto the head. Aratja is an eastern medicine, one we use over in the east. My husband taught me about aratja. It is rubbed onto the head, back and shoulders, never near the ears or the

eyes. It is only ever used externally. It is very effective. Aratja is a common plant, easily found. Every time I see one I think of its uses and what I know about it and its history and how long it has been in use as a medicinal plant. It is an ancient medicine. Our people have been using it for millennia. Modern people hardly remember it. Today's generations don't use it at all. They have forgotten about it. All they know about is the clinic, the Royal Flying Doctor Service aeroplane, doctor, sister, hospital beds, hospital wards and interstate hospitals where they go for major operations. Everyone has had an operation nowadays.

And yet, for uncounted eons our people have survived and thrived using only our traditional medicines. The oldest men alive today are alive because of traditional medicines. The same can be said for the oldest women. How else could they be alive? I think about this undeniable fact all the time, which is what is driving me to talk about it so much. The older generations are the ones who taught me. I've been taught this ancient knowledge from older people who passed it down to me. I really treasure this valuable ancient knowledge and I am glad of the opportunity to pass it on. I have never forgotten what I have been taught. I know all about these medicines because I've seen them used; I've used them myself. I've gathered the information about them during my lifetime.

The people in the old days, in my grandfather's and grandmother's times, had important health-giving foods such as quandong or wangunu, pigweed or wakati and native millet or kaltu-kaltu. They ate these foods in times gone past, as well as others, and they'd grind up wangunu with their feet. They'd do this by digging out a nice bowl shape into the surface of a hard, flat underground termite nest and then drop the wangunu into the bowl through a burning bundle of likara, or bark. The wangunu would toast as it fell through the fire and landed in the bowl, where it would be ground by the feet. First, though, a long and heavy stick would be stuck into the ground to hold onto. They'd bring their grinding stones to this place, and put them down, ready to grind the prepared seeds. The seeds were de-husked by stamping on them, moving the feet to and fro to separate the grain from the husks, in the hole, which was generally quite large and deep. Sometimes kaltukaltu would be mixed with wangunu to make a mixed-grain seed bread, which was ideal food for the children to eat.

Children, back in the days when everybody was naked, would eat this excellent food. They'd eat this food while their mother's husband would be out hunting, sometimes on long hunting trips to distant areas, and later on bringing back kangaroo meat to feed the family. The man would follow the

Aratja (hill fuchsia) is a fragrant medicinal plant. (Photo: Linda Rive / Ara Irititja 82670)

Wangunu is a prized grass seed. These tiny brown seeds are ready for grinding into flour to create seed cakes. (Photo: Suzanne Bryce / Ara Irititja 142567)

A young Nura piggybacks her brother Kawaki in Ernabella, 1948. Anangu recall their position in the family by remembering who carried whom when they were young. (Photo: Museum Victoria, Richard Seeger, RS ER 1948/4)

kangaroo for a long time until he was able to spear the animal, immediately gut it and bundle it up and carry it quickly back on the head to the waiting family. The husband would be naked too. This was in the times when everybody was naked. His wife would see him coming while she was sitting and grinding wangunu. Grinding is a long and detailed task needing care and skill. She'd be grinding and grinding and preparing the seed into seed cakes. She'd feed each member of the family, making sure the children all had plenty to eat. She'd make sure her elder sons had plenty to eat. All the time their elder sons would practise spearing with targets. The targets would take the form of a bark disk cut from a tree, called a tululu, which would be rolled along the ground and speared while it was still moving. Sometimes they'd practise with two tululu at the same time, to get really sharp and skilled. Meanwhile, their mother would be stamping and grinding, stamping and grinding, going through all the necessary stages in the production of wangunu food preparation. They'd be chopping and chopping, making new digging bowls all the time. Bowls continually needed replacing, and were always needed to collect the different seeds in.

Children used to eat armgrass millet or kunakanti regularly. Kunakanti was a very important food, but only one of many. Kunakanti, wakati, kaltu-kaltu, wangunu – these are our most important seed foods. These were strong and healthy foods and we all ate them as children. We would gather food from the mountainsides as well. Ili, or fig, is one of our favourites. We'd climb up to the tree and gather and eat the fruit, gather and eat, and gather some more, and we'd bring a big amount back to camp. All the people from olden times relied on this important fruit. The people of old ate ili figs regularly. I'm referring to the old naked people now. Those same people also ate great quantities of wayanu, or quandong fruit. They had a huge variety of food to eat.

We grew up on these good foods. Our grandmother taught us how to gather and prepare them. As we walked the country we had to always be on the lookout for them, because the meat wasn't always immediately available, but the seeds and grains were. We'd make camp near where the men could have success

A hunter scans the hills around Ernabella for signs of euros, 1932.(Photo: H.H. Finlayson / Aṟa Irititja 57634)

at hunting, and also near enough to a water source, such as a rockhole. We'd camp near the rockhole, what we call a tjukuḻa. Sometimes we'd drink all the water available in that tjukuḻa, and the whole area nearby would become hunted out in time. If this happened, once we'd used up all the resources in that area, we would move on to the next place.

The men were skilled and prolific hunters. We call men like this kukaputju. Men like this always brought home the meat. They'd bring home plenty of meat and all the children in the family group would have plenty to eat and would be growing up strong and healthily. The young boys would be turning into nyiiṉka and the young girls would be growing up into kungkawaṟa. The abundance of food gave the children a chance to grow up healthy and strong, which was important.

I now want to turn to a different subject and talk about an ailment, which we used to refer to, or call, pika lirutja. Pika

A woman separates the stalks and husks from kalpari seed, Amata, 1972. Different seeds were mixed together to make mixed-grain bread. (Photo: Noel and Phyl Wallace / Aṟa Irititja 46282)

Men rest after a day's hunting surrounded by their tools and weapons. (Photo: AA85/1/5/30, Elder Collection, South Australian Museum)

lirutja has nothing to do with snake bite. It is not contagious. You won't get it from someone else. Pika lirutja takes the appearance of burns by fire, but dry and crusty. It looks like leprosy but it isn't leprosy. There is no medicine for it. They would refer to this as pika lirutja. The skin would be dry, and maybe there were other names for it, but our people used to call it pika lirutja. The sufferer was more or less immobile. They might be able to creep around with the aid of a stick, but otherwise, could not walk. They could take a few steps but would have to sit down. Family members would have to assist them to get along to the next camp and sit them down when they arrived, or if they were struggling along behind, once they got there and couldn't see the sick person, a man would return to find them and carry them on his back and bring them quickly to camp. The man would carry them on his back into the camp and then put them in a comfortable spot. Our people used to call this sickness pika lirutja, though I don't know what you'd call it today. It was very bad and it took the appearance of very dry skin and swollen glands. (Pika lirutja is the same ailment we are referring to when we warn about mining those sacred

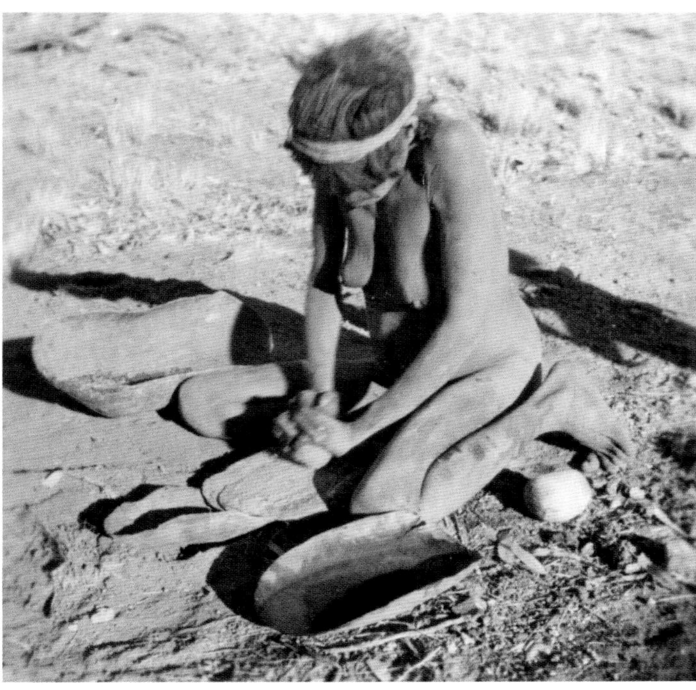

A woman prepares wangunu seed cakes, Apara, 1940. (Image courtesy of the State Library of South Australia, PRG 1218/34/1284A, C.P. Mountford)

A boy drinks from a tjukula (rockhole) near Ernabella, 1949. (Photo: Source Museum Victoria, Richard Seeger, RS ER 1949/100)

A father and son return from a successful hunt. (Photo: AA338/43/287, Tindale Collection, South Australian Museum)

Nura's Uncle Hector and a group of men and boys burn spinifex to drive out mala (rufous hare-wallaby), Kunapanti soak, 1933. (Photo: H. H. Finlayson / Aṟa Irititja 57646)

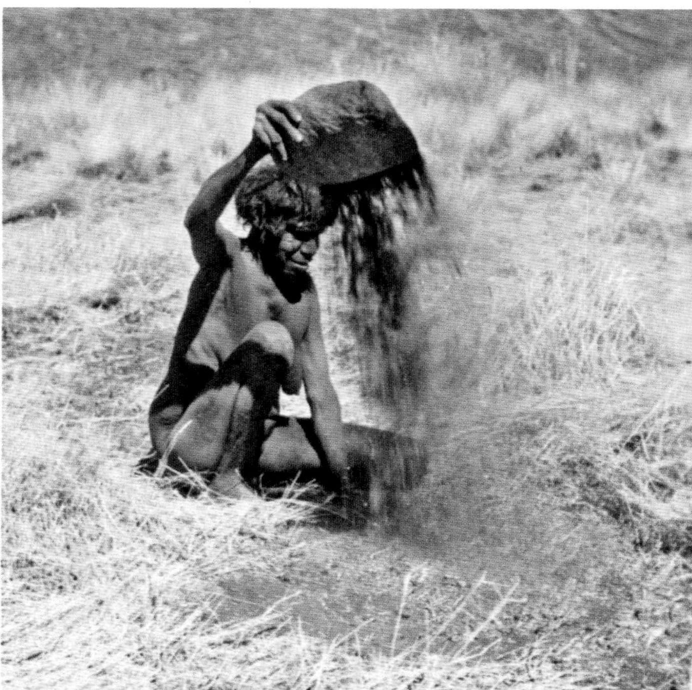

A woman winnows and de-husks grass seed, Alkanyunta, 1940. The seeds will be ground to a flour, mixed with water, and baked as a cake on top of a bed of clean, hot coals. (Photo: Image courtesy of the State Library of South Australia, PRG 1218/34/1291B, C. P. Mountford)

rocks around Irrunytju. This is what will happen to everyone if those rocks are damaged by miners. There are other rocks at Anumara Piṯi which give the same effect. This is at a place called Purtjunya. There is spring water there, and black rocks. If someone scratches those rocks they'll be covered in purtju. So anyone going to get water from Purtjunya is very careful).

I am relating my stories to you now while I have the opportunity, and I am giving this specific information out about our traditional medicines because these medicines are still relevant to the health of our people today, just as they were back in the old days.

3. My childhood

I now want to tell you some stories about my early childhood in more detail, and about life when I was a schoolgirl in Ernabella. Just thinking about today's way of life makes me very sad, which is why I want to talk about the early days now. Oh, how good those early days were! Sometimes us girls would go off separately on our donkeys down the watercourses looking for water to dig and drink. We would drink then bring our donkeys down to drink. We'd give them a drink in a billycan.

We'd ride our donkeys a long way away in search of maku, which are witchetty grubs. We would go off to dig maku, and then cook it on the fire and have a great feed; it was so satisfying and enjoyable. And it was great fun. We did this because we had been taught how to hunt and gather by our relatives, our grandmothers, big sisters and mothers. Another thing we tried out as children was mingkulpa – wild tobacco. We'd all get intoxicated from it and then we'd all vomit and fall asleep and

Mingkulpa (native tobacco). (Photo: Noel and Phyl Wallace / Ara Irititja 42059)

This photograph would remind Nura (left) of the fun and laughter of her childhood. (Photo: Source Museum of Victoria, Richard Seeger, RS ER 1948/83)

have violent headaches – all because we'd secretly tried out mingkulpa. Mother would be asking us, when we would come back to camp vomiting and sick, 'What's up with you lot? What is the matter?' But we'd be trying out mingkulpa and all getting sick, hidden away from sight! I was only a little girl then, and Nganyinytja was a big girl.

We would go to school every morning. We'd wake up from sleep and rise quite early in the morning and go off to school. We didn't have modern conveniences back then, like showers or anything, so we would wash in cold water under a hose in the outdoors. We'd shower like that until we were nice and clean and then we'd comb our hair and make our hair all nice and tidy. Then we'd be told, 'Run around the river red gum tree now! Race each other!' So we'd race off and get dry, bless us! We were all naked. None of us had clothes back in those old days. You might imagine that our leader – our superintendent – was not a nice person, who spoke in a bad way to us. But no, our superintendent was a good person who had our good health at heart and indeed, we did have good health, with no scabies, boils or lice.

Anyway, we would go to school and then after dinnertime we would leave. After eating dinner, we would always go to see the nanny goats, sometimes carrying a small billycan or an empty tin. We'd find the goats and call out, 'Hey! The goats are over here!' and then we'd chase after and grab the goats, and sometimes a goat would shove a child and they'd cry, and so we'd shout, 'Hey, goat! Don't push that little child around!' Then we would hold our goat, hold it still, and then lie down on the ground underneath it and grab its udders, and, while another child held its back legs, drink the milk straight from the teats. Each child had its turn, and we all had a drink of fresh goat's milk. We'd try to ride the goats too, to no avail! Sometimes some of the smaller children would be too frightened of the goats and would cry for their mothers, poor things! But they'd still get a drink of goat's milk. We'd all get a big drink of milk, then, with full bellies, we'd all run down to the creek for a swim. Well, more often than not, the creek or the rockholes in the hills didn't have any water, but we did have a cement swimming pool. There used to be a lovely swimming pool.

When it was very hot, we would play in the swimming pool, and then we would get out and lie down on our tummies and slide back into the pool. We children would play and splash and swim in the water, until a child would shout 'Hello? Hey, look at that!' 'There's dust coming! Quick! There's a whirlwind coming! A big kupikupi is coming!' We'd all stare and shout 'It's true! A big kupikupi is coming!' (We Pitjantjatjara people call this wind kupikupi; Yankunytjatjara people say unpalaṟa.) We'd see the approaching kupikupi with delight. 'Here comes the kupikupi! Here it is, bringing dust and prickles flying!' We would all get out of the water quickly, all dripping wet, and rush to meet it head on. We would be wet through and we'd run into the centre of the whirlwind, dripping wet, hair and all. We wouldn't be scared of it, or all the dust and prickles that would be flying around, as well as all the sand and dirt and tumbleweeds. We would be in the middle of this maelstrom, and we'd be smothered all over by the flying debris, which would coat our skin and get into our hair, until we were covered from head to foot and brown all over, hair bristling with prickles. We'd laugh and laugh so much!

When the whirlwind passed on and into the trees, we'd be standing there laughing. The wind would go, and move off into the trees, thrashing them around. When the wind died down we'd all look at one another and laugh so much at our faces. We looked like weird and strange earth-creatures with our faces

Children would play with the goats and enjoy a drink of milk, often directly from the teats, Ernabella, 1949. (Photo: Frank and Mary Bennett / Aṟa Irititja 48)

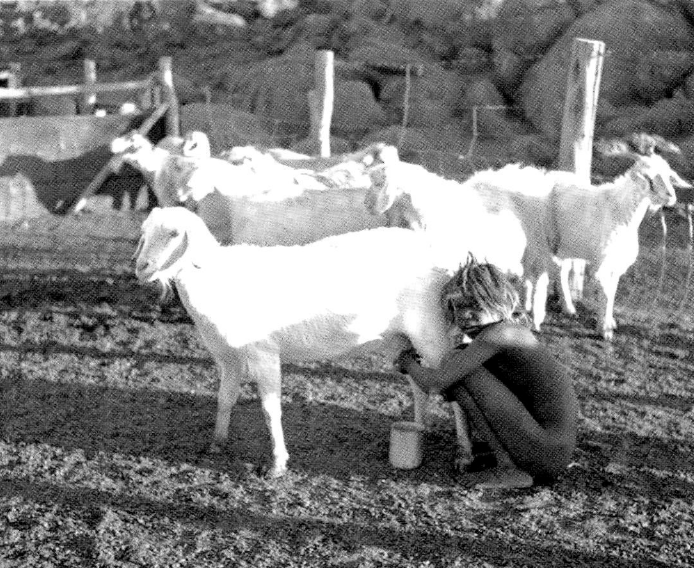

Purki Edwards milks a goat in the goat pen, Ernabella, 1949. (Photo: Source Museum Victoria, Richard Seeger, RS ER 1949/56, Seeger)

Kawaki (front left) and friends prepare to dive into the Ernabella swimming pool, Ernabella, 1961. The pool was one of the first built on the lands. (Photo: Bill Edwards / Ara Irititja 13282)

and whole bodies composed entirely of earth, sand and prickles. We would look mad, all prickly and brown and we would shout at each other, 'Look at your ears! They are all prickly! Look at those big prickles in your hair! Your head is all prickly!' We just laughed and laughed and laughed. We would laugh in the dust storms and the wind and we would laugh inside the whirlwind and we would laugh in the pool and we would laugh up in the mountains and stony hills!

Then we'd all jump back into the swimming pool again and wash ourselves off. Often, another whirlwind was coming along behind, and we'd run inside it again unless sometimes, we'd be told not to. 'Hey! Be careful! You're going to get hit by a branch or something! A great big branch is going to come flying along in a minute and impale someone! This wind is stronger and it is breaking large branches off. Watch out! Someone is likely to get killed!' Of course, we'd often ignore these warnings, but we were good children nevertheless.

Happy after our fun, we'd all get out of the pool and head out to the bush to hunt for something to eat, usually for wild tomatoes like tawal-tawalpa or maybe gooseberries like kulypurpa, or figs like iḻi, or bush tomatoes like wiriny-wirinypa or maybe witchetty grubs like maku or desert raisins like kampuṟarpa. There used to be some lovely big fat kulypurpa growing in the hills around Aeroplane Well, and we'd climb up to get them, often quite high above Aeroplane. From there we could look down at Aeroplane Well, from that great kulypurpa area, which was also near a great kampuṟarpa-growing area. We would harvest whatever we found and eat it. We'd go and gather and eat those fruits in an empty tin. We'd go with a tin and fill it up and eat the fruits. We'd always be full up on fruit. Iḻi too, we'd also eat iḻi, climbing up in the hills to find it. We'd climb up on the rocks and get the fruit. Everywhere wild fruits grew, like wiriny-wirinypa, tawaḻ-tawaḻpa, kulypurpa, all growing in the hills.

Down below was good maku country. Not maku ilykuwara, but the ones found in punti, the senna bush country. There are maku found in punti as well, and we'd go there, and dig up our own grubs. We'd dig our own grubs, or sand lizards like tinka if we were lucky. Other times we'd go to the rocks near the river-bed, to the big iḻi trees growing there, and feast on figs. There was so much variety in bush food, wherever we were we could find something to eat. Life was great back then. It was wonderful! Everywhere were beautiful flowers, all different ones, tjuḻpun-tjuḻpunpa of all different shapes and colours, dotted everywhere, so beautiful. Everything was so much fun. We'd go and find fresh water and drink it. We'd be satisfied with that and happy. In those days there was little or no tea. There were no tea bags, only a little loose-leaf tea. These days we have tea bags, but in those days there was only leaf tea and milk and sugar. Tea would come from a long, long way away. The same with flour, there was only ever very little flour and we had never eaten damper made from flour back then, or at least, hardly ever. The family would get ration flour from time to time and little dampers may have been cooked then, but not much. Back then there might be a little bit of damper given to the children by the mothers and fathers.

We would be told, 'You bigger kids watch out for the little ones! Don't throw stones in case you hit one of them on the

A woman and her baby run for shelter to escape an approaching kupi-kupi (whirlwind), Ernabella, 1959. Nura and her friends enjoyed kupi-kupi, they would cover themselves in dust, and then jump into the pool. (Photo: Bill Edwards / Aṟa Irititja 13141)

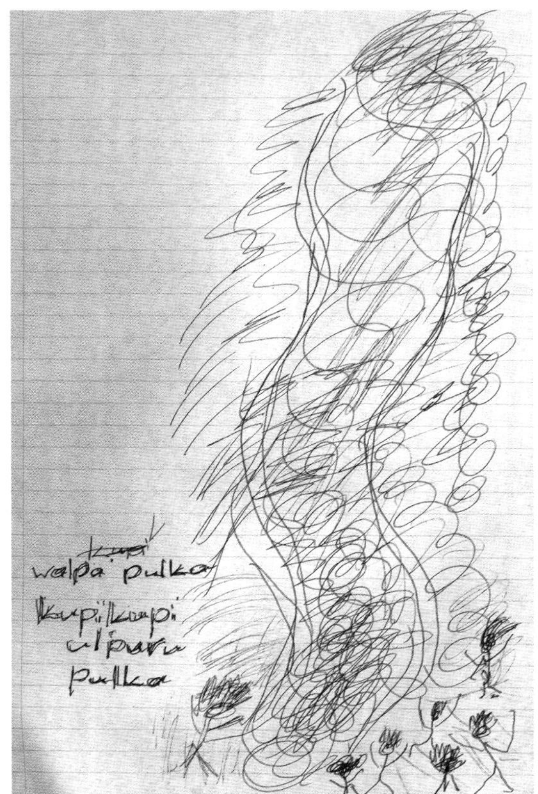

Nura's drawing of kids playing in a kupi-kupi ('a strong wind, bringing a great deal of dust'), July 2006. (Nura Ward / Aṟa Irititja 109065)

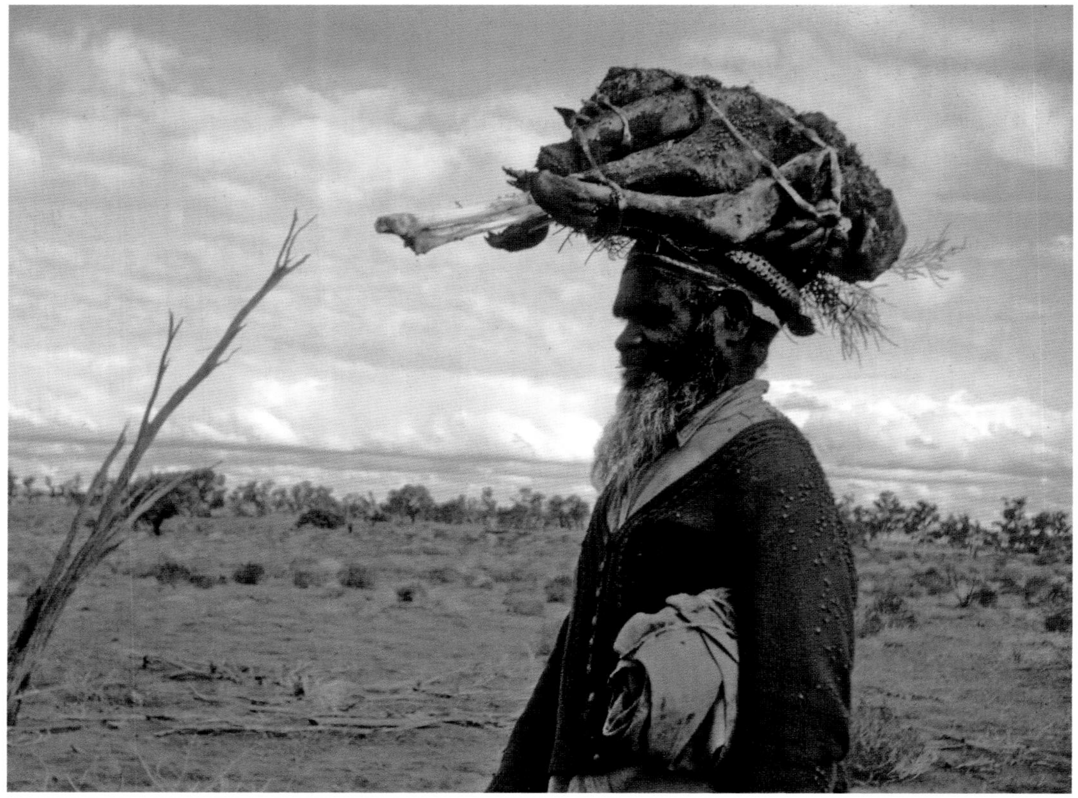

A hunter brings cooked meat portions, bound together with intestines, back to camp, 1963. Everyone in the camp received a share of meat. (Photo: Bill Edwards / Ara Irititja 13390)

nose!' So we were careful and we looked after each other. Lots of photographs were taken of us children all playing together. There are plenty of photographs of us playing on the rocks together, looking after the little ones, watching out for them and making sure none got bitten by a snake, or anything. We played together all the time, good friends, and then we would take the little ones back to their mothers. We were great kids, always looking after our little brothers and sisters.

Putja David Umula was a lovely man. He lived with us when we were children. We children loved him. He would go off for kangaroo meat. He would take his hunting dogs, and be assured of success. He'd go out hunting and he would come back with a big fat kangaroo and his shirt stuffed full of kampurarpa. He wouldn't wear trousers! But he always wore a shirt! He would stuff the shirt full of kampurarpa and he would come back and call us over 'Come and get some kampurarpa!' What a lovely man! He used his shirt as a bag if he went hunting, he'd lay it down and fill it with kampurarpa and tie it up like a bag and carry it back. We'd call out, 'Grandfather is coming back!' We'd run over to him. He'd come back and sit down. 'Children! Come here!' We'd go over and see the shirt full of the fattest juciest kampurarpa, that were so sweet – they were unbelievable! So delicious and sweet! He gave us all a share and we'd fill up whatever container we could find, such as an empty tin, and there we'd all be, all us children, gobbling up our kampurarpa! That dear man!

We ate our kampurarpa and later we ate the kangaroo he had speared. Of course we shared our kampurarpa with our parents. Our parents would have bullock meat from time to time. We always had food from somebody. Somebody would always be giving us food to eat. Our grandfathers were very loving. They just loved us smaller children. We always got something from them. Those old men loved their grandchildren. They would give us kangaroo tail to eat. We always had meat. When those old men went hunting, we knew there would be meat. When we saw them coming back we'd be there shouting, 'Grandfather! Grandfather!' We'd sometimes be told to be a bit quieter! Paniwakunu and Kurkuru were both the same, great hunters and generous men who always provided abundant meat.

Nowadays though, it just isn't the same, and life is miserable for children. Nobody watches out for the little ones any more. Older brothers don't bother looking after their younger brothers; they don't bother taking their younger brothers into the bush for learning. Older sisters don't bother taking their younger sisters out for learning either. Nothing happens like that anymore. Poor things. These days, children are hardly taught anything at all. There is only grief and sadness in the lives of my own descendants. We see young girls getting pregnant and abandoning their own babies or giving them away to others to raise. They are not capable of growing up or teaching a child, because they were never shown anything themselves.

Children play on the rocks above Ernabella church, 1959. (Photo: Doug Hooper / Ara Iritija 4467)

Children pick kampurarpa (desert raisins) in the country surrounding Ernabella Mission, 1949. (Photo: Source Museum Victoria, Richard Seeger, RS ER 1949/99)

Nura carries Johnny Briscoe on her hip while Tinpulya digs for water in the Ernabella creekbed, 1949. (Photo: Source Museum Victoria, Richard Seeger, RS ER 1949/359)

They do not know their grandmothers' Laws or teachings. Their fathers know only about alcohol or marijuana. These young girls get together with boys and get up to no end of trouble. They don't know about work or anything. This makes me so sad. The way I grew up was so different. I'd be out there climbing mountains, climbing trees, playing happily by myself, never bored, and helping others do things. Everyone saw this and everyone reciprocated in every way they could. Not today though. Some children are neglected and hungry. Nobody helps anybody with anything. What a tragedy life is today for the new generations and so different to the way my life was led, which is why I've been wanting to talk about my own life.

Oh dear, talking about those early days makes me so wistful and sad. I am sad for the young people of today. Now there is a new future ahead of us and we are all very old ladies. The new young people in the future will be all lost, poor things. Our children have shed the past from them and do not practise hardly any of the old traditions. They are not taught anything of past practices, and they do nothing about it. They all end up in the hands of the police, because of petty theft and that sort of thing, and they are all smart in new ways and have a lot of interaction with the police.

When I was growing up we had no contact with police at all. We never did. Two policemen did come later on, two white men named Jacob and Bruce, who came from Oodnadatta to Ernabella and Amata but not to Fregon as it wasn't around then. We were as frightened of them as we were of snakes! We were terrified of the police and of breaking any law, such as hanging around any houses. We were scared of being seen and scared of getting into trouble by someone reporting us. We were terrified of being taken off in chains to jail. Not like today. People today have no fear of any of that, and are confident. Perhaps it is because they can speak so much English these days. Perhaps it is because children have learnt so much English, that's what I think. Children have all got new ideas from school; they can all speak English, and they are all smart in new ways. Not like

A family of hunters lay out their dingo scalps for inspection and trade valuation, Ernabella, 1943. (Photo: Len Young family / A<u>r</u>a Irititja 30739)

us, we never answered back in a smart way. We had no English language at all, and we were nervous and scared. We were terrified! Even if we were offered a lolly or something, we'd be too scared to take it! We'd be terrified of everything.

We never had money, or lollies or milk; we never had money until dingo scalps came in. We were paid for dingo scalps – and sometimes not. We would kill dingoes for their scalps and take them to Kulgera and sell them, and we'd take them to Wapirka as well, and we would also take them into Ernabella. My father would take the dingo skins that he caught, papa mi<u>r</u>i, and he would sell them to whitefellas, to Mr Bennett and Mr Bill Edwards. He would sell them for flour, sugar, tea leaf, blankets, shirts, trousers and dresses. Food would be given out as well. For three papa mi<u>r</u>i, we would get a lot of mai, lots of mai. For three more papa miri we would also get lots of clothing to wear, as well as billycans and pannikins. We would get similar amounts to the rations, which was great for us. We'd always be really happy and satisfied by the exchange. We would get the flour in large bags, which we could then carry along with us. The treacle wasn't golden syrup, it was proper dark treacle. That's what we would get in exchange for our dingo scalps. We'd also get tins of condensed milk. We would open the tins and drink the milk.

If only we had known that it was going to lead to diabetes! Poor things! Everyone who drank and ate that food then is diabetic today – all of us. All the children that lived that life then, and ate and drank that food became diabetic later on in life. We never had cool drinks but we had these tins of condensed milk, which was very sweet. Mum would use an axe to open the condensed milk tins and we drank it. We had no cool drinks at all back then, no cool drinks and no orange juice – no fruit juice of any kind. We did have cordial though from time to time.

Nobody received wages for a very long time, until the young women began working in the Craft Room in Ernabella [1948], and began receiving wages for the first time. It was only a small amount of wages, like ten dollars, ten pounds, five pounds, that sort of amount. I used to be paid from the craft room amounts like that. One pound, two pounds. The one pound note was a green note. I remember getting notes like that. When we first started receiving wages it was only a little bit. But in the early days, my parents' generation and my grandparents' and aunties' and uncles' generations, they received only rations as their wages. Only rations, ratjina. For papa miri – dingo scalps – would be exchanged huge bags of flour. A 100 pound bag of flour was really big and heavy and would have to be carried on the shoulders. Along with sugar, tea leaf and milk, it was a substantial amount of food. A husband and wife would be needed to carry all of that food but a 100 lb bag of flour was a really big bag that needed a strong person to carry. They would carry a bag of flour like that for a very long way, even from Ernabella to Angatja! They'd carry it along all the way back to where they were camping. The children would see their dad coming along with the bag of flour, 'Look, here's dad with some flour! Here's dad with some flour! He's got a really big bag!' And there would be their father carrying this massive, heavy bag

A dingo scalp expedition arrives at Yulpartji, 1959, to meet the mission vehicle carrying trading goods. Nura was part of this group, riding her camel Ukana. (Photo: Bruce Edenborough / Ara Irititja 9506)

Men and boys prepare to dance the ngiyari thorny devil ceremony, Ernabella, 1940. The body designs were painted with natural ochres. (Photo: Image courtesy of the State Library of South Australia, PRG 1218/34/1243C, C.P. Mountford)

Men and boys dance together at a public performance of the ngiyari ceremony, Fregon, 1965. (Photo: John Fletcher / Ar̲a Irititja 19530)

of flour along! The end of the bag would be sewn shut, and he'd carry the sealed bag along on his back. I clearly remember those days, and seeing Kutjukuru's father carrying great big sacks of flour back to her.

We all learnt how to sing and dance. We would hear the men singing and dancing in the late afternoon, and we'd go over to watch. 'Come along everybody! Inma time! Come and see the inma!' We'd run over straight away, and sit down in the group. We'd never run around or just run past it. We'd run up, join the group, and immediately curl up and hide our eyes. Mother would tell us, 'Pupakati! Bow your head! Don't look! Don't look at the men!' and so we'd bend our heads and not look, until we were told, 'Right, everybody look now!' We'd hear the men start singing together and we'd pop up and look. 'Oh lovely! How beautiful they look!' It was glorious to see and hear the men sing. What a thrill! 'When is the next inma?' The very next day we'd hear, 'More inma this afternoon! Come on everybody, inma time!' and we'd rush up again and again we'd be told, 'Pupakati everyone!' So we'd pupakati, meaning, we'd bow our heads and not look, until the men lit a huge fire with big glowing firelight, and the men would start to sing again. And we'd be told, 'Hello! Everybody can look now! Look now everybody!' So we'd all pop up again and there would be the new inma! We would never dream of saying, 'No, mother, let's just look anyway, let's not shut our eyes!' No way! There is no way in the world we would think or say that! Our older sisters told us, 'Look, you kids, if you look when you are not supposed to, I'll be killed. So don't ever look, okay? If you look, then a man will be sent to kill you. Next time you are by yourself you'll be followed and when you are not expecting it, you'll be knocked on the head and killed.' Do you understand what I am saying? Our traditional way of life was very, very strict, but it was safe.

Sometimes we would hear men's public inma being sung, quite close, maybe 50 metres away, and we would see the preparations and so we'd sneak up on it to watch and listen. It would sound beautiful and we would say, 'Oh, what beautiful singing!' But the men would find us out because their dogs would hear us and they'd start barking and the men would think, 'It's those children sneaking up on us!' So they'd shout, 'Go away, you children! You will learn your own inma one day, when you are old enough! This is sacred business! Leave us be! We are dancing secret men's inma here! If you see it, you'll go crazy for me and you'll fall in love with a man!' This would scare us away so we'd run away, frightened, and we wouldn't go back. We'd only go to the women's inma, which was separate again. It was a lovely way of life back then, with all those strict rules and the gender separation.

We would be allowed to see dances only when they were danced in our home camps. The men would stamp and the women would dance their steps and we would be allowed to watch those public inma in our homes, but we were never allowed to see secret, sacred Law activities. We never went and we were very obedient. We listened and did as we were told. After we'd seen the women's dances, we girls would go and hide to try out their dance steps, and so that's how we'd learn, by watching, listening and learning, and practising. The boys would do exactly the same. Though the dances we did were real, the way we did them was only in fun. Ngalypa-ngalypa, pretend dances. We girls would never dance in front of the boys. It was always separate. Not like today. Today boys and girls do everything together, and nothing is sacred. Back then even the little children danced.

Another one of my memories that comes to me was how I was hardly ever carried around on the backs of my mother or my auntie, because I was always riding camels! I was not carried around by my uncle either, because I would only ride around on the back of our camel. I would only ride on a horse or our camel, which was called Ukana. I used to climb onto its back and ride, while my father rode his horse alongside. My father told me,

Boys dance Inma Wiilu in saltbush near Ernabella, 1949. Wiilu (bush stone-curlew) is a tall bird with a loud call. Wilton Foster (front, second from right) remembers the occasion and the old men singing. (Photo: Frank and Mary Bennett / Ara Irititja 15762)

Girls perfect their dance steps and movements in the hills above Ernabella, 1956. (Photo: Win Hilliard / Ara Irititja 20042)

Two brothers travel with their families from Yulpartji to Nyapari, 1959. (Photo: Bruce Edenborough / A<u>r</u>a Irititja 9510)

'Don't ride this horse – it is too skittery – it will jump around too much for you, but the camel is quiet and safe and you'll be able to sleep on it as you go along.' And that's exactly what I did. I would often fall asleep, head bent down, as we walked along, with me riding that camel. Mother wouldn't ride it though, and she never did.

We were warned to stay right away from camels in case they kicked. 'Don't stand near camels' legs. They kick out without warning'. 'Don't stand at the back of a horse. It could kick you in the heart and kill you'. 'Don't climb big trees a long way from home, because you could fall and break a rib or an arm and a serious injury like that could become gangrenous, so be careful'. You see, there were no planes in those days. No planes. Only Sister Donna was there to help us. So we were always well-behaved children.

We would always be warned, 'Don't try putting your hand into a hollow log to pull out a bird. A snake could be in there and it could bite you and you'll die'. We were always very careful about this when we climbed into trees to hunt birds for meat. We were never bitten by a snake because we took such good care and we were so scared of snakes. We had no medicine against snake bite back then. So we were always warned to take great care of snakes, never be kicked by a camel or horse, or be bitten by a camel or horse. We never put our hands into the tree hollows, because snakes slithered up into the trees too, and would go into the hollows to eat the baby birds, and would go to sleep inside the nest hollows. 'If you put your hand into that tree hollow, you are risking a snake biting you, so don't do it! You'll be bitten, and you'll fall out of the tree and die!' we'd be told. I always thought about that, because I didn't want to die in the bushes, and not able to be found until it was too late! Mother and father wouldn't know I'd been bitten and I'd die alone before I could be rescued! I didn't want to die by myself out in the back of beyond without my mother and father, so I was always very careful. I didn't want mother and father to have to come and find me dead somewhere. I think about my life as a hunter, as a digger of holes in order to dig out meat, and how I was always very careful of snakes, how I was taught how to kill them before they bit me. I never stop being cautious about snakes because they are so dangerous. I never forgot the way I was taught to poke a wili (poking stick) into a rabbit burrow, not only to feel for rabbits inside but to prevent snakebite on the hand. The wili pokes the snake, and the snake comes forward, and if your hand is in the burrow it will bite it. So the wili stick is vitally important, and then we need to know how to deal with the snake, and how to avoid getting fatally bitten.

So those are the kinds of warnings we were given, and we children heeded those warnings, and consequently we were always very careful. At night, we would be told tjukurpa stories about wanampi, liru, and tjangara, and we'd go to sleep with those stories on our mind, and consequently we'd think about them the next day and remember to be careful. I was always scared of a tjangara in the hills seeing me, and catching me and eating me. My auntie used to tell me that tjangara hunt children, kill them, tie them up into a bundle and put them on their heads, to take back to their camp to cook and eat. I always imagined it would happen to me, so I was always cautious, because I never wanted my mother and father to lose me to that. So I stuck to my family and I never went alone in the bush. I used to walk everywhere, but never alone.

How different things are today! Life is so different for the new generations that it is not recognisable anymore to the older people. Everyone has their own ideas and won't listen to anyone else. Everyone thinks only of themselves and does what *they* want to do. Touches what *they* want, does what *they* want. We, on the other hand, would *never, ever* be like that when we were growing up! We would never touch what we shouldn't. Father or grandfather or uncle would kill me if I touched his stuff! We never touched anything of the whitefella's or else we'd be in big trouble. We were always told, 'Take your younger sisters and brothers away from the mission buildings and go and play out in the open! Go and play and teach them games, and look after them! Teach them things! Show them what to do! Don't touch anything of mine! Leave my bag alone!' That's what we were always told, so we always took the smaller children away to the hills to play and learn things. We were always scared of

The blue Ernabella truck loaded with supplies picked up from a train, c. 1958. It was a long trip, but train supplies were a lifeline for the mission. (Photo: Annis Bennett / Ara Irititja 16047)

touching anything that wasn't ours or doing anything wrong. I knew that if I touched anything of my father's I would be killed. So we always played out in the open with all the little children.

But sometimes fights would erupt and we would see the men fighting each other with spears, and we'd see the men spear each other. They'd run the spears right through each other. The fights were always very serious. Men and women would spear each other in the thigh in a big fight. The spear would go into the thigh flesh and come out the other side. Poor things! They would spear right through the thigh. What spears! It was very frightening. We'd never got close to a fight like that. I never would, that's for sure. I was too scared. If you got too close we'd be grabbed and protected. I'd be so frightened of all that blood. I'd feel so sorry for anyone who had been speared or hit, women as well. Poor things!

A fight could erupt if a dog was hit. Say, a woman might hit someone's dog, the owner could swear and shout and get very angry. 'What are you hitting my dog for? The poor thing is probably only hungry! It didn't steal your food, it's still there!' And so a fight would erupt, and I'd always be really frightened.

If someone was very sick back in the early days, they'd have to go all the way to Finke on the blue truck, and be put on the train, and go to Alice Springs on the train. There were no Flying Doctor planes back then. If the children did get seriously sick they would be sent on the truck to Finke and then on the train to Alice Springs Hospital. After they were discharged, they'd have to come back on the train again and they'd be picked up by the truck when the truck was there picking up the loads to be brought back. Although, back then, there was a very small aerodrome of sorts, no planes ever landed there. In those days we only had Sister Donna and Sister Lipuru, who came from overseas, working for us at Ernabella, together with the Health Workers, Mayawara Minutjukur and Purki Edwards. They were the Health Workers working in the clinic in those days. They'd teach the children as well. They started work as big girls and were still working as adult women. They worked for years helping new young mothers, teaching them how to keep their babies clean, and how to feed them good food. They taught the young mothers to feed children plenty of food and porridge. They were good carers for new young mothers and children. None of the children ever got diarrhoea.

Nowadays everything is the new way, and hundreds of planes land there all the time: the Royal Flying Doctor plane; PY Media comes in on a plane; the mail plane comes and goes; and all the Aṉangu patients go off in planes all the time to the hospital, and expectant mothers fly in from the hospital with their children. Some go on the bus, which many people prefer. But we knew nothing of all that back in the early days. Not like today.

Our life was wonderful, living in the bush near Ernabella. I loved it, and I was happy. The early days in Ernabella were wonderful, and it is those days that I want to talk about some more now. We used to go to school in the mornings, and after lunch we'd finish for the day. And off we'd go! We'd go for miles on donkeys, covering great distances to the outlying camps like Donald's Well and Kelvin's Well and we'd hunt for maku and iḻi, and we wouldn't come home until night time. We didn't live anywhere near the white people then. We didn't live near their buildings. The whitefellas would already be sleeping, anyway, because they all worked so hard. We would be off hunting all day, right up until the night time, out hunting and gathering iḻi and kulypurpa, and we'd be right up in the hills, hunting meat. The nyiiṉka would always be out hunting, and they'd bring their meat back to give to us. We'd all have our own portion of meat to eat. We would be collecting kulypurpa, and we'd call our older brothers over by name, and give them kulypurpa, and they'd be calling us over to give us their meat. We'd also give them water and figs, ngapartji ngapartji. We were all so happy. The boys would give us meat and we girls would give them maku and all the figs we'd gathered. The sharing made us so happy and excited. It was lovely.

Every day we would bring some food to our older brothers. I would bring food for my older brother as often as I could, and it would give me much pleasure to do so. I'd take him some food, or fresh water, or tea, and I'd give to him and then I'd come back home straight away. I wouldn't stay with him very long. I'd come back straight away, because you see, he was a tjitji nyiinka and he was not to be around females. He was in semi-seclusion. So I'd take him food and come back right away, and leave him in his young men's camp, which is called tawaritja. I would give the food to my uncle to give to him. We never were allowed to play around where they were, because the men didn't like it, but that is the proper way of life and is how it should be and it is a good way. Today, life is any old how, and everyone's all mixed up, and also sad about it, everyone feels like something is wrong, nothing is quite right anymore. But back then, it was a lovely way of life and everyone was happy.

On Saturdays, we would go to the mission buildings and at the school we'd all be given bags to pick up the rubbish in. We'd all be picking up the rubbish until everywhere was clean and tidy, and when we'd finished we'd be called over. 'Children! Come here and line up!' We'd all line up, and then we would all be given our rations, which were small amounts each of tea leaf, sugar, and tins of milk, not powdered milk. After we received our rations we were told to run along. 'Off you go children, and no hanging around the buildings during the weekend! Do not hang around here during the weekend!' And so off we would run. Our donkeys were never very far away, so we'd grab our donkeys and off we'd go! We would go to Kenmore, which is a long way, or to Balfours Well, or to Possum Well, and we'd camp there overnight with our donkeys.

Our donkeys were lovely and quiet. They'd carry us everywhere! The men would even use them to go hunting, and when they came back with a kanyaḻa, they'd bring them home on the back of a donkey! They'd ask us to help with the hunt too. They'd tell us, 'Children! Mount your donkeys and ride up the side of that hill, and chase the kanyaḻa down off the mountain for us to

spear!' So we'd ride up the side of the mountain, throwing rocks and calling out, and the kanyala would rush away from us, down the other side of the mountain, where the old men were hiding with their dogs and spears, and as they came closer they'd all be speared. Nobody had rifles back then. This was a long time ago when the men were still hunting with spears. They would send their spears into the kanyala and we'd be up there cheering! 'Hello! Father has struck meat!' 'Grandfather's hunting dog has got one! That's our meat now!' It was great fun. The meat would be cooked and we'd be called back down again, 'Nephew! Here, come down here and get your meat!' and we'd all be given a large joint of the cooked meat, like a large thigh or a hip joint. We were given large joints of meat as payment for our help with the hunt. We'd love to get these big chunks of meat because it would mean a real feast of delicious meat. We would eat a fair bit of the meat before carrying the rest back to our homes.

And so we learnt. We learnt how to hunt and dig and get our own meat. We learnt how to survive and how to feed ourselves. We learnt how to dig out rabbit burrows and how to get meat — real meat — real, solid, life-sustaining meat. Proper meat. We were taught how to dig properly in order to sustain our energy so we could keep going until we got the meat. We could hunt and feed ourselves when we were children. We loved it! We'd be so proud when we caught our own meat! We were happy, obedient, compliant and participatory.

Mostly we kids would go a long way away with our donkeys, camping out anywhere, any way and we wouldn't come back until Sunday. We'd go all that way out and then turn around and come all that way back, on our donkeys. Off we'd go, as fast as we could, because the next day was Sunday and it always came around very quickly. We would have to be back for church on Sunday, because we were told, 'If we don't see you in church on Sunday, your father and mother will not qualify for rations. I will not be giving them any rations'. This would always scare

A hunter returns to camp with a bundle of cooked dingo pups. The ears and tails have been removed to claim the dingo scalp bounty. (Image courtesy of the State Library of South Australia, PRG 1218/34/1458, C.P. Mountford)

Nura's brother Kawaki (second from the right) and friends head out of Ernabella for a day's excursion to Wamikata, 1958. The enormous tree in the background was a popular spot to collect ripe figs. (Photo: Bill Edwards / A<u>r</u>a Irititja 13033)

us and we didn't want to be responsible for them missing out on rations, so we'd come right back for church, and we'd all go together, mothers, fathers, grandmother, uncle, grandfather and aunties would all be in church on Sundays. When church was over, they'd all be given their rations, and then they'd take the rations home to camp. We were never allowed to stay around the buildings, or throw stones at the buildings, or pinch anything, or take anything from the garden, because the whitefella mayatja had eyes in the back of his head and he never missed a thing. He kept a close eye on the mission buildings. So we always kept right away, and we were never allowed anywhere near the vehicles either. We were all very well behaved and honest.

Come Monday at school, anyone who was seen would be told in no uncertain terms, 'You were seen on Sunday, hanging around the buildings, and you were seen close to the vehicles, because you were sneaking into the garden to steal the tomatoes. Your mother will not be receiving rations now, because of you. She won't be getting any rations'. If that happened, we'd all be desperately unhappy for her, because we knew that is exactly what would happen. We were always terrified of breaking the rules for this reason. If we'd had money and could have purchased our own food then it wouldn't be so bad, but we didn't have money back then. If a child was caught red-handed in the garden, then on the Monday at school, his or her parents would be called in and told, 'Your child was caught stealing from the garden,' and then that child would be spanked in front of the parents. The spanking would be hard, and it hurt. We were always terrified of it, and so we would always try to go as far away from there as we could.

If I missed church on Sunday morning, because I might have been out in the bush, and if I missed church then my mother and father would not be given any food. My father and mother wouldn't get any food, poor things! They wouldn't get any food if I missed church. That Ron Trudinger was a tough man. He would say straight out to the wati fathers in Pitjantjatjara, 'Hey! You fellow! If I find your child hanging around the houses on the weekend, then you will not be allowed to get any mai. You won't be given your flour!' So if anybody hung around the mission houses on the weekend and were found making a big noise, then he'd say, 'I had no sleep, with all your noise. Why don't you take your child away out in the bush and teach her things? Take them away! Go away and teach her singing and dancing! You older sisters should be teaching the younger ones, so you can practise for when you are parents yourselves! Teach her things! You boys! You should be out there dancing with your older brothers, fathers, uncles and grandfathers, dancing their culture! You should be out there following in their footsteps! But if you stay here and hang around these houses and if you throw stones at the sheet of iron, then you are bad. That is a very bad thing to do. And don't pinch anything from the garden! Don't you go pinching tomatoes, watermelons or rockmelons, because if you do you'll be going to jail!'

The policemen were tough, and they'd act straight away. Mr Trudinger was a very strict teacher. He would not tolerate theft of any kind and children would be spanked on the bottom for pinching something. Only the boys were spanked, not the girls. Never the girls. But the boys would get a real hiding! Rodney Brumby got a right old walloping, and Pantjiti McKenzie's old husband, he got a good hiding too! Lionel and Tommy Manta, they both got spanked! They were shouted at, 'Your brother is like a dog trying to get into that yard! Don't go into that yard!' And they'd get a good hiding for it! This is a true story! He really did that! But he was teaching us. That was his way of teaching. Our early superintendents were very good people, though. Our earlier community advisers, store managers and teachers were all very good.

We never hung around houses. We were always so busy off in the bush. Nobody ever stayed in the community or in the sight of the whitefellas. Nowadays nobody has any shame and does what they like in front of white people. So whitefellas see this and form their own opinions and think things to themselves about us, wonder what our children are up to, see us throwing stones at houses, hear us screaming and shouting, see all our problems. Back then, nobody had any problems or made any trouble. The whitefellas always had a nice quiet weekend,

A<u>n</u>angu teacher Nganyinytja and Bill Elliott at the outdoor Ernabella school, 1951. The children were only allowed into the mission complex for school. (Photo: Source Museum Victoria, Richard Seeger, 1951/161)

because we were always gone from the community. Only when school was open did we come into the community for school.

On Mondays we would go to school and if we had been seen looking for birds' nests we'd be told off, 'Hey, you children! Hey! Last weekend you were all very naughty. Don't touch those birds' nests! Leave them alone! Don't damage them or throw rocks at them!' You were throwing stones into the yard. You were throwing stones at birds. Why? Why do you kill those birds? They are only just birds! Poor things! Leave them alone! You can't murder those birds for nothing! Don't kill those birds! Don't swear at those birds! Don't you go about swearing! Birds don't swear at you! Birds don't steal food from you! Birds eat their own food!' That's what we'd be told in no uncertain terms. I clearly remember being told these rules. I learnt to keep away and look after the kids.

One time, me and two other small children sneaked out and ran away from Ernabella, and we walked all the way to Kelvin's Well. When we arrived we found the old lady Ampintangu and her husband had just been out hunting, and were just returning with some meat. One of the children I was with was Ampintangu's daughter, and I was bringing her back to her. Ampintangu said to her daughter, 'Daughter, come and sleep here in our camp, because the men are about and you are going to be killed by them if you don't come inside now!' So, all three of us slept there and we were told, 'You children stay right here and don't go anywhere! And daughter, you stay right here and

Children on a school picnic at Itjinpiri rockhole, 1950. (Photo: Frank and Mary Bennett / Ara Irititja 4866)

don't follow those big children again, or else you're going to be bitten by a snake! So stay home here!' The next morning I got up and said, 'Hey kids, come on, let's keep going! Hurry up! Let's go to Kenmore!' and so off we went, heading for Kenmore, me and those two other kids! When her mother came back to camp she saw that her daughter had run off again! 'Where have those children gone now, for goodness sake?' She looked around and she saw by our tracks that clearly we had left again. 'Those kids are heading for Kenmore!'

Meanwhile, we walked all the way to Kenmore. We arrived at Kenmore and we sat down there in the camp. I went to my uncle's camp and found my uncle sitting there, and I told him I had walked there, but Ampintangu had followed us and had grabbed the other two and had taken them back with her, while I was able to stay put. However, the next morning the whitefella came out and got me and I was taken straight back to Ernabella School. So there I was, back in Ernabella.

Another time I sneaked away secretly again, by stowing myself away on the back of Frank Quinn's truck. Frank Quinn was the whitefella who went to and fro between Finke and Ernabella with the store loads. I hid on the back of his truck and I rode to Mulga Park, but when he stopped to open the gates, he saw me and he told me off, 'You are a very bad girl for sneaking onto the back of my truck without telling me! What are you doing that for? You should tell me if you want to ride on my truck! So what are you going to do now then? Are you going back to Ernabella?' But I said, 'No way! I'm not going back there! I want to find my father and mother!' 'Well you are a very naughty girl for sneaking on the truck like that! Bad girl!' He nearly put me off the truck right there and then, but I started crying too much, so he relented and let me stay, and he took me on to Mulga Park. I suppose I should have asked him for a ride, but I didn't. I just got on that truck without asking.

We were taught the ways of our families and kin, how to live properly. So, we lived great lives of love, care, learning and teaching. We hunted and were always full of good food. We heard and learnt from great stories. We were never neglected or left behind.

We were not allowed to gamble. The men would be told, 'You are a bad man for gambling. Stop it! You must come to church! You are not looking after your mother and father!' This is what would be said to the young men. Anangu used to have a very good way of life and the young men did not play around the camps. They lived separate lives. Their lives were secret. They went to sacred sites and they were warned to not sing out publicly. We girls were warned to keep things secret as well. 'Don't let them find out,' we'd be told. 'Don't damage the Law. Keep yourself clean and healthy. Follow grandmothers' Law. Be careful'.

My kami Napatjari was wonderful! She would cuddle me in her arms and tell me great stories, especially women's stories and women's Law. I would listen intently to these stories, and think hard about them, and then I'd ask questions. Oh yes, I would ask questions! How, why, how, why? I was told, 'You stay with your auntie, stay with your mother, stay with your older sister – always live with your older sisters – and learn the Women's Law.' Being women together, in that way we would learn, and in that way we would always be healthy.

4. Travelling the country

When I was still a child we all lived with our fathers and mothers in the ilytji; that is, the bush or the scrub. We would go hunting for dingo scalps and my father and mother taught me many skills. We would travel to many places and I was taught about the land. Grandmother and grandfather also taught me a lot. They told wonderful stories, and we always had plenty of meat and food, which had been hunted and gathered from far and wide. At night everyone told stories of what had happened, until we fell asleep. My father had many wonderful stories too, and we listened and learnt.

We would all go on holidays together, and nobody would be left behind. Everyone would go, and we'd all hunt together and then make one big camp together. We were always together, because we were all related; our togetherness affirmed our relationships, and we'd always enjoy each other's company greatly. Nobody ever camped separately; they'd always camp near each other, especially their mothers and fathers. Everyone shared around the meat, and nobody ate by themselves; we'd always eat together. We'd eat kangaroo meat, euro meat and rabbit meat. We'd love to see our big brothers arrive back in camp with the meat. Donald's uncle would arrive back in camp to join up with his group and all their children. It was a lovely way of life. Seeing all those photographs on Ara Irititja made me so happy. Seeing them and remembering them gave me so much pleasure. I can picture those happy days in my mind still. It brings me joy, can you imagine? We lived such happy lives then. It was wonderful.

Back then everywhere seemed so lush, with beautiful plants and beautiful grasses, such as ipiri. Tragically, everywhere we look now is smothered in buffel grass. Everywhere is covered in buffel grass today, but back then there were beautiful grasses and shrubs, ipiri and tjilkala and wangunu, kaltu-kaltu, kunakanti. Everyone foraged for food amongst these grasses and plants when they dried out and the seed ripened. And they'd grind the seed and we'd eat the ground seed. We'd be taught which ones were good, and if we weren't familiar with the ones we were eating we'd be shown them, and they would be explained to us. This is how I learnt so much about food plants and all of our beautiful flowers and blossoms. I just love flowers and blossoms so much, and I remember how many there used to be. I wish everywhere would bloom like that again. But I don't think it ever will again, because buffel grass has choked out too much of the land now. Buffel grass is a tjanpi maliki to us — a strange new grass.

We were often taken around to visit distant places, shown the waterholes and told their names, and we would be reminded: 'Never forget this place. You must remember all these places when you are grown up. Don't forget'. We were shown Palpatjara (a big creek just outside of Ernabella); Alkala (on the Kenmore road); Kalikali (near Turkey Bore); and Ininti. These are all lovely and important places, which we were taken to and had explained to us. It was wonderful to travel to these places. We were also taken to Wamikata; Tjukula; Alalka, and Itjinpiri. We know all those places now. They are our places. We would travel to the north, and to the south, to Aliwanyuwanyu and to Kunma Piti. Then we'd go north to see Alilitjara. We would go to Atarka, to a place named Atarka. We would go to Ngarutjara and visit those areas. We would go to places in between, like Tjata Unngutja. We were shown Tjata Unngutja, and had the name explained to us and told all the stories. We were shown everywhere, and told all the fascinating stories associated with each place. And so we learnt.

We had donkeys and camels to ride. My mother had her own camel. Just the one! My father had one camel and two horses. I would ride the horses, and my two older sisters would ride the camel, and my mother would lead a donkey. Everyone had an animal to ride and we'd travel around like that. So we'd all be going along, riding donkeys, camels and horses, going on holiday around the piriyakutu (north-westerly windy season in September). We'd always walk around at piriyakutu, and it was always lots of fun. Sometimes we would want to go much further, and so that is exactly what we would do, we'd go far, far away, walking to Angatja. My older brother Leslie didn't walk to Angatja though, he didn't go; Leslie Mingkili didn't go. He stayed home and my daughter looked after him, because she loved her uncle. She knew what to do. She'd go and visit her

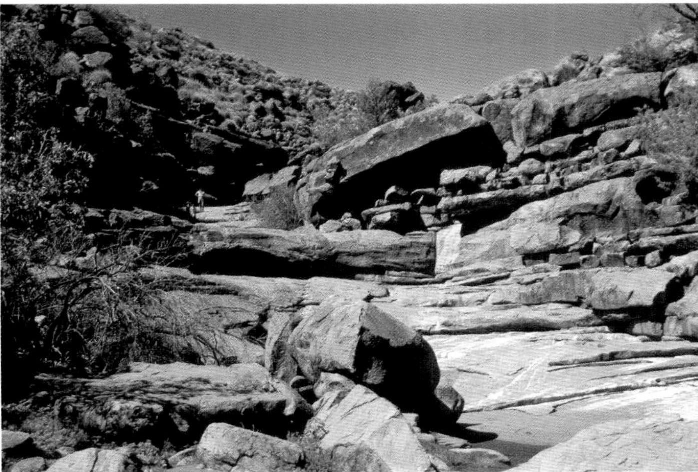

Nura's father taught her the location and name of important sites and rockholes. Kalikali, seen here in 1962, was one of those places. (Photo: Margaret Bain / Ara Irititja 37031)

older brother as well. But this does mean that she doesn't know the Angatja area quite so well as I do. But everyone knows the country and all the places in it, and they know who is related to whom and who is related to what country. So everyone lived a contented life, and there was no sadness. Everyone shared meat and food, nobody was hungry. Everyone reciprocated with meat and food. There was plenty for all, food, tea and meat, and other foods, and we'd all have our share. On another journey we walked all the way to Wingellina, so we could visit my old mama tjilpi, old Eddy. I remember us walking all that way to visit his dad, and what a great trip that was, and how well he looked after us. My big sister Anmanari Alice Wilupara Nyanitiya – Fairy's mother was with us that time. She wanted to go and visit another of our fathers. She was just like Miltjitjanu, exactly like him, short! They looked so alike! Father and daughter.

We used to go on long holidays every year, as we always did, during the piriyakutu season. All the families would spread out into small family groups and went away travelling in their own particular directions. Small family groups would travel around their own country, as we did. Our relatives took it in turns to take the younger ones, and we'd move around, living with all our relatives at one time or another. I did that, and I would go on a journey and I'd stay with a relative, and then I'd be returned to my own mother and father. This worked well when my mother and father had work and were very busy. They actually loved to work, and they were hard workers! My father knew how to ride horses and he could put on quite a show, riding horses in a really fancy style, rikina way! He would look handsome on a horse!

We would travel east to the Kenmore area and go to Alkala to camp, where there were a lot of kangaroos. The men had their own hunting dogs, and they'd set the dogs onto the kangaroos who'd be hiding in the thickets, and the dogs would bring them down for us. They were ferocious dogs, and a great help with the hunting. The men would bring the fresh meat back to camp for roasting. It would be cooked and shared, and we'd feast on that delicious meat. This was at Alkala. Come late afternoon, we'd all be settled down and that's when the storytelling would start. The first ones were the alpiri, speeches focusing on where we were going to next and how we were going to get there, and the hunting and gathering strategy along the way – say we were going to Glen's Well. The older people would tell funny stories, or pretend stories about the travelling way of life. We would fall asleep to the sound of storytelling.

I learnt who my entire extended family was, who all my grandfathers and grandmothers were, and I also learnt a great deal during the early morning alpiri speeches, and the early evening speeches. 'Tjamu, tell us a story! Tell us a story!' So we'd all gather around him, and he'd tell us a story. We always listened intently to the stories, and slowly we would get too tired and eventually we'd fall asleep. That was lovely, to go to sleep to the sound of stories like that.

We children were very obedient, quick to understand and do what we were told. The stories we were told would be all different sorts, some were purely historical; others were eyewitness accounts of some event that our grandparents may have seen. Other stories were more like 'once upon a time' fairy stories, just like your grandmother may have read to you. We believed everything that was told to us and we would laugh at some of the stories too! The same with inma. We would laugh all through some inma and we would be astounded at some portrayals in

A school picnic at Wamikata, 1958, still a favourite place today for picnics and games. On this occasion a cricket match is about to start. (Photo: Bruce Edenborough / Ara Irititja 9539)

the inma, like Minyma Kakalyalya, for instance. 'Poor thing! Why is that happening to poor Kakalyalya?' and we'd be told, 'Minyma Kaa<u>n</u>ka beat up Kakalyalya!' This happened because they shared the one husband between them, and Kakalyalya and Kaa<u>n</u>ka had a big fight. What a terrible story! We'd worry about the poor things in that story!

Grandfather and grandmother, and my older brother and older sister, could all tell wonderful stories and talk about history, and relate the Law to us. Grandfather Tjamu, in particular, was a brilliant storyteller. I couldn't get enough of them! He'd ask me, 'Granddaughter, did you listen to my stories, then?' 'Yes, I was listening to you!' 'That's good!' That is what he would say. 'Listen then, all you children, and I'll tell you a story!' So he would tell us a story during the night time. He would tell us stories about anything: about the stars. We would ask him, 'Where is the Seven Sisters, the Kungkarangka<u>l</u>pa?' He would answer, 'Just look up and see that small cluster of stars there!' 'But how did they get up there?' 'They once lived on earth and then they left the earth behind and flew up into the heavens, and there they are now, living as stars.' He would tell us great stories about the Kungkarangka<u>l</u>pa, but when we became women ourselves we learnt a whole different set of stories about those Seven Sisters, and we would dance and sing women's-only songs

At a theatre production of *Ochre and Dust* in Adelaide, 2000, Nura tells some of her life stories. (Photo: Heidrun Lohr / A<u>r</u>a Irititja 128891)

A father rests with his children after a day's hunting, Ernabella, 1949. (Photo: Barbara Bills / A<u>r</u>a Irititja 4790)

A man looks after his children. (Photo: Image courtesy of the State Library of South Australia, PRG 1218/34/1304, C.P. Mountford)

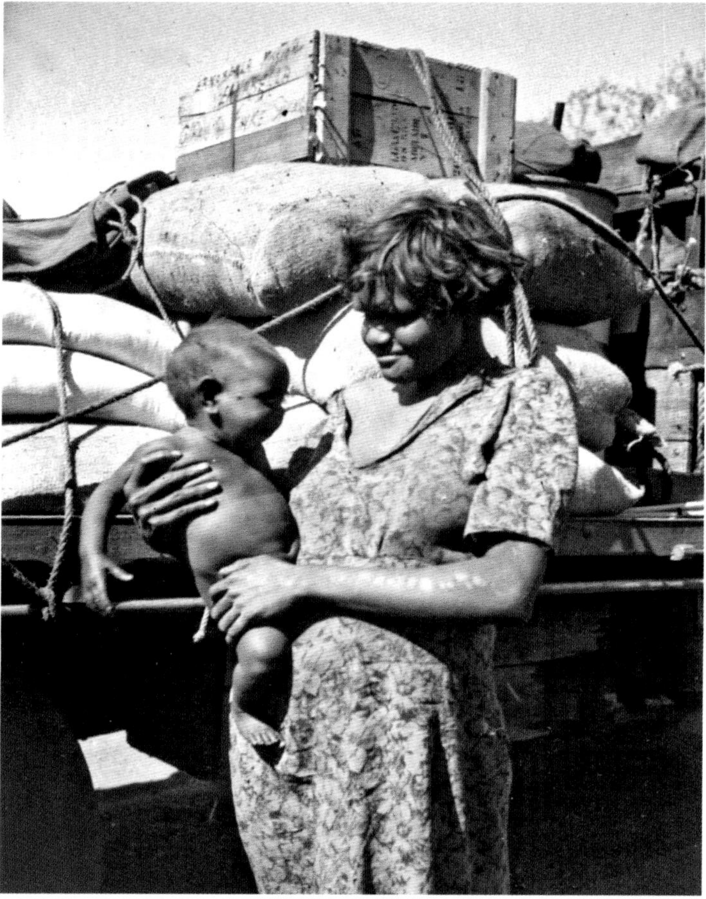

Anmanari Alice Wilupara, stands next to Frank Quinn's truck holding her son David, Ernabella, 1949. Anmanari passed on her knowledge of bush medicine to Nura. (Photo: Frank and Mary Bennett / A<u>r</u>a Irititja 12929)

and dances about them. They are beautiful songs and dances. I love them.

Ku<u>t</u>a. Kangku<u>r</u>u. Ngunytju. Mama. Tjamu. Kami. Grandmothers' Law is very beautiful. Grandmothers speak plainly and authoritatively. Our grandmother told us wonderful stories that were both educational and entertaining, and so we learnt a great deal from her. Without this, I would have become a sick and ill person. But I didn't, because of the care that was taken of me by my grandfather and grandmother.

So this is the type of life I have led. A life listening to the daily public addresses of a<u>l</u>piri from both men and women. In the morning we'd all get up early, and we'd receive instructions for that day's hunting. The senior men would tell us children, 'Climb up to the top of that mountain there, while us old men go around to the other side and wait at ground level with our dogs. We'll set our dogs onto the game, and we'll have our spears ready too! We'll stay here with the pre-initiate boys while you big girls take the young ones up to the top. Take good care of the little ones, mind you, and teach them about things as you go! Stick together and make sure they don't fall off their donkeys!' So we'd go up to the top, chase the game down, and then descend, and then later, sure enough, we'd see the old men coming back to camp with the game meat bundled up on their heads. They would have set the dogs onto the meat and speared them, but they wouldn't cook the meat there. They'd bring it back to camp, so it was always a good sight to see them arriving. We'd always be excited!

You know how the cockerel will crow every morning? Well, a<u>l</u>piri is just like that – it has just the same timing. Men calling out to the whole camp, just like the cock's crow: 'Good morning everybody! Now hear this! Is everyone awake? Is everybody listening?' 'Yes! We are awake and we are listening!' 'Right then, listen up! This is what we are going to do. We are all going hunting today. We are all going to such and such a part of the bush and we are all going to rendezvous at such and such a mountain. Everyone is to go to such and such a mountain. Everyone is to go up to the top and chase down all the kanya<u>l</u>a, the hills kangaroos. Everyone must chase them down to ground level and then sic the dogs onto the younger ones. Everyone must go up to the top of mountain first. The older brothers must help their younger brothers. Older brothers, you must look after your younger brothers. Climb up in pairs. Don't go alone and don't leave any young ones unattended, in case anything happens to them. Go up together and watch out for each other, work together as a team. Stick together because if one of you goes to the side and is bitten by a snake, the other could be going along and not know one of you is in trouble, and will soon be sitting down, and soon after that, lying down, and then, the inevitable will happen, following a snake bite'. That is the sort of thing that will be said publicly during alpiri, followed by the women saying much the same sort of thing.

The women will be addressing the group saying things like, 'When you are digging holes, don't go putting your hands straight into the hole. You are bound to be bitten on the hand by a snake before too long if you do that. Use a wili, poking-stick instead'. This is what the women would call out, and everybody would hear it. We would listen and the messages would sink in. We always heeded these messages and instructions. Everyone would be included in these public addresses first thing in the morning. Everyone in the camp would be awake and listening intently to the news of the day. Everyone would be listening and be ready to carry out their instructions. Everyone would appreciate what was being said, too. 'What he is saying is true. I agree entirely with what he is saying'.

Young people of today have not been handed down the old teachings. Women's sacred Law has not been taught. Women's Law, culture and stories. In the past, *all* women passed down the teachings to the younger women. Everything was kept strong and cohesive. It was beautiful. Their grandsons and granddaughters were strong and responsible and beautiful. They were beautiful and good. They listened well and learnt strongly. Their mothers and fathers lived harmoniously and had productive lives and their children were the same. The fathers were strong father figures, and they were powerful men. The mothers were strong women, powerful women, in a womanly way. They taught their children well, and passed on their skills properly. The fathers were the same, teaching their sons everything they needed to know to be strong. It was a good way of life. The men would make spears and give them to their sons. They'd also make miru — spear-throwers — give them too — well, no, not miru, but nganamiru — their first training spear-throwers and with these they'd train their sons in the art of spearing. 'Spear that. Right, now spear that emu as it comes past. Stay hidden. Don't stand up and allow yourself to be seen'. They'd practise like that, trying it out and getting it right. They'd keep at it for a long time until the real thing. Then the day would come when a boy would spear something for the first time. He would have proper grown-up spears, and he would be spearing successfully.

A man teaches boys to make weapons, Ernabella, 1937. (Image courtesy of the State Library of South Australia, PRG 214/45/B96, J.R.B. Love)

Today of course, we have rifles. The rifles are fired and animals are hunted and brought back. Nobody does it the traditional skilful way. Nobody digs rabbits any more. None of the younger people have any of the traditional skills. They were brought up in the age of petrol sniffing and drinking alcohol, and all those modern things. They all drive cars, they are all car-drivers, driving along, music blaring, speeding up the roads, listening to music. They never hear the natural sounds of the bush. They have radios stuck to their ears, or they are listening to music on the tape recorder; they have lost the art of listening. All they hear is the noise of music and cars. They've all got these things stuck to them and their heads are nodding up and

(Left to right) Tjariya, Charlie and Nura: older girls played a big role in the care for younger siblings. (Photo: Richard Seeger, Annis Bennett / Ara Irititja 18979)

down to the beat of the music. Their heads are filled with this racket and they are consequently damaged because of it. Even their thinking is different. Meanwhile, their younger siblings are in the store buying sweet things and eating things loaded with sugar. Rubbish stuff, rubbish food. It makes me so sad.

Every community today is filled with rubbish things. Everything is rubbishy. Every place is rubbish and every thing is rubbish and our people are completely impoverished. Everyone's lungs, hearts, brains, kidneys, liver and every other organ has been damaged. The children get tired too easily, and can't do anything for themselves anymore. They are lazy. Hopeless. Children today go, 'Can't do it. Don't know how to. Don't want to. Not interested. Can't climb mountains. Too tired'. I feel like saying, 'Well stay hungry then!' I wish children would participate more and *do* more today. Just think of the mountains they could climb! They don't know about kanyala. They never go up into the mountains to see those animals. They don't know where to go and where not to go. They are all too tired and bored nowadays. All the children are diabetic and feeble nowadays. Everyone is diabetic and alcoholic. Poor things. All the children are addicted to lollies and sugar. Nobody eats good food like we did. There is no good food available. Everyone's got sick kidneys, lungs, liver. Everyone bumbles around slowly. Most people live half their life in hospital, alone and separated from family. Families are not cohesive. Nobody has any get-up-and-go or mobility. Nothing. Everyone's a mess, sick and tired. I feel sorry for everyone. Everyone's driving cars around, bludging petrol money, puffed up and arrogant, caring only for Number One, not doing anything for anybody else. Everyone's having car accidents and getting killed, or committing suicide, losing their lives from car accidents, hanging themselves, dying from marijuana, alcoholism, and accidents. All families are suffering endless grief, and a massive human tragedy has been visited on our people.

Despite everyone's best intentions, we have failed in our upbringing of today's new generations. We have failed to pass on the traditional teachings, and consequently the young people of today know nothing. Our older sisters' teachings were not taught, and our grandmothers' teachings were not taught. Our older brothers' teachings were not taught and our grandfathers' teachings were not taught. The boys of today know nothing. They've just cleared off, knowing nothing, hiding away and living their own private lives, going their own way, with all their new ideas. 'Oh, I think I might knot this rope and hang myself'. They do not hear the voices of the birds singing.

How different this is from the energetic and participatory way we lived! Some of the old men are trying their hardest to keep the good old ways alive, by telling the old educational and cultural stories. 'Come and listen to a story!' 'Coming! Wait! We are coming to listen! Lovely!' They love sharing the old stories and making each other laugh. Some of the old stories are so funny. The men have their stories and the women have their stories. We grew up hearing those stories, which were told to us last thing at night. They were great stories and I loved them!

Now back to what we did on our holidays. We'd hunt around Donald's Well and other places, where the hunting was good and there were beautiful lush plants and grasses, wildflowers, clean soft sands and beautiful weather. The piriya-kutu weather is always abundant, especially if it has rained earlier, and it is the season for witchetty grubs and plentiful meat. The women would go digging rabbits, and would get many, and us young girls would be watching and learning as we helped. We'd gut and cook the rabbits and feast on the meat, and then later the men would come back to camp with kangaroo or euro meat bundled up on their heads.

From time to time, some men would come back empty-handed, but there was always plenty of meat to go around because we were all hunting and contributing to the meat and food. We were completely contented and secure in that way of life. There was absolute co-operation with everything we did.

We would also hunt around Gilpin's Well, because it was an abundant place and there was water and lots of ironwood trees exuding edible gum. Us children would climb the trees for the gum. Sometimes we'd be told, 'Come down you children! Don't eat it too dry! You'll choke on it! Bring it down and grind it up properly, before you eat it!' So that's what we did. We always did what we were told, regardless of our age — child or young woman.

We little children stayed with the older girls, and they'd teach us all about digging out rabbits and how to open them up properly and gut them. We'd gut our rabbits, then pierce them through the ears with a strong wili stick, and carry them back to camp on their carrying stick. We'd call out to the others, 'Get a fire going and let's cook these rabbits!'

We had all sorts of animals travelling with us. We had camels, donkeys and horses. We would dig maku. Maku are found in all sorts of different plants, and during piriyakutu we'd dig them out of the stems of tjilkaḻa shrubs. Tjilkaḻa are those round roly-poly plants. We'd pull them up and ease the grub out of the stem.

Meanwhile the men would be hunting with spears and they'd be roasting kanyaḻa on the fire. In those days one or two of the men even had rifles, but most were still new to it. Most men hunted with spears and spear-throwers. They'd go to the kangaroo areas with their hunting dogs, and spear or club the meat after the dogs had brought them down. They were really expert at this. It was great.

In ages past, with kangaroo hunting, the old men would spear the maḻu, bring it back and then somebody else would cook it. Someone else would cook the kangaroo and the hunter would give out the meat. The cook would not eat the wiṯapi (spine portion of the kangaroo meat), though. Of course, he could eat the wiṯapi section, but not this time. He'd eat the two feet, or the tail, or a little part of the lower back. The man who cooked the meat would only eat those parts. The man who did the hunting, the spearing, would get nearly all of the cooked meat returned to him, and he would then have the pleasure of handing it all out. Each special portion of meat would be given to a particular person. He would call out people individually by

A young girl expertly guts and prepares rabbits for cooking, Mann Ranges, 1969. (Photo: Noel and Phyl Wallace / Aṟa Irititja 43180)

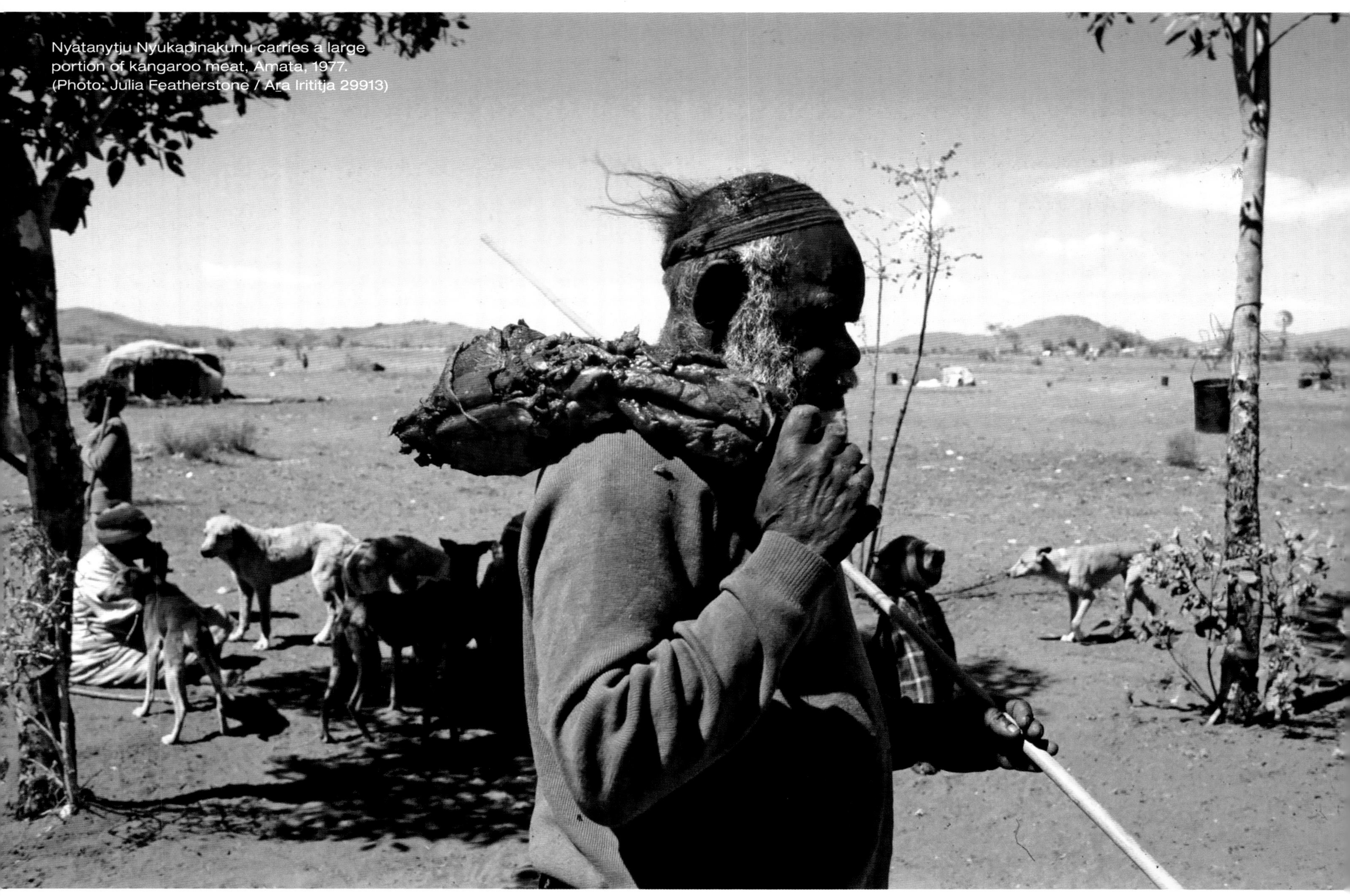

Nyatanytju Nyukapinakunu carries a large portion of kangaroo meat, Amata, 1977. (Photo: Julia Featherstone / Ara Irititja 29913)

name, and they'd come up for their specially assigned portion of meat. His relatives would each receive a particular portion of meat, according to who they were and what their needs were.

Not today though; now the hunters go out any old way, in any old car, shoot what they can, and then bring it back and those who are around might get some of the meat. If you happen to be standing around you might get some, adult or child. There is no polite waiting until your name is called out, and the correct piece of meat given to you; no waiting to see if your name is called out and the thrill of going to get your assigned piece of meat. It used to be that if your name was called out, you'd be the one to go forward to get your meat. I remember waiting for my name to be called out. We all did, we all had a chance to be called forward to receive the portion. You'd be listening out for it, and if your name was called out you'd be so happy! 'How lovely! I've been assigned a piece of meat! I'm going to be the one to bring the meat back and share it out!' because the meat portions are big, and are shared out between a lot of people. Everyone would receive some meat from the one kill and everyone would sit and eat their meat together. Nobody ate their meat alone. It was always something that everybody did together, children and tall girls, too, everybody.

Let's say there might be some children who'll be waiting hungrily, but their fathers will be sitting nearby thinking, 'Oh no, I didn't get any! I missed out! We're sitting here hungry but I didn't get any, and I can't give any out'. The father will feel bad about it, and then he'll get angry, because his children will be hungry. 'Why didn't you give me a portion when you can clearly see that I have hungry children here?' He'll get really angry about it, and he could end up spearing somebody over it. 'How come you just gave the meat away to the people around you and not any to me when you can see my hungry children waiting?

Jeannie Ampintangu, Anne Karatjari, Nura and Tjikalyi take a drink at Arkala waterhole, 1982, with friends Beth Mitchell and Ali Beale. (Photo: Beth Mitchell / A<u>r</u>a Irititja 123376)

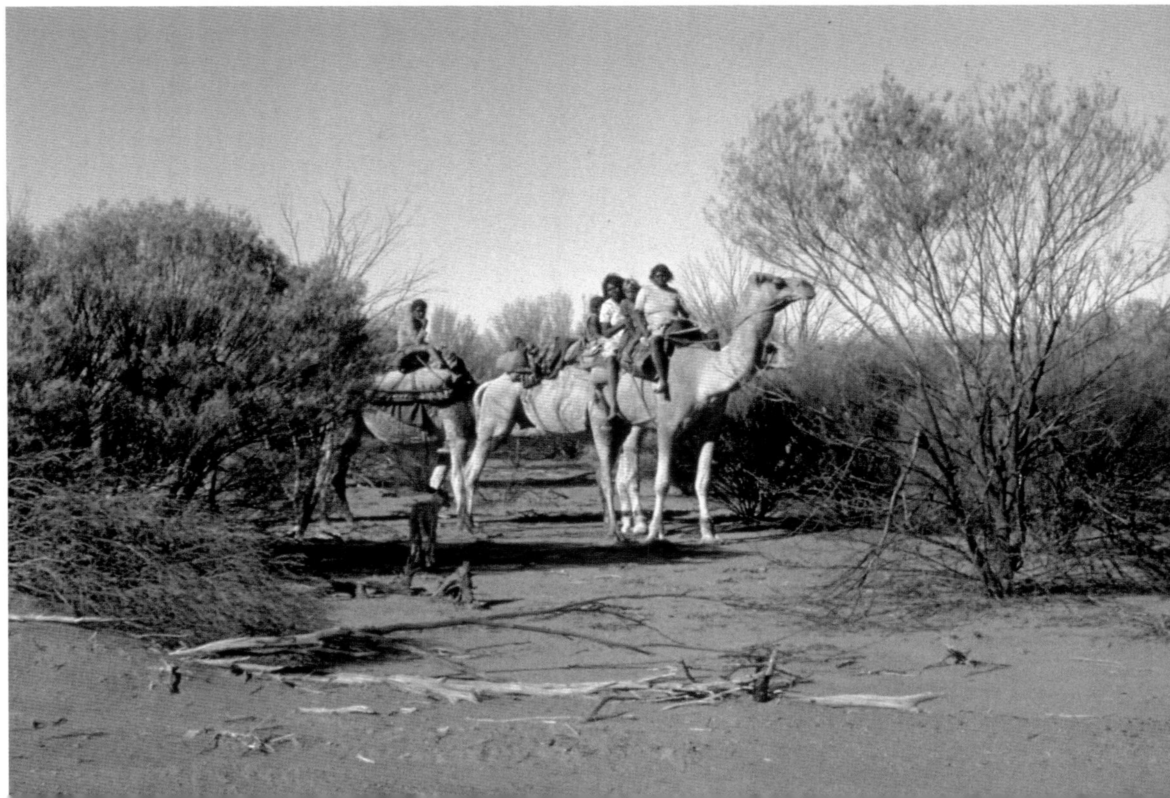

Nura and her daughters ride her camel Ukana in country around Ernabella, 1965. (Photo: Aileen Johnson (Jennings) / A<u>r</u>a Irititja 6651)

You must see that I am in need here. ' He could well spear the man just like that, or hit his wife, even though they would be his relatives. It would be, 'You gave meat to your wife, and your mother, and your grandmother, and your older sister and your auntie. What about my hungry children too? You should be a bit more considerate to those around you. Surely you must have seen me sitting nearby, hungry and waiting for meat?' He'd be sad and frustrated about it, and he'd start a fight over it. The Law is that serious. It is an important aspect of our Law. We had many laws like that.

There was so much lush green growth back then. The women would go along and be exclaiming, 'Oh my goodness! Just look at all the kunakanti grain! Oh, quickly, let's harvest it and singe it dry!' So that's what we'd do. We'd all be there harvesting the grain then all sitting together preparing it by singeing and toasting, before setting off again for Kenmore. We'd go via Pailka, where we'd stop, because of the big waterhole there. There was a big karu with a big tjukula and a number of smaller warku (rock hollows full of water). Kangaroos and rabbits would come here to eat grass and drink water. There were abundant tjala (honey

Nganyinytja and her mother Nyuringka Nyunmiti prepare kunakanti (grain), 1967. The result is a delicious paste, like peanut butter. (Photo: Noel and Phyl Wallace / Ara Irititja 41222)

ants) here too, which we'd dig out in great quantities. We would move along between all the different warku and look for food.

One time I remember my father checking out where an emu had been drinking. 'An emu has been here, look, this is where it stood to drink. Right, you women, get the children and make them go to sleep in the windbreak!' Then he and another old man climbed up into a tree, while us children were sent off to be very quiet in our windbreak home. We all lay down quietly and had a nap, so the men could listen out clearly for any signs of the emu coming. They had to be very careful in case the emu saw or heard anything. The men hid up above the waterhole and waited for the emu to come up and drink. They speared the emu while it was drinking, driving their spears downwards into the meat. Finally we children were woken up. 'Children! It's okay, you can come back now! Come here and look!' That is what they always did, they would always shout out if they speared something. My uncle had done the spearing! Amantari's father, that is, had speared the emu, and had followed it to where he'd caught up with it and killed it. We were calling out, 'Uncle got the emu! Uncle got the emu!' And there it was, the big bird carcass. They said, 'Well, here it is, poor thing! And look, there is the spear that got it!' And there was the spear that had killed it, which had been broken and pulled out. He'd bundled the big bird up, and carried it back to us.

He and his brother-in-law had started to prepare the bird. They'd plucked all the feathers out and gutted it, with its two enormous thighs and its thick layer of fat. Emu fat is called kanpi. They let us look then told us to go away and play and not to hang around them. 'Off you go you children! Don't hang around here!' They always said that – as it is the Law. The men's Law. So off we went. We had to get them a piece of wood, a bit like a shovel but what we call a warika. We call it a warika, and it is their way. They use two warika to move the hot coals around in the fire pit when roasting meat. But we were not allowed to stay around to watch. 'Off you go, children! You are not allowed to stay here!'

We were hungry and thinking about that meat, so we were excited when we were called back. Oh, and that meat was roasted to perfection! Properly roasted meat is called tangka. So tender! So delicious! We were all given a portion and we chewed on the delicious meat and kanpi until we were full and satisfied. This is how we lived back in those days. We killed our meat with spears; in fact, all large meat animals were speared by our skilful hunters.

A flock of emu at Walannga salt lake, 1994, a popular site for hunting emu. (Photo: Stewart Roper / Ara Irititja 75242)

Everyone was fed with this bountiful meat, and all the children had plenty to eat, and everyone was well fed and content. Where there were two waterholes, this way of getting meat could be done using one waterhole, while people drank out of the other. They'd drink only out of the one that was safe to drink from, while the men speared meat using the other one. In this way plenty of meat would be available. Sometimes the meat was just speared.

Nobody does this anymore though. Everybody hunts from cars now, and the animals all run as soon as they hear a car engine, which means that they get chased in cars and shot with a rifle if the car gets close enough. Children of today have a very limited experience of wild-caught meat, and definitely no experience of kuka walkalitja. They wouldn't even know what it is. Not very many people even know what walkalpa is nowadays.

A hunter carries an emu back to camp for cooking, Mann Ranges, 1940. (Image courtesy of the State Library of South Australia, PRG 1218/34/1204B, C. P. Mountford)

Girls played for hours with milpatjunany (storytelling) in the sand. (Photo: Source Museum of Victoria, Richard Seeger RS ER 1949/368)

Our forebears lived like this. They knew how to live well in these lands, in the days before us, and the older ones would teach us these techniques of healthy survival.

Well after my mother and my auntie were full up from that emu meat they went off for more rabbit meat. I went with them, and I got two, two little ones. When we got back everybody was singing. While we dig out burrows we also sing. We sing as we dig, children and all. We would dig with our hands, anything, and the whole family sings.

Anyway, it was soon time to depart, and we left for Ulalpa. We were guided there by one of the oldest men, who knew how to get there. When we got closer he warned us about the bullocks, and the white men who owned them. He told us that the white men would shoot at us to make us run away from their bullocks. So we had to make sure we skirted around the bullocks, in case one of our dogs bit one or chased one. There were fences as well, and we had to be very careful.

By this time we had eaten all the emu meat up, so we were without meat by this time. Two women went and dug out honey ants and shared them out. We had a lovely feed of honey ants. Later, two young men went ahead and speared a ngintaka. There were numerous ngintaka in that area, and those two men brought back two ngintaka that they'd speared. We were pleased, 'Excellent! Look what uncle has brought back! Two big fat ngintaka!' The ngintaka had a big layer of nyiti fat on it. Nyiti is ngintaka fat. They were cooked and shared out.

Next, we moved on, one group following behind another, walking in lines behind one another, and then fanning out at an angle, taking shortcuts. We travelled on into an area rich with blossoms and flowers: punti inunytji, the cassia and senna blossoms, kurku inunytji, the mulga blossoms and tjulpuntjulpunpa, the wildflowers. It was beautiful and lush with ukiri, which are the green grasses or green growth. What a magnificent place! Anyway, we set the dogs out to hunt for us. They were ferocious, and quickly helped my father bring down a kangaroo. He gutted it and pinned the stomach hole back up again with a tipinpa (that's the word for a sharpened wooden stick) and twisted off the legs, then put the stomach bits off to one side, and brought the uncooked kangaroo back to us. That's what those old shepherd men used to do, bring back fresh meat to cook back in the camp. We had so much to eat! Honey ants! Kangaroo meat! Kampurarpa!

Some of the men decided to go and hunt down dingoes, and followed their tracks. We went on with two camels to the waterhole for water at Ulalpa. We'd had a lot to eat, first the ngintaka and then the kangaroo, and don't forget we'd been travelling with that emu meat as well. That was typical, to travel with a supply of meat. We had emu, kangaroo, rabbit, ngintaka and any meat that *could* be carried *was* carried for the children to eat during the day, to keep them happy and well fed. Another thing we were fed on as we were travelling was maku lunki, which is a type of cossid moth witchetty grub that would be drawn out of their holes and fed to us as we went along.

Anyway, we camped near the waterhole, but at some point we said, 'Hey? Where are those two men? They aren't back yet!' They'd been following a pack of young dingo pups into the sandhill country and had killed six, and were still on their way back through the sandhills with their six dingo pups. We were lying down resting, when we heard them coming back. We were camping at Tiil. Later, the men went out again, and picked up more tracks and followed more dingoes, while another group of men went in a different direction. This time they came back to Tiil with five dingoes.

Some men were really good at getting dingoes, whereas my uncle was best at getting kangaroos. He was a kangaroo man, and a great hunter! Anyway, those men got all those dingoes and brought them back and shared them out between us all. Another typical thing that was done – they all swapped their kills. They were returning late in the evening, so they camped just before they got back to Tiil. We knew where they were because they'd kicked up dust. They camped in the senna bushes near the rocks. They'd also got another ngintaka, got it out of a shallow burrow, clubbed it, speared it and cooked it.

Anyway, at some point somebody said, 'Hey, look, our tea leaf is finished, and our flour is getting low. Let's go!' So we moved on. We came to the bore where an engine was running. That's what they did at bores – run an engine; it pulled water up for the bullocks. That's where we all met up with the others again; we were all back together and shared tea to drink, and the meat we had. The dingo skins were shared out, five each, or five and five per group, making ten. There were plenty of dingoes around and we all got some, each group. So we'd all be more or less equal. That's what we always did.

We had lots of meat to eat, particularly rabbit meat at that place. My goodness me it was a lovely place! Itjanu everywhere! Verdant, lush growth as far as the eye could see and fat animals! Lovely! So there was plenty of meat to eat. We met up with another family group. Nura Rupert was in that group, and Iyawi Wikilyiri. Iyawi was only little then! We found each other by following each other's tracks. They'd been to the north. We had dinner together and then all began returning home, via

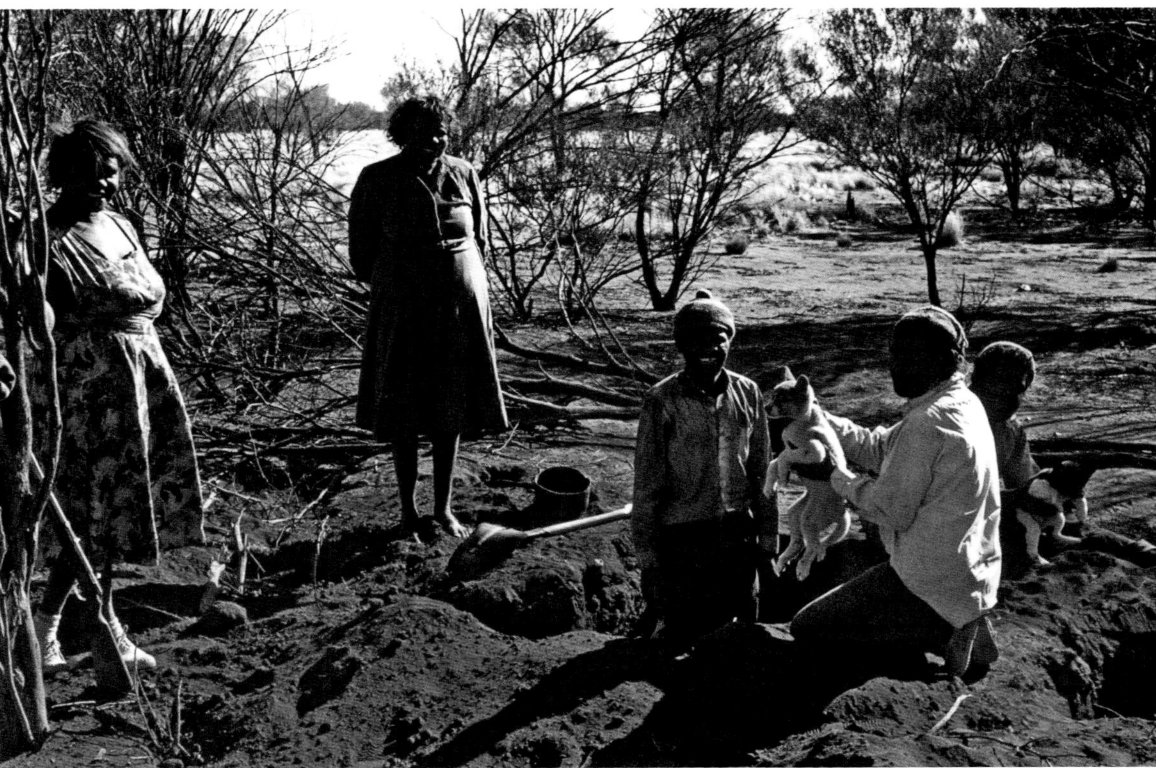

Dingo pups were dug out of their burrow, killed and eaten, but occasionally kept as pets, Amata, 1969. (Photo: David Driver / Ara Irititja 57634)

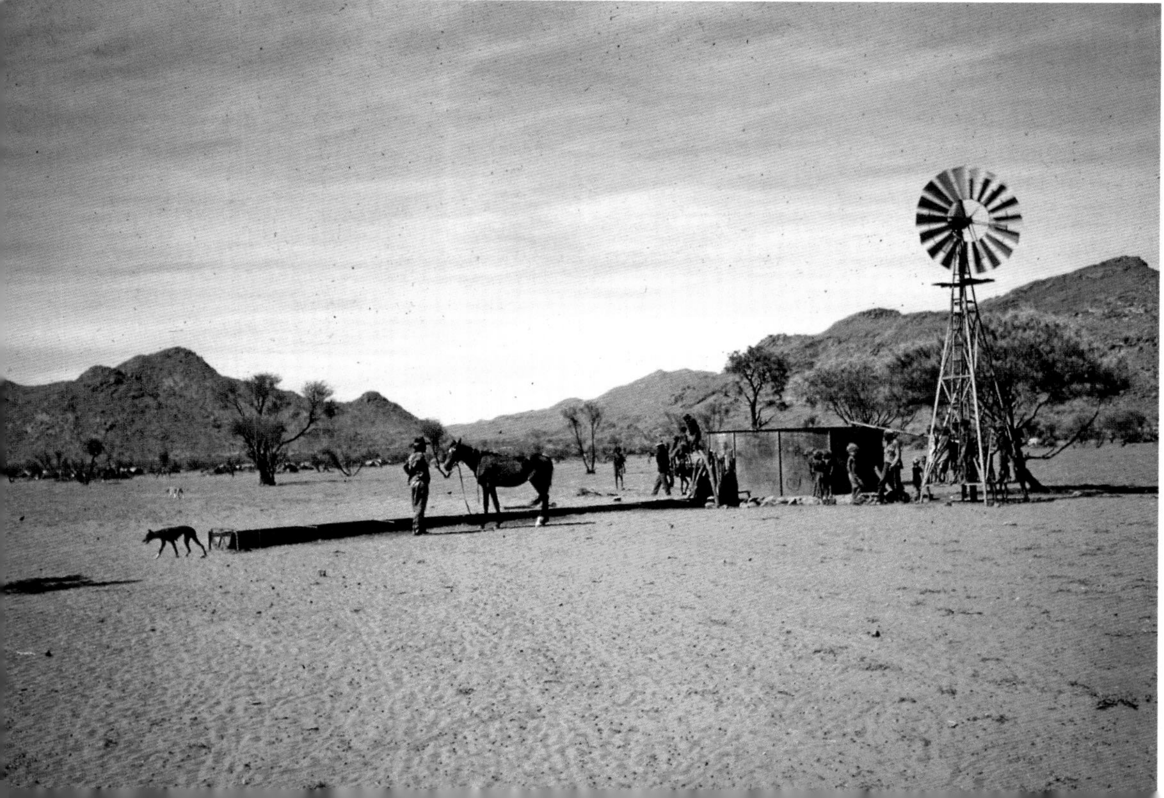

Aeroplane Well and then back into Ernabella. What a lovely time we had! We were all so happy and content, well fed and coming home laden with dingo skins to sell or trade. So that's what we did when we got back and it enabled us to buy flour, sugar, tea leaf, milk and all sorts of things. We were well off then!

Our old grandfather and Amantari's grandmother had stayed behind, and we went back to their camp. They'd been busy spinning wool to sell and had been getting rations in return while we'd been gone. They would sell the wool to the craft room. All the oldest women had stayed behind, and had been spinning wool in their windbreaks. They'd been drinking goat milk as well, as there were lots of goats at the time. We arrived at Ernabella and I started to go to school then. It was such a long time ago now! My mother would go and get a big bag of wool and she joined the spinning group, spinning up the wool. We were all back at school and it was fun to be all back together again, so healthy and happy after our holidays. There were some horses and I would watch the men break them in. We'd climb up onto the high rocks and watch the men come in; the horses would all be bucking around, all around this area.

We just loved going on holidays in the cold weather on camels and in the piriya season. We loved the piriya time, and also the hot time, particularly if there were lots of flowers blooming because we all loved flowers. We had walked back through so many flowers that our feet were black, completely black! And they looked great too!

Also, we had learnt so much; we had been instructed and told so many stories that our minds were really active and vibrant. All of us children were the same. We really thrived on the input and being taught so much, and we enjoyed learning all the Tjukurpa. We would be all pulled into line and reminded

Older ladies spinning locally grown sheep's wool for the Ernabella craft room, 1958. Nura's father and mother are seated far right. (Photo: Bruce Edenborough / Ara Irititja 9557)

A bore and tank at Wamikata Bore, 1960. The establishment of bores and tanks in the Ernabella and Musgrave ranges meant water for families travelling with donkeys and camels. (Photo: John Fletcher / Ara Irititja 12813)

of what we'd been taught. 'You children! Remember what was said! Do you remember?' 'Yes! We remember what we were told!' We were told all about hunting, the young men especially. They were told how to track and where to hunt up meat and dingoes and all the smaller animals that young people used to hunt. Nobody had cars then! There were no cars at all! None of today's paraphernalia! The only vehicle we ever saw was the food truck. That same truck was used to purchase the dingo skins off us as well. So that was good. We loved getting those goods in return, especially the sugar! Oh dear! If only we'd known then what sugar would do to us later in life! Poor innocent things we were!

One time my grandfather Louis Wirultjukur went to Coober Pedy, and he came back here with his own Landrover. He was the first one in my family to own a truck. He was a bore sinker. My family were so surprised! Then he got a green truck and he brought that one back. He had two. A red truck and a green truck – a Bedford. We were thrilled to go riding in a vehicle! The whole family got to ride in it: mother, father, and everyone else, every weekend. We'd go out for weekends or overnight camps in this truck. We'd go to Kunma Piti. We'd go to Ngatun to dig maku. We'd come back, go back out camping, come in, then go back out again. I was just a child. Not a kungkawara. I was still only little. You know the photograph of Kawaki and I – it was that time – when we were all little children together.

I am going to tell another story about a long time ago, when we were travelling away from here, from Ernabella. Many years ago when I was a kungkawara tjukutjuku, I walked three times to Warburton and back to Ernabella with my mother and father, and Pantjiti McKenzie, Ruby Williamson, and two brothers, Larry Nelson and Tjiwiri Dan Nelson. We used to call Larry Wati Wara because he was tall. Dan Nelson was a wati wiru mulapa, a good man. The two brothers were teaching us about their country as we walked through the Mount Davies area.

We left Ernabella and set out. The next place we came to was Donald's Well. From Donald's Well we left again, this time walking with a larger group of people who wanted to come as well. We changed our route and went along a different route – iwara kutjupa – because we had all decided to attend an inma.

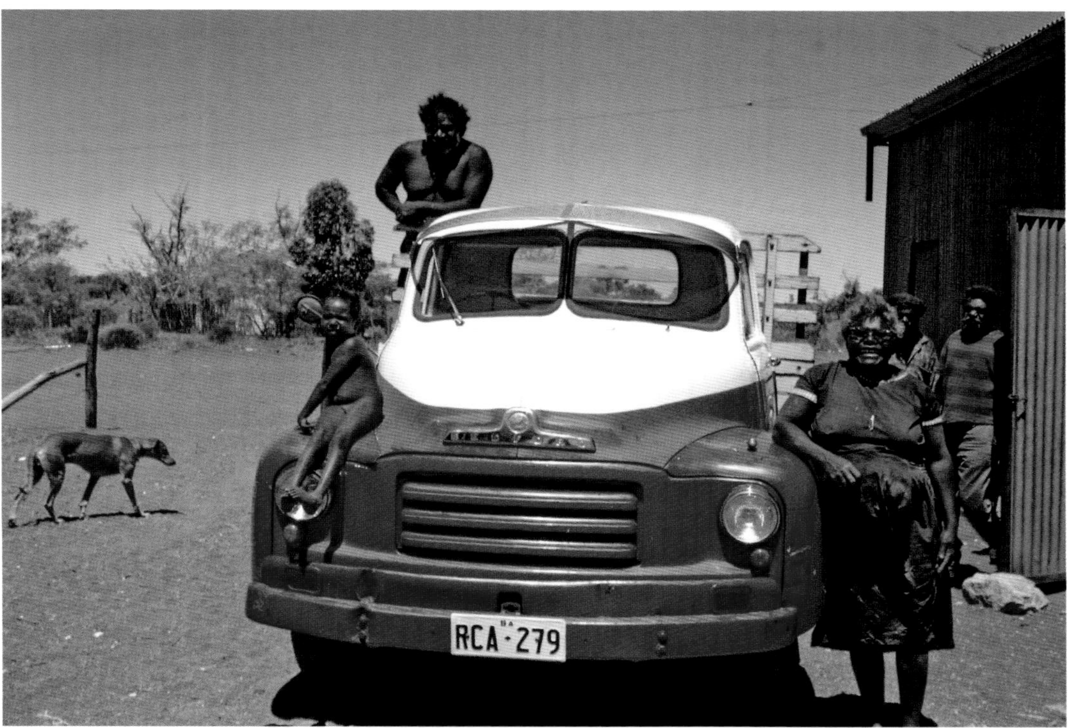

Nura's grandfather Louis Wirultjukur stands on top of his red and white Bedford truck, Fregon, 1969. He was the first of his family to own a vehicle. (Photo: Joan Stell (Nielson) / Ara Irititja 19811)

Inma Kurangara. We were travelling to this inma. Everyone who wanted to come joined us, and we travelled along as a large family group. We kept going, continuing on our way as one mob. We were travelling with donkeys and camels and horses. We came to Mulga Park, and from Mulga Park some people split off to go and hunt dingoes for their scalps. They were hunting the younger dingoes, the baby ones, so they could get their scalps for the bounty. Afterwards, they rejoined our main camp at Mulga Park.

We based ourselves at Mulga Park for a while, until one day a white man arrived, who worked there; he had been away to Wingellina Mining Camp and Blackstone Mining Camp, where there were a lot of white men working as miners. There was mining near Pipalyatjara and Blackstone back in those days. The man asked us if we were walking all the way to Warburton, and we said yes. He had a motorcar, and he offered us a lift to the other side of Blackstone in his motorcar, so some of us got a ride with him but my mother said no, she was going to ride her donkey there. So she rode all the way to Blackstone on the back of a donkey! She was coming up behind us on her donkey, with the others in the group. My father, however, travelled with me and many other kungkawara, including Mutitkali Ruby Williamson, Pantjiti McKenzie, and Karilyka in the motorcar with the whitefella, as well as another old man's mother and father.

We arrived at Blackstone Mining Camp, and my father got some work there with the miners. We stayed there then, waiting for the others to arrive, camping near the mining area, and going out hunting for meat every day. Local men were living there, and they were hunting every day. One of the local men was Pirpantji Nelson's father, Tjiwiri Dan Nelson, along with two of his brothers, all three of whom are Pirpantjiku mama — they are all fathers to Pirpantji. They were full-time hunters, living on their land, and providing for their family. Pirpantji's grandmother was living there also, as well as his kuntili Mayara. Pirpantji's father would walk to Blackstone on a regular basis, to that big high sandhill this side of Blackstone.

One day when he was hunting on that big, high sandhill half way between Mount Davies and Warburton, he spotted a kuniya python. 'Hey, a kuniya has gone into this hole here,' he said, and he called out to the others to run quickly to see the kuniya, 'Hey, quick! Come here and help me catch this kuniya!' They dug out the hole, digging deeper and deeper. They ended up digging out three sets of burrows until they found it curled up in the bottom. Pirpantji's father — he was still only a young man at the time — seized the kuniya and pulled it out. As he was pulling out the kuniya, it spat at him. Kuniya do this. It looks like vomit, but it is a kind of spit: wita we call it. Pirpantji's father was still gripping the kuniya, while it was spitting up, in the hope that it would be released. This is why they do it. But Pirpantji's father was confident and tenacious and held on tightly. The others were shouting, 'Hey, what a beautiful big python! This is great meat!' He curled it up and carried it back to camp on his head, where a fire had been made in preparation. I was looking at this huge snake, because I had never eaten kuniya before, and I was thinking I would refuse to eat it, but I was firmly told that there was no other meat to eat, and I had no choice. It was true. There was very little meat to eat at that time, there was no dingo puppy meat, nor ngintaka meat. All our familiar meat animals were very scarce at that time. There were no malu, nor kanyala either. Of course, there were plenty of malu and kanyala in other distant areas, but none in that particular area at that particular time. Any kanyala would have been on the mountain tops anyway. I was told that kuniya was regularly eaten and it was good meat. It was my first time eating kuniya and I liked it. Taste wiru! I never forgot what they taught us, those two brothers.

It was very dry around the region, with ailuru (drought conditions). Even then, we still travelled and lived in the area, but some people were suffering. There was very little meat to eat. We have a few animals that we refer to as ailuru kuka — or meat that is available during ailuru: kanyala, waru, kuniya and tjala. Euro, rock wallaby, woma python and honey ants. Kangaroo, malu, are not ailuru kuka. Malu go a long, long, long way away during ailuru, yet our hunting men would still walk a very, very, very long way to hunt them. They would tell us children, 'No, on this occasion you cannot accompany us. We must go a very long way and stalk a kangaroo for hours and hours until we can spear it and bring it back to you to eat. You must all stay home and wait until we bring the cooked meat back to you'. They would be gone for a very long time, if they were hunting kangaroo during ailuru. Yet kanyala will stay on in the rocky outcrops and on the tops of mountains and will survive any drought; in fact they'll be fat! They have the ability to eat tjanpi awilyura and tjanpi tjiri, which are huge, tough spinifex plants, and thrive on it. Waru is the same; waru are rock wallabies that have very long tails. They might be small but they are born survivors and good meat too! Kuka wiru! Tjala are everywhere in the mulga forests, and will survive a long drought. We can always eat tjala during a drought, along with kuniya. Python meat is good meat.

And so we still travelled; we have the ability to survive drought conditions. Full-blown drought can kill though, as we found out later; the poor people south of us, around Kata Aḻa and Piralyungka, were suffering terribly from a severe ailuru.

We stayed in that area for so long that my dress wore out and split open right down the back. I had no idea what to do, so it was suggested I try and mend it. 'Go over to the whitefella camp and ask them if anyone has a needle and cotton you can borrow.' So off I went to the whitefella camp. One old man was there – Ebony Sylvia Benson De Rose's father – and his wife, Kanytjupai, Sylvia's mother – and he gave me a needle and cotton. He was working there on the mining site. We were camping nearby.

Taking my needle and cotton back to the camp, as I was nearing our camp, I saw some donkeys and camels arriving. My mother and all the others had arrived at last! They all moved into our camp and settled in, glad to be reunited again. In the next few days it started raining hard, and it got very cold. We were all very cold, so we decided to shift camp and move towards Blackstone (Papulangkutja), to a location named Wiṯapi Waṟa. This is Kanytjupai's traditional homeland. We made our new camp here for a few days. We'd decided to keep going, because there were so many dingoes in this area, that there would be good returns with the bounty on so many skins.

So we stayed here, going out on regular hunting forays to get papa miri – dingo scalps. We were all busy and occupied and had no time to be homesick. We were a long way from home, but we were happy to be there, and nobody had any thoughts about wanting to go home or anything, even Kawaki, who was still quite young. He had plenty of friends to play with, because there were a lot of other children there.

After some weeks, we decided to continue heading west. So we set off and walked to Jamieson, traditionally known as Mantamaru. We set up our campsites at Mantamaru and it was here that the inma started. The songs that were sung! Oh, the songs! The songs were incredible! Many of the songs were new to us, so we were fascinated to hear them.

There are some big hills near Mantamaru; one of the biggest is named Wirkura. We made a new campsite here at Wirkura, and it was here that Wally Dunn's younger brother was born, right there. My father told everyone that a new boy had been born. To everyone's surprise, a second baby was born in the same place! Pantjiti Cooper – who's now a very old lady – also had a baby boy! Who would have believed that two baby boys could be born at the same time in one camp? I was Wally Dunn's younger brother's kami, so I helped to look after him, carrying him around, and cuddling him, keeping him warm. I looked after him really well. But it was terribly cold at that time, really freezing cold, and very sadly, Pantjiti's baby boy died. It was too cold and wet for a tiny newborn baby to survive. This happens sometimes in the desert. Everybody was crying and weeping for the loss of the poor little baby, and sharing Pantjiti's grief. We stayed there for a short while grieving, as anyone would, but that afternoon we were told we were all going to move on and leave that sad place behind.

So we departed, and set off walking west. We walked until we reached Warburton. The Warburton people knew we were coming, and so many of them had walked east to meet us, and to walk along with us for a while. Someone brought us some rock wallaby meat and someone else brought us some possum meat. Waru and wayuṯa meat – rock wallaby and possum meat. My mother knew all about possums and she had already been hunting them for us, and we had been eating wayuṯa as we travelled. My mother knew the intricacies of hunting possums: how one had to scratch the tree trunk and call out 'Shhh! Shhh! Shhh!' She'd say, 'Yes, it looks like there are definitely possums hiding in here!' So she'd dig them out, cave in their hiding place, and grab the little possums and pull them out. Baby possums are called witjitji. She'd pull out witjitji, kill them, and cook them for us. Oh my goodness, the taste of young possum is delicious! Wiṟu alatjiṯu! We would eat every last little scrap of this delicious meat, before continuing on our journey west.

Somebody had given us another camel, and we were all riding together on the one camel, mother, father and us two children. There were other camels and many donkeys coming along as well, in one large group.

It continued to rain heavily. It was difficult, but hunting had to continue. There were more kangaroo and rabbits as we went west, and the men hunted them with spears every day. In the middle of the day, when we had stopped and made camp, the men would come back with kangaroos that they had speared, big cooking fires would be lit, and the meat roasted. Everybody would have enough to eat, and we'd all feel satisfied with full bellies, which is a good feeling. Sometimes, after a big feed, we would keep going. We were all well fed and nourished and so we were all very happy and content. Nobody had any thought of how far away we were from home. We were happy to be where we were, and enjoying our journey so much.

At last we arrived at the big watercourse that flows through the Warburton area. We made our camp there, and then we walked into the area where the buildings were. Arriving at the mission, we were greeted by the white missionaries, and our names were written down. The Warburton people, though, greeted us in their particular way, by singing songs and calling out, 'Shhh! Shhh! Shhh!' and waving leafy branches around. We had never seen anything like this before, so we were watching in awe as they sang and danced.

That afternoon, everybody began to build windbreaks and great piles of firewood in preparation for the inma. When the singing began we joined in. But the rain kept falling. It was cold. We returned to our campsites and tried to get warm, but the rain was falling very heavily. It was a Saturday, and on the Sunday, the minister came and called in on our camp. He was Mr Wade, and he had been out at Warburton Mission for a very long time, and he was already an old man. We didn't know him, of course, but the locals did. As he walked past our camp, we asked the locals if he was the famous 'Hallelujah' man, and we were told that, yes, indeed, he was Hallelujah. 'We've named him Hallelujah,' they said. 'He sings like this, Hallelujah, Hallelujah, Hallelujah, Mount Calvary, Hallelujah, Amen'. The old ladies told us how they went to church together, regularly, so they could hear him sing, and how they were learning the songs. There were a lot of people living in Warburton in those days. Young men and young women were going to school there, and their families all lived there too.

The rain continued to pour down, all day Sunday and all day Monday. On Monday a plane flew overhead. Ron Trudinger was in that plane, and he had flown over to come and visit us and see how we were getting on. The plane circled all around, but on seeing all the water and floods, had not been able to land. It had almost landed, but seeing the airstrip covered in water, it had gone back up and had to return to Ernabella. It just couldn't land. Later on, he telephoned Warburton Mission to let us know that he had landed safely back in Ernabella. Remember, this was in the days before radios, so we didn't know it was Ron Trudinger at the time, but we found out when we got back to Ernabella. Ron had flown out to see all the school children.

The big inma that had been sung had been learnt by our families, and it was intended that we take the song back home to sing, which we did. Kurangara is the name of that inma. After that, it was time for us to return home. On our homeward journey we made a big camp at Wayuta Piti, which is Jennifer Mitchell's father's place. We slept there for quite a while. Rama Sampson's mother, who was an older lady at the time, joined us there. When she arrived, she was carrying her child on her back, giving him a piggy-back ride. Tjangala's mother and father were there also. Rama's mother is my kami. She had been hunting rabbits and she came in with four, and immediately set about cooking and sharing them. Another old lady cooked a number of rabbits as well. Rama's mother gave me some good rabbit meat to eat.

There were four of us kungkawara travelling on that journey. We were always hunting wayuta. As we passed each itara tree, we checked it for signs of resident possums. If we found two or three itara trees growing side by side, the chances were great. My mother and father hunted possums all the time.

On our return to our home country, a terrible thing happened to father's kangaroo dog. My father had a big kangaroo dog, who was long and lean. He would bite kangaroos that father had speared, and bring them down for him. He was a good hunter. An old man had speared the dog dead, mistaking him for a dingo. He'd seen the dog off in the distance and speared him. Oh dear, he was father's foremost hunting companion, that dog. My father came upon the remains of his scalped dog. He was furious and upset. He started shouting and shouting at the old man who had done it, but my mother implored him to stop it, 'Stop it! Stop it! Don't! Don't! He's an old man!' The old man had scalped the dog and just left him, and my father was devastated. 'Don't! Leave him be! He's just an old man!' pleaded my mother. But my father still hit the old man. 'That was my dog! That was my own kangaroo dog you have killed!' he shouted. 'You have speared him!' The old man had five dingo scalps, which he tried to give to my father, as compensation. But my father said, 'No, don't worry about it. I am a working man and I am able to find paid employment. I can make my own money. You keep your scalps for yourself and earn yourself some money'. The old man was terribly ashamed about what he had done, and how he had killed a man's hunting dog for its 'dingo scalp'. Poor thing!

We camped there for a while, and then we kept going on our journey homewards. We came to Sylvia Benson's mother's place at Patjinitjara near Blackstone. She was living there with her white husband and she was expecting a baby. When we arrived at Patjinitjara, a vehicle was departing from there to drive to Mulga Park, and so we got a ride the rest of the way to Mulga Park.

On the same vehicle, there was a group of thin and bony people. Nyurka-nyurka. The poor things were terribly emaciated; they were skeletal. They had come up from Kata A<u>l</u>a, where there was a serious, life-threatening drought. I was as thin as a bone when I came back from that walk to Warburton; I was nyurka-nyurka, but not starving. Pirpantji Nelson's grandmother and grandfather had been at Kata A<u>l</u>a, but they were doing alright; they were not too thin. At Mulga Park, flour was being given to starving people, and it was to this place they were being taken.

On arrival, the flour was handed out and everybody was rushing to make dampers, so that they could eat something. We were very hungry too, so we were also anxious about getting some flour to make a damper to eat. Once cooked, everybody gobbled up their dampers, stuffing them in our mouths, but

Nura's much-loved Musgrave Ranges were walked by her extended family and ancestors. (Photo: Stewart Roper / A<u>r</u>a Irititja 75200)

A senior man tests the straightness and accuracy of his traditionally made spears and spear-thrower, Amata, 1977. (Photo: Julia Featherstone / Ara Iritija 29924)

it did nobody any good because the white flour and baking powder in the dampers made everyone's stomachs blow right out, and cause awful stomach cramps. It was painful and horrible. Kura.

We stayed at Mulga Park for quite a long time, until it was time to return to Ernabella. We went back in another motorcar. Later, some camels from Mulga Park arrived at Wamikata, and the men started work there clearing the ground for a big inma. Everyone wanted to hold a big inma there. During this time four senior men came to Ernabella to collect more people. The inma was a big attraction and hundreds of men, women, young men, young women, and children left Ernabella to go to Wamikata. Everyone went!

Ron Trudinger was asking around, 'Hey! What's going on? Where has everyone gone?' He was told, 'Everyone's gone to the inma.' Ron Trudinger was astonished, 'No! There's no inma! If anyone wants inma there is plenty of inma here in the church! Why has everyone left and gone somewhere else for inma!' But we all went, and camped there for that night. But Ron Trudinger arrived and he told everybody, 'Come on you lot! Get back to Ernabella immediately! You children, you should be back in school in Ernabella! And you parents – you nanny-goat keepers – you should be back in Ernabella watching those nanny-goats!' He was furious! He singled me out in particular: 'YOU! You are a tjitji karangki! You are mad for inma! You only want inma! You are always going off with the adults chasing inma!' He told me off so much! 'Are you a senior man?' he yelled, 'Is this your inma? Is this your inma here? Is this your mother's inma? Did they bring you here? Are they happy you are here?' He yelled and shouted at me, in the same way that a senior wati would shout. He was particularly angry that school children should be there at that inma. But, everybody who was there, every single Ernabella resident, wanted, more than anything else, to be there at that inma. There were literally herds of people there, all gathered like herds of bullocks. It was a huge event. Not just people, but camels and donkeys too. Everybody wanted inma. We all wanted to be there for those special nights of inma. They wanted to witness the Inma Kurangara. But we school children were told off severely for being there.

Despite that, we were picked up every day in the white mission truck and taken back to Ernabella for schooling. School finished at midday, and so we children immediately started walking back to Wamikata, or rounding up our donkeys to ride back. We went back to the big inma as soon as possible. It was such good fun. These were very enjoyable times, and beautiful too. The country was blooming with flowers. It was so colourful and beautiful, with blossoms on all the bushes and carpets of wildflowers everywhere. The flowers were pretty, and the blossom was fragrant. We call blossom inunytji. There was no drought in this part of the world!

But during times of drought our people had to keep moving, and remain vigilant for every opportunity. Once, we were suffering a bad drought and we were perishing from lack of water, but we were lucky, in that somebody we were walking with knew the land intimately and was able to take us directly to a rockhole holding water. We were shown the way to this

Children at play on the Wamikata hillside in the heart of the Musgrave Ranges, 1958. Wamikata is a popular spot for picnics and games. (Photo: Bill Edwards / Ara Irititja 13031)

rockhole, so we could know it ourselves. However, I have never had to be placed in a hole in the ground to save my life, which is what we have to do sometimes in cases of extreme heat and danger of heat stroke; we dig a hole and place a large shelter up above it, and go into the hole and bury ourselves with cool earth. We do this if we have no mina, no water. This is called nyari<u>l</u>pa, which is the cooling-off and recovery hole. We never sit out in the open in cases like this, out in the sun when we have no water to drink. We go into these holes, and this gives us strength to carry on and we feel well again.

I certainly know about it, and I have heard about it and I have seen it. My grandmother used to tell me all about it and my grandfather used to talk to the boys and tell them about it, while grandmother would talk to the girls. We would be told, 'If you ever go out by yourself digging rabbits, and if you start to feel weary after spending all day digging, and when you are coming back, if you get back home and light a big fire and start roasting all those rabbits, but if you are tired and you can only make it some of the way back home, you can dig a deep hole and bury the meat and you can also bury yourself. Dig yourself a deep, wide hole big enough to fit yourself in, you'll be okay, because you will cool right off and you will be okay. Once you are cool enough you could get out and cook the rabbits so you have some meat. This is what my grandmother used to teach us. She would teach us about this nyari<u>l</u>pa — that is, how you dig to save your life from burning up in the desert, by digging a deep, cool hole and burying yourself in it. You cover yourself with cool earth and you'll survive. This is a good wi<u>r</u>u way survival technique, an action to take in order to save your own life. You dig a cool hole and place yourself in it, or if your little baby child is burning up in the heat, put the child inside. You bury the child in the cool earth and they'll sleep there quite happily. They'll sleep happily and when they wake up they'll feel revived and will want to suck ipi. The mother's ipi, too, will also cool down and be better for the child in this way. We were brought up on cool breast milk, because our mothers would keep their breasts cool in this way.

A carpet of wildflowers, Mann Ranges, 1967. (Photo: Noel and Phyl Wallace / A<u>r</u>a Irititja 41443)

If you are starving hungry with nothing to eat, as you are going along, then you dig deep in the ground for honey ants. A few tiny honey ants will go a long way towards lessening hunger. They are full of sugar and they are a real pick-me-up. In the same way that diabetics get a boost from sugar sometimes, starving people get a boost from a few honey ants. Tja<u>l</u>a are good in that their natural sugars enter the whole body and revive it. I suppose back in those days we never had any sugar as such, and so a little bit of sugar did us good, unlike today where we have sugar all the time and can never know what good it could do. But we love honey ants very much and they are a lifesaver, along with a drink of water and kangaroo meat. In my own experience, I never went without food. My father would always bring food to us in the mornings. My father, my grandfather and my uncle would always go hunting first thing in the morning and by mid morning they had speared something, cooked it, and brought it back to the children.

Pantjiti McKenzie digs to reveal a deep hidden chamber of honey ants, Ernabella, 2004. (Photo: Sometimes and Freedman / Ara Irititja 39443)

Honey ants. (Photo: Sometimes and Freedman / Ara Irititja 39254)

Highly prized honey ants, 2000. (Photo: Amanda Rankin, Watarru community / Ara Irititja 24625)

I mentioned before that many years ago, maybe 1958, our family were way out west hunting dingoes with one of my old mama tjilpi, old Mr Eddy. I remember, on that journey, we had been walking over near Kalka and we were not far from Kalka Mountain. There was a fairly severe drought at the time and there was no plant life at all, just bare ground, and there were no kangaroos at all, just kanyala. There were no ngintaka walking about on the rocks, nor tinka. There was nothing but dingoes. Everybody was hungry and there was no meat for anyone to eat. Old Mr Eddy was concerned about us all being hungry, so he took the risk of feeding us with this dingo meat which had been killed using patjina or poison, a blue dingo poison, or bait. The poison is put onto a small amount of meat and left out; the dingo eats it and dies from nerves in the stomach.

Mr Eddy had been out poisoning dingoes near Kalka. He put the poisoned meat down, and walked back to Kalka. When he went back later he'd got five dingoes, all dead. He took the scalps off them first. The scalps are really the two ears, the face above the eyes, the whole back and the tail, all torn off in one piece. So he got the dingoes, cut off the ears, cut off the tail, opened up

Eagle chicks were eaten, despite not having much meat on them. (Photo: Stewart Roper / Ara Irititja 75240)

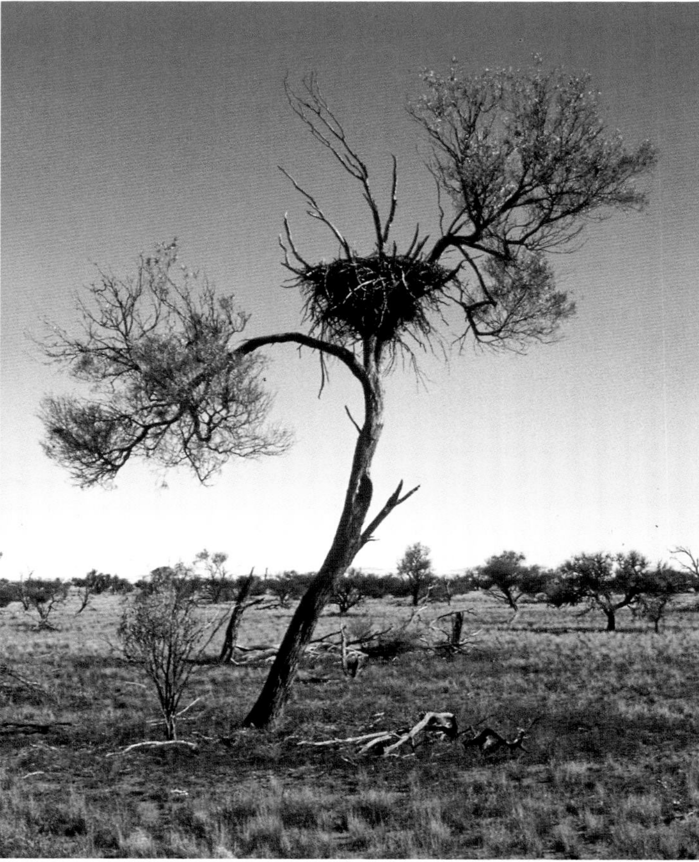

A large wedge-tailed eagle nest in a mulga tree, Oodnadatta area, 1976. (Photo: Alan Morris / Ara Irititja 10704)

the abdomen and took out the guts and threw them away. One always does a thorough job of cleaning out and throwing away the guts and intestines of any animal that has been poisoned. Then one roasts the animal whole, after pinning back the legs and pinning the stomach hole closed.

So this was done, and I was given a portion of the meat and I ate it. This is the one and only time I've ever eaten papa patjina. There was a severe drought on at the time and very little else to eat, no meat anywhere. The meat was really fat, and it was really good, a really good meat, just like kangaroo! That's the only time I've ever eaten it, and it was my one and only experience of it. It had been cleaned and cooked, with the guts thrown away, as well as the mouth and throat parts. However, we were a bit confused about the meat because old Mr Eddy initially tricked us, and told us that he was cooking cats. But we couldn't work out why he was cooking it with no skin on it – because he'd already removed so much of the skin. 'What do you mean? Why are you cooking this cat naked?' He said he had thrown away the skin and the stomach. I was upset because I wanted to keep any cats he caught as pets, and he'd told us he had five cats. So we ate what we thought was cat, but when he later confessed it was papa patjina I was mad! 'You tricked us! I wanted to keep those cats as pets!'

During a drought, meat would always be given to children; they made sure the children, at least, were fed. They would be looking at nests: eagle's nests, walawuru nests. They'd be listening for nestlings chirruping inside the nest. Kutunpa is the name for baby eagle nestlings or fledgelings. If our old people couldn't climb up the tree, they'd spear them, cause them to fall down, and then eat them. During a drought this is what our people did. Sometimes they'd spear the mother eagle as well, or the father. During severe drought, we had to. It was meat, and it had to see us through the dry times.

An alternative meat was ipuru, the spinifex pigeon, which lives up in the rocks; it is an orange-coloured bird, a rock-dweller. Children kill them with rocks and eat them, as they do another pigeon, the aralapalpalpa, or crested pigeon. Both these pigeons are good to eat; they have a good lot of meat on them, the same as the walawuru or eagle. We eat all these birds because they've all got plenty of meat on them. We also eat nyii-nyii, the zebra finch, and patilpa or Port Lincoln parrot and kiily-kiilykari, the budgerigar. We always listen for the sound of the chirruping coming from hollow trees and branches. If we hear it, in we go and pull out the baby birds, which are taken and eaten immediately.

On other occasions we'll hear the birds chirruping in the hollow trees, and we'll send the children away, saying, 'Children! Hear that loud chirruping noise all those birds are making in their hollow trees? Well stay away from it! There are so many baby birds that snakes will be there too. If you try sticking in your arm you'll be bitten. So leave them alone!' And so we scare the children off these dangerous situations. 'You'll be bitten on the hand by a snake. It is there waiting for you. It will bite you from out of some tiny crevice. If you put your hand in there, you are risking snakebite, which could mean death. So leave them alone!'

Another meat bird is the cocky, or kuwirkura. Cocky is good meat, a bit like kiily-kiilykari; they are all very good meat, especially during a famine or drought. Children hurl rocks and kill them for meat. Older children will kill small birds and give them to their younger siblings. Eggs too, such as nyii-nyii ngampu, or zebra finch eggs, are given and eaten, cooked first and eaten.

None of these meats are eaten anymore though. Nothing. Children of today might kill birds for fun, but don't eat them. They will raid a bird's nest and take the young and play with them until they die, and once they're dead they'll discard them, but they don't take them for food anymore. No more.

We ate birds, though. We were self-sufficient, getting our own meat, even when we were very small. Nganyinytja was the same, bless her, she ate birds, and she taught us how to catch them and cook them. All through an ailuru we continued to get meat. Ailuru is a tough time of famine when there is almost no meat or food to be had. No plants grow, the plants are all dried up, and there is just bare earth and open spaces. When it is like this, we have to eat what we can get, yet we were able to get meat some of the time.

Our predecessors ate langka meat in the past. Langka is the blue-tongue lizard. They would hunt and kill langka if they found one, tinka too. Tinka, the sand goanna, survive droughts, and so they are hunted during that time, and eaten. Kuniya, the woma python, live during drought too. Kuniya is hunted anytime, and eaten during drought; however, we do not kill and eat other snakes. We never eat liru or poisonous snakes, only python. Another drought survivor which we always used to see is the tjirilya, which lives among the rocks. The tjirilya or echidna, would be killed, cooked immediately and given to the children to ensure their survival. Children suffer greatly from lack of food; they risk starvation, so we always make sure they are properly fed, and of course they are learning important survival skills during this time. They learn that they can eat kiily-kiilykari and cocky. Even though kiily-kiilykari are tiny, they have some meat on them; other birds are bigger, with more meat on them. We used to hunt all of these birds when we were young, and we ate them all.

The eagle only has a little meat on it though; we'd clamber up into the trees to get them, but if we couldn't climb the tree, if it was too difficult, we'd get someone to bring a spear and spear them from below. They would be speared and dragged out with the spear down to the ground and then hit and killed. They move very quickly so we had to be fast to get them. The parents hear their chicks being killed and they fly up and then dive down to see what is happening and they call out, 'Why are you killing my children? Why are you killing our children? They haven't even grown all of their feathers yet?' This is what we say of the eagles, what we say they are thinking. It is an eagle story. Eagles love their children dearly.

Nyii-nyii don't seem to mind too much, they don't give the appearance of caring if we destroy their nests and take their eggs. But the eagles cry for their children, 'Why must you take my children? Why must my children be killed?' They fly up and then descend quickly to see what is happening and then they come in to land again. We say to them, we respond to them, 'This is how it must be. People are starving, so this is how it must be.' But the eagles do not like it.

Another meat we hunt for is the turkey, which in our language is kipara, which seem to survive the drought alright. Turkey meat is permanently available, as is walawuru, both adult and chick. Aralapalpalpa and ipuru, which are both pigeons, are also a favoured meat. Other meat birds, as I have said, are nyii-nyii, kuwirkura cocky, kiily-kiilykari and patilpa. They all have good meat. There are many, many other birds and animals which are good for their meat, too many to mention. Many other birds are eaten, such as the tjalpu-tjalpu black-faced wood swallow and the piil-piilpa yellow-throated miner and mininy-mininypa yellow-rumped thornbill and the ikarka spotted bowerbird and the kaanka crow. Even the crow! Crow is

Budgerigars provide a small amount of meat which can keep hunger at bay. They provide hunting practice for children. (Photo: Stewart Roper / Ara Irititja 75262)

Bush turkey is a large bird and a favourite meat. They can survive droughts and were a vital survival food. (Photo: Stewart Roper / Ara Irititja 108764)

not normally eaten, but on occasion when there is nothing else, we will eat kaanka.

I remember my father cooking crows for us once, and eating them. We ate those birds, and I remember they were quite fat! They looked healthy and he had said, 'Look, I'm going to get those crows for us to eat', because we were on an overnight trip, which meant we were away from everyone else, and we had nothing else. We were with Iwana and Angela and that is when we ate crow. We were on Mulga Park Station and there were bullocks everywhere. And that crow meat was all right, we were just giving it a try, and it was just fine!

Now here is another story. It is about kuka walkalitja, which is meat which has been poisoned with walkalpa, emu poison bush. This tactic was employed during tough drought times when there was almost no meat to be had anywhere else, and all kangaroos had left the area to find food further away. We children were told, 'Children! We are now going to a place not far from here. It's not far from Intjara. Near Intjara is a walu – a flat rock face. There's a walu near Intjara and that is where we are going. Just to the one place.' We'd be told 'Children! Make sure you look for all the footprints. There will be bird footprints and tracks everywhere. We've made a hide there.' They'd made a hide, and we were made to go to sleep inside it. We were told to not get up, not to pop our heads up, not get up or walk around. We were to lie still and not move. We weren't allowed to do anything except lie down. 'Go to sleep now. Don't move. Just sleep.' So, like the obedient children that we were, we did as we were told and went to sleep. We knew that we had to do exactly as we were told, and that is what we did.

They had put a poisonous plant called walkalpa into the water – emu poison bush. The water was looking black. Walkalpa leaves, which had been finely ground, had been tipped into the water and mixed in. The purpose of this was to knock senseless any emu that might come by and drink the water. Three or two emus might come by and drink this poisoned water, and if they did, each would be affected. Even dingoes would be affected badly by it, because it is poisonous. They'd drink it and soon they'd behave as if they were intoxicated. It was a strong poison, similar in effect to dingo bait. The emus wouldn't survive it. We were told that the men would spear the emu before they died of poisoning, though. They'd be hiding in a tree and watching from above, and would spear them soon after they drank. They'd see the emu as soon as they arrived, and watch them crouch down to drink. As they were drinking, they'd be speared from above.

So during drought emus were hunted in this manner. I've experienced this myself and eaten the meat of two or three emus, which were hunted with walkalpa and considered kuka walkalitja. I've eaten emu meat on at least two occasions that were kuka walkalitja. Both times the emu had ingested walkalpa but had actually died by the spear, poor things! We didn't have rifles back in those days. The emu would drink the walkalpa and then run away with the first spear still dragging on the ground, but were followed on foot and finished off with another spear. They'd die with the spear in them. They died by spear, not by dog. We didn't have dogs to bring them down. Sometimes dogs were used, but when we didn't have dogs – or even rifles back then – only walkalpa and spears were used. We were always confident that we'd get our meat; and we always did, such was our skill. So on two occasions I've eaten walkalitja emu meat. Emu were hunted either by walkalpa or spear, or both.

It was important to not eat the stomach parts, or to slit the stomach open and allow the contents to get onto the meat. The animal must be gutted and cleaned a long way from people because the stomach part will be poisonous. The animal must be carefully gutted and properly cleaned out before preparing to cook, because of the risk of ingesting any of the poison and the risk of death. This is important. The people always used to take the greatest of care with all stomach parts and its contents, because the watery liquids in the stomach are toxic and can kill. Children were always looked after while the animal was being prepared in this way; they were not allowed to go near any parts that may have been affected and certainly never eat any parts that are near the stomach. Children were always shooed away. They could eat malu or kanyala – that would be alright – but not kuka walkalitja. Only the men and the senior men were allowed to eat kuka walkalitja.

During a tough ailuru, I would never know where our next food was going to come from. I never knew what we'd be eating next, if at all. Even so, there were always rabbits around; we'd hunt and knock out a couple of rabbits. Same with ngintaka, the big perentie lizard, although they were usually around on their last legs, thin and bony. They rarely had any meat on them during drought. However, the euro hills kangaroo always remained fat and healthy. Kanyala always fare better in a drought. They always kept meat on themselves. They seem to manage on kulypurpa, a kind of wild gooseberry, which also seems to persist through a drought. Kanyala eat kulypurpa, and any other green vegetation, which they might find high up or in the foothills of the mountains and ranges. So kanyala fare quite well, and remain fat and healthy.

At a place called Inytjara, we used to live for quite a while, 'we' being Umuka, Nellie, Tjarpurai and her two daughters, and all our families; we used to live around there, basing ourselves at Inytjara. We lived on fat kanyala meat, which had been speared. We also ate a lot of wild fig and roasted rabbits, which we dug out of their burrows. I hadn't eaten ngaltatjiti at that point, but I had eaten emu walkalitja.

I want to talk about mingkulpa now, because it is so important. It is part of our tradition and culture. Our Law. Anangu elder men and women are the holders of the Law about mingkulpa and they keep that Law alive together. Mingkulpa is also known as wild tobacco. Mingkulpa is really important for keeping our mouths moist, because without it our mouths dry right out, we feel parched and our eyes get dry and sunken. Poor us! I'm a bit dry now! Anyway, this is part of our Law.

The strongest mingkulpa is found growing in rocky areas and around caves. That is the best and strongest plant. There is another plant that grows in the woodland. Mingkulpa is eaten by our people. By that I mean it is held in the mouth. To get mingkulpa supplies we go to find the plant, pick the plant and bring it home. When we arrive home we take all the leaves off and then grind them up. This is our Law. To compliment the mingkulpa we use white ash from burnt kurku bark. Kurku is our name for the common mulga tree. Old men take off the bark

Staple foods maku (witchetty grubs) and wiriny-wirinypa (bush tomatoes) in a bowl made from a car hubcap. (Photo: Suzanne Bryce / Ara Irititja 27377)

from the kurku and burn it to make a nice white ash, which is then mixed with the mingkulpa to make a very pleasant and effective tobacco mix. It looks good too! The green and yellow colours of the two mixed together always look good. And the mix is quite powerful as well! It is what we call pikati, or aggressive!

We used to say if there was no water, we could use mingkulpa to keep our mouths moist enough. We'd be told that if we had no water our mouths would dry up and our eyes would sink in and it would be no good for us. There is nothing better than a good drink of water. The whole body responds to it and we feel immediately better. If there is no water, mingkulpa will help enormously, but nothing can replace a big drink of water for all the good things that it can do to the body. One immediately feels better and one can begin to sweat again. Only water can do this, although mingkulpa is of enormous help to enable someone to carry out an important task without water. If someone had to go

hunting for meat but had no water, they'll be very thirsty and weak, a condition we call upa. The whole body looks drawn and stressed when it is suffering a lack of water. We have a word for what it feels like, which is kuṟupiilyurukatipai. White people use the word dizzy. So thirst manifests as dizziness and if it progresses to the end, the person will die. The whole body shuts down, eyes, arms, legs and stomach, all through lack of water. Mingkuḻpa has an effect on the body just like a drink of water. Mingkuḻpa is like water. Wonderful!

When one is starving and cannot see straight, one cannot think straight either. As soon as one gets a good meal, it is remarkable how quickly you can recover. A good feed in the stomach can do wonders for a starving person. A starving person is a sad sight to see. Their eyes fade and go dry and papery. They look thin and papery, and the person is weak and helpless. 'I am so hungry I just don't know what to do', and they'll be just lying there. 'I'm so thirsty, I cannot think straight. Please bring me some water'. All we can do in that situation is dig up some moist earth and plaster it on their skin to cool them down. It will make them cooler at least and they'll feel a bit better. But with no water to drink, at least mingkuḻpa, or a substitute, will help sustain life a bit longer.

If someone is dying of thirst, they'll be asked to bring water as soon as possible. They'll be asked to search every last place where water could be, and bring it to the thirsty person. Bring it carefully and not lose any. If no water is available at all then it is bad news for the sufferer. It could mean goodbye. The sufferer will be sitting very quietly inside the shade of a shelter. They'll be thinking, 'What am I to do? What can I put in my mouth? A little mingkuḻpa would help'. They'll be out of ideas and options.

The old people will keep a kapuṯu or ball, of this mingkuḻpa on their lips for a long time. They'll keep it there for a long time

Nura grinds a pure white ash of leaves and bark with tinned tobacco, Black Hill, 1999. Tinned tobacco is considered a poor substitute when mingkulpa is not available. Mixing the alkaline ash with tobacco helps to release the nicotine, and give it 'bite'. (Photo: Heidrun Lohr / Aṟa Irititja 182443)

and then, if they are walking around, they'll put the kaputu behind their ear and hold it there until they are ready to put it back on the lips. They use it to keep the moisture and spittle flowing in their mouths. We call this wita. The old men swallow the spit from time to time and it gives them a lift and makes their eyes bright.

In the very olden days before there were bags, mingkulpa used to be carried around in a bundle of wipiya. Wipiya are emu feathers. The wipiya would be bundled up and kind of sewn together, and the mingkulpa would be put in the centre and wrapped up. These bundles were the Law of the old men. They all had their bundles and they would carry them around by tying them onto their heads with their headbands, or puturu. They'd get the string of their puturu and wrap it around and around until it was secure and that is how they would walk around. They would use the leaves from the kurku tree for their ash, although nowadays we use the bark from the kurku tree or from the itara tree. The itara tree is the river red gum. But back then they used kurku leaves, and they would also suck the leaves, and sometimes they used the bark for ash as well. These

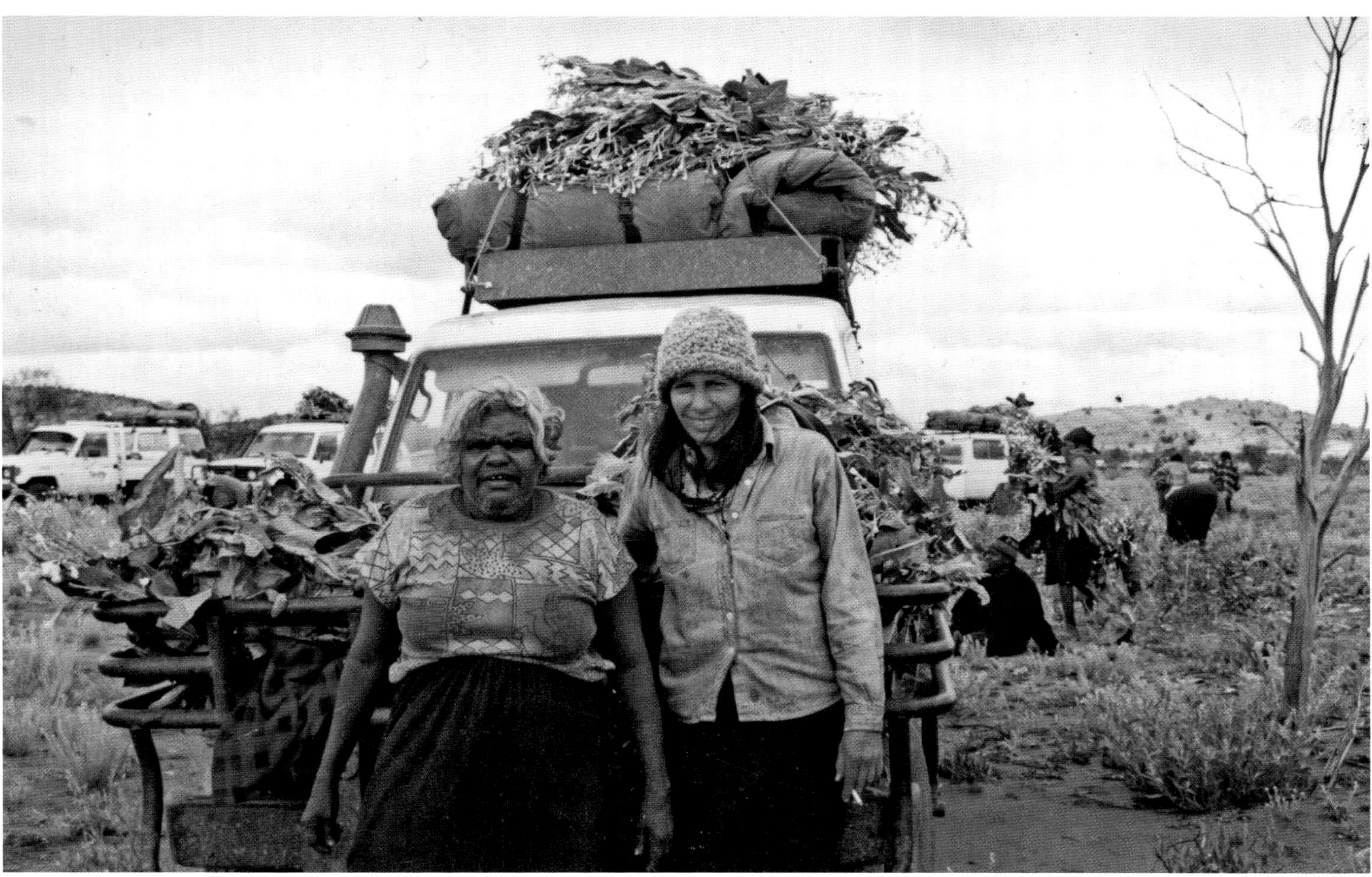

Nura and Ali Cobby Eckermann dry out a large haul of mingkulpa on their vehicle, Watarru, 2001. (Photo: Thisbe Purich / Ara Irititja 128934)

old people were very strong. They had to be tough. Mingkul̲pa was vitally important to everyone, as was water.

Many years ago my mother would collect her mingkul̲pa and carry it around in a little yakutja, or bag. Just a little one. She used to carry it around with her. As I said earlier, I was only a child when I first started out on mingkul̲pa. I remember trying it out secretly at first. We'd all get intoxicated from it and then we'd all vomit and fall asleep and have violent headaches, all because we'd secretly tried out mingkul̲pa. Mother would be asking us, when we would come back to camp vomiting and sick, 'What's up with you lot? What is the matter?' But we'd be trying out mingkul̲pa and all getting sick, hidden away from sight!' We would chew it and get sick and then go to sleep in the bushes, sleep like a baby, sleeping just like my little granddaughter Jasmine here! That's how I first learnt how to use mingkul̲pa. I was warned, 'Watch out for that stuff! It is powerful!' Urtjanpa leaves, or kul̲at̲a leaves, which is what we call the spearbush, is fairly harmless. We learnt to use it when we were children. We used it all the time when we were children, until we were old enough to be given mingkul̲pa.

The flora of Ernabella includes thryptomene, wildflowers and the popular tall spinach-like mingkulpa plant. (Photo: Bill and Allison Elliott / Ar̲a Irititja 18205)

But I kept trying mingkul̲pa until I got used to it, and then the addiction set in! After that, of course, I couldn't get enough of it! We used to beg from our grandmothers, 'Grandmother! Please give me a little bit to try!' It is usual to see someone pleading for mingkul̲pa if they see someone with a nice amount.

We used to say, 'I could do with a bit of something for my mouth because it is dried out. I could do with some wit̲aku. Give me some wit̲aku, somebody!' What I mean by this is, I am saying I need some relief from my dry mouth. I want to create some spittle. Somebody would give us something for our mouths, and as soon as we had chewed, the moisture in our mouths would return. 'Oh, thank goodness for that! I feel revived again! Lovely!' It would feel like a big drink of cool water, nice and wet.

When there was no mingkul̲pa to be had we used kantur̲angu. Kantur̲angu is a tall tree, known as the desert poplar. Kantur̲angu are those tall trees you see in the sand dune country. They are plentiful in sand dune country. When they are covered in nice new fresh foliage, we gather the leaves and grind them up with unmut̲a and they really pack a punch! With tawal̲tawal̲pa, we grind it up with unmut̲a and it really takes the skin off one's mouth. It takes the skin right off one's lips when we use it. Tawal̲tawal̲pa is wild gooseberry and unmut̲a is the native cress.

Mingkul̲pa has a similar effect to cigarettes, but different and better, in that it is wet and moist, rather like having a drink, and is a great thirst-quencher. White people's law is about cigarettes and tobacco. Tobacco, or baccy, is chewed or can be rolled up in paper and smoked. This is black tobacco. Young men used to smoke tobacco rolled up in newspaper. Cigarettes are strong and powerful but they are also horrid, what we call nyampa. This is true! Whereas mingkul̲pa is strong and pleasant. Mingkul̲pa is addictive in the same way that cigarettes are. The difference though, of course, is that mingkul̲pa doesn't damage the lungs like cigarettes. We are not inhaling smoke. Mingkul̲pa is held in the mouth and is kept

Women depart with their families on a long journey around their traditional country to collect bush foods and hunt dingo scalps, Yulpartji, 1959. (Photo: Bruce Edenborough / A<u>r</u>a Irititja 9509)

in the open until it disappears. All we take in is the enlivened spittle, which is swallowed. No smoke or anything else gets into the lungs. No smoke goes into the lungs. Smoke going into the lungs is very bad for you. It causes asthma and coughing fits and bronchitis. Mingku<u>l</u>pa never causes bronchitis or asthma. Mingku<u>l</u>pa causes no harm. Healthy people use mingkulpa, whereas cigarettes are bad. If one takes apart a cigarette and rolls the tobacco into a ball and puts it in the mouth, then it still gets into the lungs and still causes coughing. Cigarettes cause coughing. White people invented cigarettes and A<u>n</u>angu invented the use of mingku<u>l</u>pa. Mingku<u>l</u>pa grows in the bush and A<u>n</u>angu have always harvested it for their use. The use of it is an A<u>n</u>angu invention.

Now I am going to tell a story about a journey our family made when I was a kungkawa<u>r</u>a, a big girl, not long before I was married. I am going to name all the places and water sources where we went, places I have seen with my own eyes.

I have been to Yulpartji, and then from Yulpartji to Nga<u>l</u>pu. At Nga<u>l</u>pu I remember sleeping overnight, and then the next day, leaving Nga<u>l</u>pu and going to A<u>r</u>altji. Spending the night at A<u>r</u>altji, and then the next day leaving A<u>r</u>altji and travelling to Umpukulu. Staying at Umpukulu and then travelling from there up to Angatja. From Angatja we go to A<u>t</u>al and from A<u>t</u>al we go to Mu<u>t</u>inga<u>r</u>anytja and from Mu<u>t</u>inga<u>r</u>anytja we go to Tji<u>t</u>api<u>t</u>i and from Tji<u>t</u>api<u>t</u>i we go to I<u>r</u>anykatjara and then on to Nga<u>n</u>tjapi<u>t</u>i, where, as you may know, the vomiting event

A woman cleans ngaltatjiti (kurrajong seeds) ready for grinding into a paste, Ilpil, 1933. (Photo: AA122/1/1-p58/2, Hackett Collection, South Australian Museum)

occurred, where Wati Ngintaka vomited up all those edible ngantja (mistletoe berries). The next place we go to is Irurpa, where there is a cave. Irurpa is my father's own place, a really lovely place. Tourists go there all the time. Irurpa is a good tourist destination. From Irurpa we go to Tjanpara and from Tjanpara we go to Wiikirkin, which is another lovely place. Wiikirkin is known for its abundant food plants including wangunu, although nowadays like everywhere else, it has been invaded by introduced grasses. Everywhere you look you see introduced weed species. But in the recent past, it had an abundance of food bearing indigenous plant species. There used to be food plants growing abundantly on the plains, and masses of ili trees growing all over the rocks and ranges; but today the place is desolate because of the weeds.

This journey we undertook started from Amata, a long time ago. We people departed from Amata and we travelled to Yulpartji. We arrived at Yulpartji and stayed there while we waited for a new load of stores to arrive. The white people had a store truck and they were bringing it to Yulpartji, and we were to get food stores from them as rations; no, not as rations; I mean, in exchange for dingo skins, which we had hunted. Finally the store truck arrived, and then we began the trading for the skins. When the trading at Yulpartji was complete, everybody loaded up their donkeys, camels and horses with our supplies.

Our family had six horses and three camels, and once they were loaded up we set off on foot, walking to Ngalpu. We arrived at Ngalpu, which is not far from Yulpartji, but we were really heading for Angatja – Angatjanyakitja. We were heading for Angatja, and Nganyinytja's father was with us, as well as Nganyinytja, and we were going there to see the place and to look at their country. Nganyinytja was with us and many other Anangu.

Anyway, we camped at Ngalpu, and the next morning the women got up and went over to the water hole. Two or three women went to get water, and when they got there they exclaimed, 'Hey, look at this crow vomit! A crow has brought ngaltatjiti (kurrajong seeds) and vomited up pellets of ngaltatjiti next to the water in the waterhole here!' They saw all the pellets that the crow had vomited up around the water and they said, 'Look at all these pellets! There are many ngalta trees growing on the plains. Perhaps they are loaded with seed at the moment?' Anyway, later on the women were told, 'Tomorrow morning, all you women go to see if there is indeed a lot of ngalta seed available from those trees dotted about!' The women responded, 'No problem! We'll go and check them out!'

The following day the men got up and went over to Yulpartji to track down dingoes and hunt them for their skins, to kill them, skin them and bring them back, while other men hunted for meat to eat. Meanwhile us women and girls walked to the ngalta trees and did see that they were loaded with ngaltatjiti seed. There was a lot of food. So the women were soon busy chopping out the seed pods, chopping, chopping, chopping, and knocking them down onto a tarpaulin. Then they were threshing, threshing and threshing to get the seeds out. It was my first time seeing how this was done, so I watched and learned and helped by breaking the pods open as they were handed to me. We processed the seeds and then we departed, heading for Aratji. Aratji is just this side of Angatja, very close.

We arrived at Aratji and there we sat down to do the rest of the preparation while others dug for honey ants. I was, at the time, still only a kungkawara, which is a big girl, and there were four of us kungkawara there: me, Tjikalyi Colin, Yuminiya Yakiti and Nungalka Stanley. Tjala were being dug up for us. Leah's older brother was there at the time, I remember. Anyway, plenty of tjala were being dug up, and I was watching but suddenly I noticed that the women were now cooking the seeds that they had collected. I couldn't help noticing how greasy the ground was around them. It was like butter. I asked about it, and I was told, 'These ngaltatjiti seeds grind up very greasily, they are a greasy seed and that's why the ground looks like it does. They are like butter'. Anyway, we were not given the cooked food while it was hot. It was put aside and we had to wait until it had cooled down enough to eat. We rubbed our hands together in anticipation, and when we got to taste it, we were really excited, 'Oh, this is a lovely food! Yummy!' We were very satisfied with our meal of ngaltatjiti and thought it delicious.

A traditional wooden bowl filled with ngalta (desert kurrajong) leaves and ngaltatjiti (seeds). (Photo: Suzanne Bryce / Aṟa Irititja 27211)

We all stayed at Aratji overnight and the following morning we got up and moved on towards Angatja. We arrived at Umpukuḻu and stayed there one night. The following day we travelled onto Angatja, so we could get water from Angatja waterhole. After that we moved onto Aṯal. We were told to keep moving because Aṯal was so close and it was a good place to stop. I remember my father — my *two* fathers — no, my *three* fathers — telling me all about our country and our places, how Angatja, Aṟatji, Aṯal and Umpukuḻu all formed part of our lands, and how we were connected to them. We had been walking through our lands and I was seeing all these places and living in them. So anyway, we stayed at Aṯal and ate the rest of our food, and then the women left to get more. They went back to get more ngaltatjiti — more of the same food.

I stayed behind to look after the youngest children in our group, eating arnguḻi all day. There were plenty of arnguḻi bush plums for us to gather and eat. Of course we didn't just eat the ripe fruit, we processed it first. We would mash up the fruit in a dish and then drink the mashed fruit, and lick the bowl after. We did not have anything else to eat apart from the bit of flour that we had with us, the arnguḻi mash and the ngaltatjiti, because the women had, as yet, been unable to find any wanguṉu or kunakaṉṯi.

Later, we children were told, 'Come on then, it is time to move on! Let's go to Tjitapiṯi next!' So we moved on, passing through Muṯingaṟanytja. We stopped to look at Muṯingaṟanytja, and we were told the story associated with it. Those of us that had never heard the story before and were rather taken aback, asking, 'My goodness, really? What a story! Is it all true?' We were assured, 'Of course it is a true story. It is Tjukurpa!' It was so good to be shown and told the true stories of our land and to experience them first hand. I was staring hard at the places as we passed them by, now that I knew more.

By and by we arrived at Tjitapiṯi where we were to camp at an established campsite. The women were already there and had come back from some good grounds where they had been able to harvest a plentiful supply of kunakaṉṯi. They'd threshed the seed on the hard ground surfaces called putu, which are found above flat termite nests. They had been foraging for kunakaṉṯi, and been in ideal country for the harvesting and processing of seeds.

I saw the seeds and I asked them, 'What's this, a strange kind of spinifex?' 'Yes, it is similar,' they told me, 'come and help.' So I helped with the harvesting, which was good for me because I was learning important skills. We filled up the bowls with seeds, and later as we were returning with them, we saw the men arrive back from hunting. They were carrying dingoes and kanyaḻa, or euro. 'Oh look! Here are the men with dingoes, and they've also got a kanyaḻa! Well done old men!' There were about three or four old men — my own father, old Nyimi (which is an affectionate name for an old man) Muyuru's father and Matjangka's father, and we were all at Tjitapiṯi.

This happened at Tjitapiṯi. We were not far from that big salt lake that's in that area, which is called Paṉṯuwaṟa. It is like a kind of claypan, not far from Ngaḻpu. It is also not far from

Ngintaka Ulkapatjunkunytja. While we were in that area we were all shown Ngintaka Ulkapatjunkunytja, and had the story explained to us.

After that we went to Irangka, and after Irangka we continued on to Ngantja Piti. At Ngantja Piti we stopped and were told the story of how Wati Ngintaka had vomited out all the ngantja (mistletoe berries). 'This is where it happened,' said my father, 'now, let's keep moving and get to my place.' So we continued on, and kept moving until we were close to Irurpa, to where the big creek line is there. From there my father showed me his country. 'See all that? From this creek line here, over to there, is all Irurpa area. This is all my country, see? I was born here'. Nowadays, tourists visit Irurpa often, but back then only we went to Irurpa. It is my father's birthplace, and obviously it was a special time for me to be shown it by my own father and to camp there for a while near the sand dunes.

We stayed there many days, and each day the men went hunting kanyala. They'd hunt them with hunting sticks and spears, bringing them down and killing them for meat — not only kanyala but also kalaya. An emu was speared not far from the salt lake and brought back for meat.

Dora's older brother, Arthur — my older brother — climbed up the rocky hillside of Irurpa to look out and get a view of Tjanmata — Tjanmata Piti. He could see Tjanmata Piti off in the distance, and after he'd seen it, he threw some alputati into the air. Tjaka — it is a traditional practice to pull up an alputati and a tjanmata plant and throw it into the air. It is like a game, but it is what we do. We throw alputati in the air for others to see — and we saw it from down below near the salt lake. We called out, 'Hey brother! What are you throwing those flowers for?' Because he had thrown them without saying anything, and then descended immediately afterwards, and I didn't know why. He told us he'd thrown them to signify his intentions to go and visit the place. It was also as an expression of a need to do what our ancestors always did, which was to help create more tjanmata in the natural world. Our ancestors were responsible for helping tjanmata to reproduce and grow, thus providing food for us to eat. There are individual and special stones at that place, which must be activated to make this happen. I'd go there but it is a bit far over the top and on the other side were Tjanmata Piti, or rather, Kunakanti Piti and Kaltu-kaltu Piti. Wati Ngintaka had created all these places; he had vomited seed up during his journey in all those places.

Anyway, we were told that soon we'd be moving on again. 'Come on all! We are off to hunt more meat! It is time we hunted more meat!' We went past Pantuwara, to a place called Tjanpara. What a lovely place Tjanpara is! It was stunningly beautiful with endless green grasses and masses of pretty flowers! It was absolutely lovely, so green and lush! For many of us it was our first time there, and we were surprised and delighted. None of us were homesick for any other place or person — we were all so excited to be there in such a gorgeous place. We were happy. We had no other thought in our heads other than how good it was to be in such a bountiful place.

We stayed at Tjanpara for two days, until it was time to move on again. Our next destination was Wiikirkin. We got to Wiikirkin, and camped there and while we were there, one young man came up on his camels. That young man was none other than Cookie — bless his heart! Peter Nyaningu — Cookie — had come by himself from Kanpi to Pantuwara via a narrow valley, or a gap in the ranges. So now here he was, with us, and happy to see his father, because Cookie's father was one of our group. He and his wife had been travelling with us since the beginning of our journey. The group was made up of my mother and father, Nyuringka and her husband, and another two, old Mr Ken and his wife, although they'd actually left the group previously, to travel to other places. They'd gone towards the sand dunes and sand plains. Our group, however, stayed on, and continued to hunt and forage in the area.

There was a huge amount of kunakanti growing. Huge! Of course a great deal was harvested. Lovely! Kunakanti is one of our oldest traditional foods. It was harvested, processed and ground up to eat, and it was delicious. I remember eating some and asking, 'What kind of nyampa or tasteless stuff is this anyway?' and I was told, 'This isn't nyampa! This is proper mai. This is our ancestor's food. Miri tjutaku mai. This is what our

A woman cleans ngaltatjiti (kurrajong seeds) in a bowl made from a car hubcap. (Photo: Suzanne Bryce / Ara Irititja 27216)

ancestors lived on'. So this mai was processed and prepared, cooked and handed out to us, and for many days this is what we lived on.

When it was time for us to move on again, we headed back towards Pirurpa. By now it was cooling down and the weather got quite cold and wet, chilling us all. We were in search of new food areas and we were heading back towards the ngalta trees. 'We're going to head back to the ngalta trees, in order to gather ngaltatjiti seed from them'. We had a good store of kunakanti with us, carrying it in a big yakutja, which is a big bag that one of the camels carried. Once at the ngalta trees, another large store of ngaltatjiti was collected.

Everyone carried a small bag, each filled with seeds, but the camel carried the large bags. We had with us both cooked and raw seed, wanka and warutja. Of course, I was nibbling the seeds as I rode along on the camel. I ate the toasted cooked seeds, which were very delicious. They taste rather like peanut butter. They were lovely! That's the sort of food we ate, and it was always delicious. We continued travelling continuously at this point, carrying with us our large store of kunakanti, kaltu-kaltu and ngaltatjiti, and this saw us well fed until we arrived back at Ernabella. There we gave everybody a good feed of the seed food, especially the children. All the children had a good feed, but it wasn't just the children who got some; the grown-ups did too. The old men and the old women also had a good feed from it. Everyone had a solid meal of our traditional food, which was enjoyed all round. Wintalyka (mulga seed) was another vitally important food used. It would be cooked and eaten. I can remember eating many a meal of wintalyka around Mulga Park, where wintalyka is abundant. Kurku trees are abundant in Mulga Park.

Once upon a time, nobody would miss a chance of harvesting this traditional seed food. But nowadays people will walk right past it, while they head straight for modern foodstuffs. They'll walk right past that lovely food, while it ripens and falls to the ground untouched and unwanted. In the past, the women would harvest any wild food they saw, without hesitation. They'd never miss an opportunity to go harvesting, and they'd always bring in a huge harvest. Their biggest food bowls would always be full. They were very skilled at the work, and would carry large volumes of seed about in their yakutja.

The new generations of today do not know how to forage. We used to walk the land in groups, and each and every woman was a skilled forager who could provide for her family. Every person would be well fed and nourished every day, by their efforts. Harvesting wild food is a thing of the past, and this is a tragedy.

5. Married life

I'm going to move forward into the future now; time went on and I grew up. One time I had a lucky escape when I was a young girl, the first time that I came to Alice Springs by motor-car. I was with Old Corrigan. He brought me into Alice Springs and dumped me here. He left me here all alone! I was only a girl! He left me at Mission Block. I ended up going everywhere and staying there for a while. People were living at Morris Soak and I stayed there too. You see, I was stuck in Alice Springs and I had no idea how to get home. I didn't know what to do!

I was getting to know the Arrernte people. I stayed down at the old Farm with my cousin and her husband. The Farm was at Ilparpa down near Old Timers. Not that there was very much at Ilparpa back then. I stayed there for a while, with that old woman Goodwin, at her place. I stayed there for quite a while. This was when Albert Namatjira was living there. My older sister, Namatjira's wife lived there. Yurpiya lived at Ilparpa. This was the first time that people were allowed to drink so openly, because that old man had been the winner. Old Namatjira, my brother in law, because he was the winner. He was drinking. Everyone who was drinking was fast forgetting everything about their parents and family. Their heads were going bad. They were saying bad things. Things were all going bad for them. But I was stuck in Alice Springs. I hadn't really had any experience of Alice Springs before that. I was there amongst people and drinkers; I didn't know what to do. That whole drinking scene was all around me. It was awful. I was in danger. It wasn't good. I knew I was in danger. The drinkers were fighting. Nobody hit me though. They were drinking wine and getting cranky.

So I was so lucky that my malanypa, which is my cousin or younger brother, came along. So lucky. He rescued me and said to me, 'Come on, come back with me. Hurry! You can't stay here with these Arrernte people!' He said, 'Come with me and we'll go on the train together'. I couldn't agree more, 'Oh yes, absolutely! I want to go with somebody who knows what they are doing!' So the two of us travelled together on the train back to Finke. We were asked, 'Where are you two getting off?' and he replied, 'We want to go to Finke.' I asked him, 'Where are we going to?' and he replied, 'We need to get off at Finke. The Ernabella truck goes there.' I was thinking, 'I hope he knows what he is talking about!' But we did indeed get to Finke and there was the blue Ernabella truck waiting for the load to arrive on the train. The train pulled in, and the load was unloaded and piled on the truck. We were asked, 'Do you want to get a ride back on the truck?' So we loaded our swags on the truck, my younger brother and I, and off we went, back to Ernabella. The blue truck went via Kulgera. Luckily all this transportation worked out for us. Who knows what could have happened to me there? My life might have become a sorry mess if I had stayed.

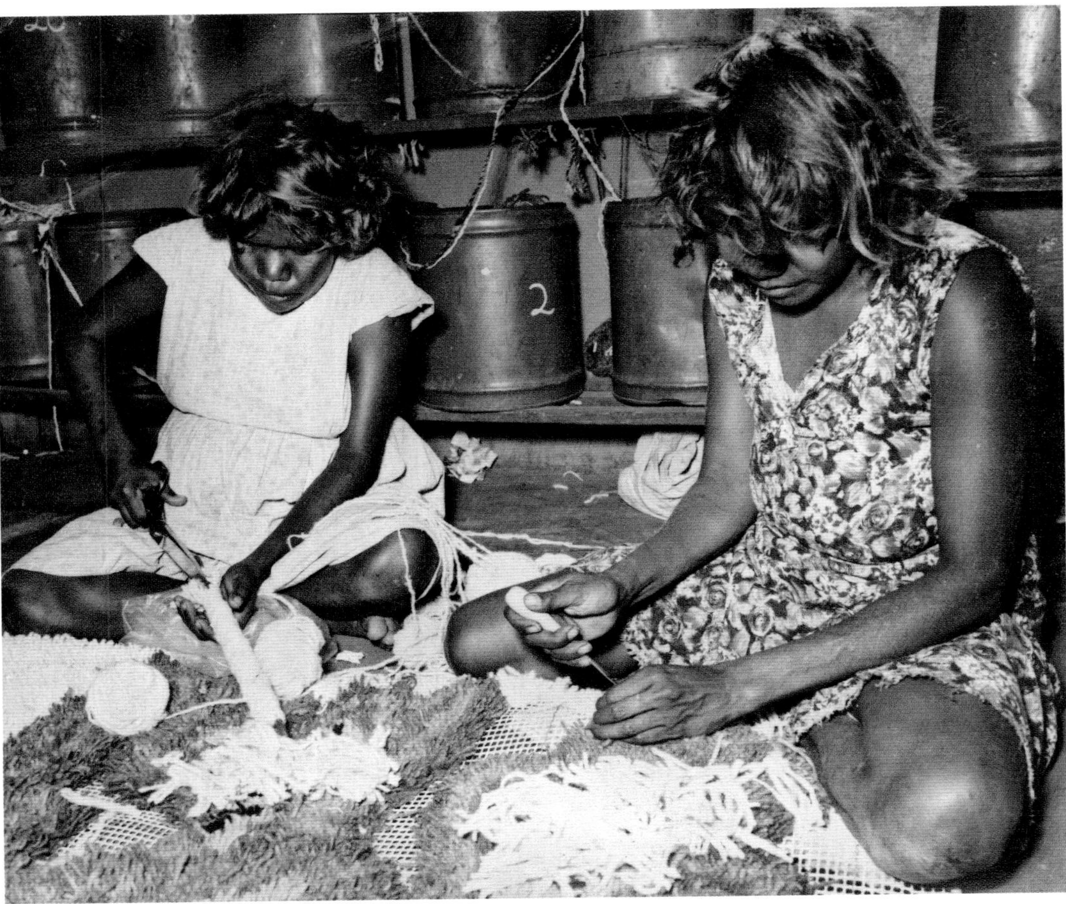

Nura (left) and Ivy Ingkatji hooking rugs in the Ernabella craft room, 1960s. Rug making was a local industry: the wool, from Ernabella sheep, was sheared, spun and hooked or woven by the community. (Photo: Bill Edwards / Ara Irititja 180244)

I remember one day when I was a tall young girl — a kungkawara — going to Mulga Park to see my father and mother, who were living there. My younger brother was not with me that time, because he loved to go to school so much, he would mostly stay behind. But I was a bush girl and I loved the bush, so I would go. Father was working on Mulga Park. I moved there and got myself a job working with him. He taught me lots of different skills, and we would sometimes travel away together. The brothers, Dave and Ted Pukuti, taught me many new things; they were really good teachers and really good white people. I was the only girl working there, except my friend, Katanari. Nelly Patterson was there, but she was still just a little tiny girl then. They didn't live near me though. I lived close to the house in the stockman's camp. It was a nice place.

One time we went to Atila or Curtin Springs and camped there for quite a long time until the work ran out. I was still a kungkawara when I was living and working on Curtin Springs Station. Old Peter Severin was there then. He's still my friend, old Peter Severin. He's a good old man. I used to work there for a while when old Peter was young; he was always a decent man. His son Ashley was only a little kid at Atila. When I lived there, Ashley was just a little boy. Anyway, I was working with his father for a little while, not long, and then I went back to Mulga Park. I worked at Mulga Park for ages, on the bullocks and on the station. Sometimes I would help out when there weren't enough men. I used to help with the mustering; I helped to take the bullocks over to Curtin Springs, handed them over there, and then we all returned. We used to take the bullocks, count them in, make sure they were all there, leave them, and then come back. It was great work. Sometimes there were not enough men to do it.

I returned to Ernabella for Christmas, for a little holiday, and then I got a ride back to Mulga Park with Frank Quinn, Peter Nyaningu's brother-in-law. He's a white man, Tony Quinn's father, an older man who had come in to Mulga Park from Blackstone with his loaded truck. He was servicing the mines out there. There was a lot of mining activity at Blackstone and Pipalyatjara at the time, and he used to take the mail out to Blackstone Mining Camp. He'd arrived back from that trip, so I got a ride back to Mulga Park with him, because I was missing Mulga Park. I didn't particularly want to hang around with the big girls. I wanted to be off on adventures! On another occasion I jumped on and got a ride into Ernabella. When we arrived I went straight back to school. Not school — what I mean is, I went straight back into the craft room, where I worked. When I started work, I'd be paid only two pounds. The girls who worked in the craft room would be paid two pounds or five pounds, two pounds, three pounds, ten pounds. We dealt in pounds back then. We used to think a pound was a huge amount of money! It was! It was a lot of money back then, one pound! We worked in the craft room and we were paid in pounds, but the old people received only rations, back then in the past.

Frank Quinn was an important link in the Ernabella economy, driving his truck to and from the Finke railhead and the Blackstone mining camp, delivering supplies and mail. Here he is with his truck loaded with bales of Ernabella fleeces, bound for the interstate market, c. 1954. (Photo: Bill and Allison Elliott / Ara Irititja 17946)

Talking of Mulga Park, once, we were there on a trip away — and we were on our way back when we encountered another

whitefella with a load of stores; he was going around trading stores for dingo skins. Sometimes people would jump on the vehicles and ride back, but not me. I wanted to stay with father and mother and keep on walking with them. I wasn't homesick for Ernabella, and in no hurry to get back. I just wanted to keep walking with my family, all of us all together. On that particular trip we were on our way back from Amata. We camped at Wiilu – or rather Pi̱ṯiyaṯu (Pi̱ṯi Aṯunytja). From Pi̱ṯiyaṯu we went to Wiilu, which is the other side of Cave Hill. I remember asking, 'So when are we ever going to get to there? Come on warpungkula! Hurry up!' I was told, 'Kuwaripa! Don't make me hurry! Not yet. You've got to slow down or else you'll be bitten by a snake'. I was told by hand signs that once the weather changed and the western winds had started to blow we would get there. For now, we were still walking around in the cold weather. It was beginning to warm up though, and sure enough, it was warm by the time we arrived at Pi̱ṯiyaṯu. There was a large number of old men living at that place, a lot of people. We joined them and my father got some work with horses and bullocks. We stayed at home, while he went out to work going out on rounds with the horses and bullocks.

I then came back to Ernabella but my father still rode horses and went mustering bullocks on Mulga Park. Once the work ran out, he returned to Ernabella. I did not go back to school because I was a big girl, a kungkawa̱ra, so I started working in the craft room with Mary Bennett.

I learnt many new skills in the craft room because we were always making or doing new things, for instance, spinning wool or weaving, or painting cards. It was interesting work. We made so many lovely things. We also made moccasins out of skins. Many women and a lot of the big girls were working there, some weaving blankets out of wool on large looms, others making the moccasins. We made a lot of floor rugs, which could be sat on; these had many stages of preparation. First,

Nura carrying freshly cut spearvines for her grandsons, accompanied by her blind dog Mutjaru, Black Hill, 1999. (Photo: Heidrun Lohr / A̱ra Irititja 128922)

the women would get their one ounce of wool and they'd spin it up into yarn, and then we'd take the yarn and wash it until it was clean. Next, we'd dye it, then we'd cut it, and then it would be hooked into rugs. It was a lot of work, for not much money, really. We didn't get much, maybe five dollars or something like that. We didn't really understand the value of money though, and so back then we thought five dollars was a lot. For years, five dollars seemed like a lot of money – enough to buy flour to help mother out with food provision. We had enough to eat.

As well as working in the craft room, I also helped out in the health clinic at Ernabella. I started to learn all there is to know about clinics then, which I loved. I learnt a great deal during my early education: at school, in the craft room and in the clinic, as well as outside. I enjoyed it all. I'll tell you more about that later.

We lived mostly at Donald's Well, and then we'd go into Ernabella. I remember seeing the soil being pushed around, when they were clearing it to make the Ernabella Football Ground. My father was the boss in charge – mayatja-mayatja – at the time, and he was also the football mayatja then. We lived there, and life was good, all living together. All the grandsons and granddaughters would come to visit and they all knew who their grandfathers and grandmothers were. They all knew who their mother's younger sisters were, in other words, their own younger mothers, or ngunytju ma<u>l</u>atja. Everyone knew who everyone was. As I got older, I left Ernabella again and moved to Kenmore.

While living at Kenmore, I met and married my husband. My older sister was my husband's pikatja, or 'promised' partner. So he was really betrothed to my older sister, and she was referred to as his pikatja. However, it is normal for a man to marry his pikatja's younger sister. That's normal in our custom. An older sister may be the betrothed, but the younger sister may become his actual marriage partner. An older sister's promised husband may well marry the younger sister. My husband's country was in the Indulkana and Amuroona area. That is where he was born.

My husband Bully Ward Tjarutja was a tall man. He had a son called Albert. He looks like our daughter, Jeannie. We used to camp at Kelvin's Well Creek, not far from Black Hill. My husband was a very good man. He was very generous with his money. He was strong in his work ethic, and he was a great teacher. He was my teacher, and he taught me a lot. The two of us were living and working together, side by side, at Kenmore. He was such a good man to me, my husband. I picked up a lot of skills as we went along, such as how to build yards, how to put up a fence, how to dig a bore – anything and everything. I would watch him, and he would tell me what to do. So I could take over and turn my hand to pretty much anything. I helped him with his work while learning at the same time.

Nura with husband Bully Ward Tjarutja. (Photo: Guthrie and Irving / A<u>r</u>a Irititja 36264)

Later on, I was even taught how to drive a motorcar. He would teach me how to turn the steering wheel, how to apply the brakes, how to drive it down steep sandhills and up the other side, all in four-wheel drive. So that is how I learnt how to drive. There were huge sand hills around that country and along the boundary fence, which we were building. We were putting up the boundary fence between Victory Downs and Mulga Park, and there were many big sandhills along the way. Fortunately, the motorcar had four-wheel drive. It was a Blitz wagon, eight tons and I was driving it! I was just a slip of a girl too! But I used

Nura stands beside the rusted body of her husband's yellow Blitz truck, Victory Downs, 1999. When her husband taught her to drive she became one of the first Pitjantjatjara women to drive a vehicle. (Photo: Heidrun Lohr / Aṟa Irititja 182456)

to drive it. That truck is still there at Victory Downs, near the houses. I can easily show you.

When I was still learning how to drive I drove in a restricted kind of way and only stayed in a couple of gears, and I was told to not touch this and that and to drive very slowly. But as I got better I began to be able to drive with both feet and both hands, properly co-ordinated. My husband taught me how to drive properly as well as shoot and how to work the cattle. Just as I had become greedy for shooting the rifle, so I became greedy for driving the truck! I would work tirelessly, I enjoyed it so much. I'd take the truck into the creeks and into the sand dune country. I'd drive among the woodlands. I was told to be careful amongst the woodlands and not to damage the vehicle or the tyres, and to drive slowly in case I had an accident.

Not like today, where inexperienced people get behind the wheel of a car and drive like the clappers and have accidents. Back then we took our time and drove slowly and carefully, building up our skills. People are over-confident with driving these days, and should take more care. I'm often saying, 'Take more care. The police will be after you if you keep driving like that. Or you'll run over someone or smash into another car. You'll smash into a horse or a bullock or a camel. What about your brakes, are they working? I bet you don't have proper brakes. You'll run somebody over if you are not more careful, and end up in jail.' That is the sort of thing I'm always saying. It is, after all, white man's law also. It is white man's law. I'm often saying, 'Slow down and come to a stop. Don't go slamming on the brakes at speed or else you'll go into a spin and crash. Be careful crossing those creeks. There are big ghost gums — pilpira — growing around the creeks, and you'll easily smash into one with the bonnet, and then you'll go straight through the windscreen.' I always advise younger people how to drive more safely because that is how I was taught — safely, and in a good way — in a wiṟu way. I always try to live in a good way. If I'm travelling away by myself I always take extra special care and drive carefully. We can go any time to Victory Downs and see that same old Blitz wagon that I used to drive, an eight-ton four-wheel drive vehicle. I used to drive it myself, going up and down the gears. It is still there.

My old husband taught me how to shoot a rifle, bless him, that old man! As I have said before, he taught me everything. He used to take me over to the dam and he taught me over there. He told me to shoot one of the ducks. I fired and fired and fired but I kept missing, while he got one every time. I just couldn't do it at first, but at last one day I got the hang of it and I shot a rabbit. I shot a rabbit, and then I got really good at it, and from then on, even though I always had a crowbar with me — I always travelled with a crowbar — there was no turning back and I became a proper shooter. I would shoot anything, and I even got greedy for kangaroo! I would shoot kangaroo too. I shot rabbits and ngiṉtaka — perentie — there was no stopping me. I used to drive the truck and shoot guns. I learnt about horses the same way. I learnt how to be a good rider and to be able to ride everywhere safely and without injury.

For a long time my husband and I lived and worked together on Kulgera and Erldunda, putting up fences and building yards.

We also put up a long boundary fence this side of Finke; we made that long fence. After that we moved to Tieyon, or Tjayawara, close to New Crown — not on New Crown, but near New Crown. We worked all around that area.

I am remembering another story now, of when I was a kungkawa<u>r</u>a. We were working together, enjoying ourselves, my husband and I, building the big boundary fence. It was a big job. We were hand-hewing the wooden fence posts ourselves, cutting and shaping them ourselves, loading them onto the Blitz wagon and carting them. I drove the Blitz wagon over high sand dunes, loaded up with wooden posts. I used to drive while my husband stood on the back throwing off the fence posts at regular intervals in a big long line. He'd throw them down one at a time until we'd thrown off the entire load. I'd drive to where we'd previously made a mark to indicate this was where we wanted a post dropped. We'd have marked with our feet the direction the fence was heading and so a post would be dropped there. I'd drive on to the next mark and drop the next post, and so on. Then we'd knock off and go back to camp. Next day we'd be back early, digging the holes and setting the posts in the holes, backfilling them and we'd fence about one mile. I'd be praised for my hard work, 'You did a good job dropping those posts! They are in the right spot!' After that we'd go and get the fence strainers and the wire. Old Manta Frank, he'd measure out one mile of fencing wire. I'd drive the Blitz along the mile, while he rolled it out. We'd finish that length, and then we'd knock off.

After we'd finished that job, we went up to Kenmore and were living and working at Kenmore for a long time doing all sorts of different work. We'd be building yards, trucking things, building windmills. My husband would be up the top of the windmill, putting all the parts together. I never missed out on any of this work. We always worked together on every project. He taught me so many skills. He was a great teacher.

When I was younger and living with my husband, we used to hunt together all the time. We'd go hunting on our camels, and we'd get five, six or four dingoes at a time, or seven. I had my own female dingo, which I grew up. I took her to Kenmore with me, but she used to attack the calves and make the mothers bellow at her. She also used to kill chickens. Brian Harrison's older brother was the owner of the station and he would say that he wanted to shoot that dingo of mine. I was sorry for her, and I said, 'No, don't shoot my dingo!' He used to chase that dingo in his car, so I'd call her over to me.

Nobody hunts for dingoes these days even though dingoes are easy to hunt. Everyone's too scared of them because we live in houses now. Our communities are now composed of houses, chickens, bullocks, sheep, horses and donkeys. Nobody hears the call of the wild dingo anymore, or even thinks of them, and yet they used to be one of our favourite meats. When our people think of meat today they think about chicken and lamb. Yet their forebears were skilled hunters of kangaroo and euro as well as rabbit. But the people of today's communities are disconnected from all those ancient skills and don't bother about doing proper hunting. They've all forgotten how. They only know about their

Nura and husband Bully build a wiltja, Mimili, c. 1980. (Photo: Catherine Winfield / A<u>r</u>a Irititja 39689)

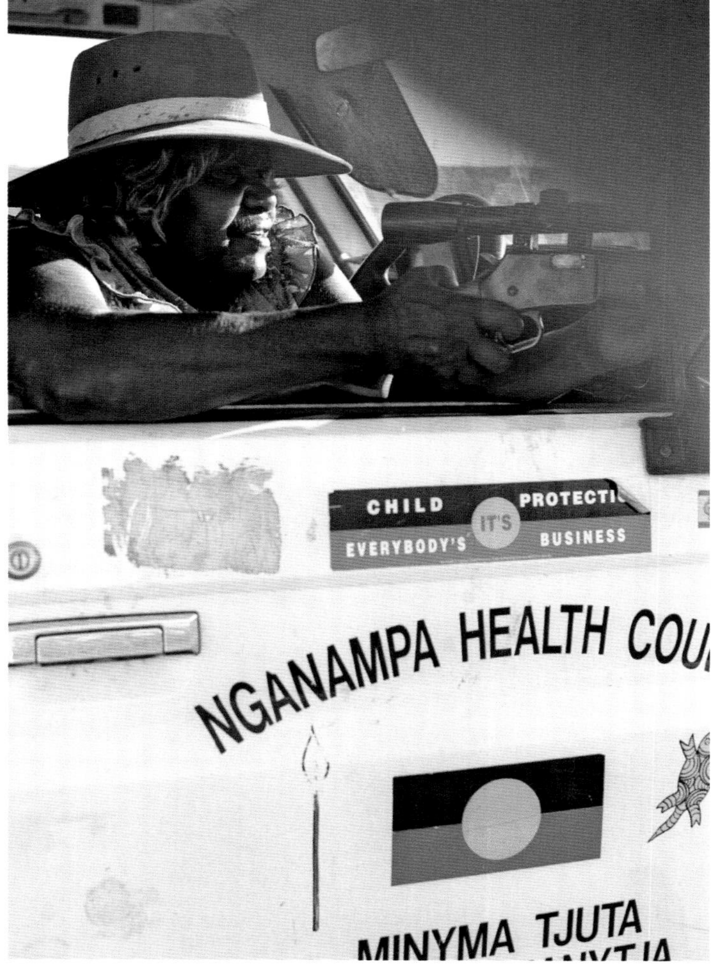

Nura hunts for meat on her way to Kalka for a women's health meeting. (Photo: Suzanne Bryce / Ara Irititja 124051)

pet dogs, never hearing the call of the wild dingo. They have lost the art of hearing the wild bush sounds.

Anyway after a long time building fences and yards on the stations, I decided to return to Ernabella for a while, and after that I went over to Kulgera. I was expecting my baby, and my baby arrived while I was at Kulgera. Baby number one was born at Kulgera. Not long after that I went to Mount Cavanagh, otherwise known as Watjula. I have two daughters, Ann Karatjari Ward and Jeannie Ampintangu Ward.

Ann was born in the bush near Kulgera. My older sister accompanied me and showed me everything. That was Clem Toby's mother – she was a very good midwife. She helped me. She told me 'I'm going over there, because my feet are burning.' I said, 'No please don't leave me! I don't know what to do!' But she was tricking me and then suddenly the baby moved! I said, 'Hey! I think the baby is coming!' Then later on the baby started coming. I told all the women, 'You all go away!' I was burning up. There was also another midwife around, Muni, who was the policeman's wife from Mount Cavenagh. She was a white woman, a white Yankunytjatjara-speaking woman. She'd had six children in the bush. She told me she'd help and I had a surprise, because I'd never given birth in the company of a white woman before. That policeman's wife's name was actually Ann, and this woman Ann said to me that seeing as my baby daughter was born at her place, then I could give her the name of Ann if I liked. She gave her name to Ann. I was delighted. She was not an Aboriginal woman. She was a white woman. She was a white woman but she knew a lot about women's issues and she spoke fluent Yankunytjatjara. She knew about birthing of babies who were born in the bush. She told me she'd had her own babies in the bush too – on the dirt even!

After that I went back to Wapirka for a while, until one day someone suggested we all go hunting for dingoes. 'Come on everyone! Let's go hunting dingoes! We should go hunting young dingoes!' In those days it was usual for people to go hunting dingoes for their scalps or skins. So off we all went hunting dingo, down south. I have forgotten the names of all the places we travelled to because we were away for a long time, but I do remember that this was when I developed a serious problem with my right breast. It happened because my baby had a sore mouth and problems sucking milk.

In the end I said, 'Come on, we need to go and get me some medicine, quickly. I need medicine or tablets'. My husband said, 'What kind of medicine do you need? Don't worry. I will get something from the store.' But while I was waiting, my breast became terribly swollen and engorged. It was huge and it became really hot. I developed a fever and became delirious

Nura teaches her granddaughters the correct dance steps and gestures, during an inma festival, Ernabella, 1976. (Photo: Mike Last / Ara Irititja 6867)

and very ill. In the end I had to demand to be taken to Ernabella, 'Quick! I need to get to Ernabella for a needle! I am very ill!'

So I was taken to Ernabella. But unfortunately the motorcar broke down half way. We were stuck half way, miles from help. We camped the night, and early next morning my mother had an idea. She went and dug out a rabbit burrow and came back with a brace of baby rabbits, newborn, their eyes still shut, and all with very dark fur. She also had their mothers, which she cooked. She opened up the guts of each of the baby rabbits while they were still uncooked and fresh, and opened up their stomachs which were full of their mother's rabbit milk. This fresh rabbit milk she then rubbed all over me: all over my head, neck and throat, and breasts. 'Mum! What' are you doing?' Yet it worked; I cooled down, and started to feel much better. The milk on my breasts was really cooling, and although it was a really hot day, with hot sun, my breasts were cooling. My breast had been completely engorged and tight and I hadn't been able to feed my baby at all. But my mother's idea was brilliant and it began working, although I didn't understand at first. But I was so ill, and my breast was so huge that it had torn my dress open and my breasts were hanging out of the rip, they were so enormous and tight. So that is how I recovered initially from that terrible situation, and all without Panadol or needles. Eventually we got going again and finally pulled in at Kenmore. By time we got to Kenmore I was much better, well on the road to recovery. When we finally arrived back at Ernabella I was

Nura with her two daughters, Jeannie Ampintangu (left) and Anne Karatjari (right), at the Ernabella hospital. (Photo: Hancock family / Ara Irititja 76142)

almost back to normal; I said, 'I am practically cured. The problem has been fixed. I'm fine now.' Just to be sure, I was given some tablets by Sister Mark or Ann.

What my mother had done for me was what women have done for each other since time immemorial. These traditional women's medicines have been used for centuries and they are very effective. We have wonderful bush medicine of our own here. Women have great ideas and ways of healing each other.

Another of our traditional medicines is from the faecal matter found in the gut of the anumara type of witchetty grub. You cut the grub open and squeeze out the kuna, or dryish faecal matter, and you rub it onto itchy rashes. For really bad rashes, this is the medicine to use. If you have small children you can keep them in really good health by using common remedies like these.

My youngest daughter Jeannie was born in Ernabella Clinic. By then I knew what do to. She was put through the smoke. When a new born baby is put through the smoke, all its strengths come to the fore. They become strong in themselves, their blood becomes strong, their bones become strong, their brains grow, they lose their fear and they tend not to cry as much. They grow up strongly and they are hungry for breast milk, which we know is the best. They grow up strong and live strong lives.

If you put the child's feet in the smoke it makes them strong and it helps with their balance. Children who do not go through the smoke do not have the same sense of balance, and are prone to tripping over. The mouth goes into the smoke and the two hands. The older sister helps with that. Baby and the older sister will go in, or else it might be baby and the youngest older brother. The mouth goes in as well. Smoke makes them warm, gives them a warm nose, and spreads out their skin and makes them good and strong. We smoke the back to make the lungs spread out and be strong. It is a good practice, good Law, good stories or Tjukurpa.

My generation knows all about those traditions, but I am afraid some young mothers of today don't like the idea of the smoking, and say, 'No way! Don't bother with the smoke!' Why?

Are they scared they'll get burnt? Their stomachs, breasts and blood, what will happen to it? Well, laying the body upon the smoke will be better for them. They should do it. That's what we always tell them. 'Listen, you young mothers, when you've just given birth, you should stay right away from the men. The men will smell you and your baby and it is not right.' You should keep away. The men will say, 'You need to be concentrating solely on your baby. Stay in camp and make sure your baby is going to be strong and healthy. Put your baby through the smoke and make sure you and the baby are both well and strong'. Then later, when the baby is older, his umbilical cord will be ready to come off. The father can cut the cord off. You need to take the cord off but do not do it straight away. Don't be too quick about it, or else it will affect the baby and his father. The father risks his own health if the cord comes off too quickly. So the father has to cuddle the baby a lot, and that is what makes a strong baby and a strong father. We have so many Tjukurpa on these subjects.

Birthing is a private women's business. We used to give birth in the wild bush. But we all knew how to do it and we are very knowledgeable from ages of experience. It was a good way, the proper way. You know what I am talking about. This is women's birthing knowledge. I talk about it but I always tell the truth and the way it is. It is the way women give birth, how they do it, how they use fire and what they do at night, and what they do about the blood and how they look after themselves. Only women can do this together. It is women's business. Uwa.

Both my daughters are grown up now and have their own children. I have helped to give birth to many children, and they all went through the smoke. My great-granddaughter and my granddaughter were born at Congress, or rather, Alukuṟu. I assisted at their births too, and they were put through the smoke as well. Vivian's baby was coming, and I got a phone call to go and help, and my grandson was born that way. As soon as he was born I put him through the smoke. And I can tell you he never goes into hospital for any illness. He has never been evacuated on a plane! He is strong. He is a football player. Look at all the other children, though. They are all weak; they've all got diarrhoea. They go to hospital all the time, and they are all on formula; they are sick all the time. They are born and go straight onto the drip. I always say, 'Get that child on the breast straight away!' They say, I can't, no breastmilk!' Maybe a grandmother will say, 'Daughter, you have got to give your baby breastmilk! Keep it up or else she'll refuse you!' And it is true, if you don't they do refuse.

The grandmother is the first one to see the newborn child. After the child has been smoked and is strong and well, the child is presented to the grandfather. The grandfather then embraces the newborn close to his body. This is called ngampaltjunkunytjaku, and in doing so, the grandfather passes his good qualities onto his grandchild. Fathers only see their babies after they have been smoked, and after the grandfather has embraced them. Grandfather first, father second. This is the correct way. Sadly, most children born today are not being smoked and are going home far too soon.

A brand new baby is embraced by the grandfather or grandmother in order to ensure that the baby has as strong a body as the grandparent. If a grandmother is a wonderful loving and caring grandmother who always brings water and digs for honey ants and rabbits for other people all the time, she can bestow that generosity of spirit onto her grandchild with her body. The grandfather does the same, and so this is a grandparents' story, the grandfather and the grandmother both embrace their grandchild. A small newborn baby is embraced like that, pressing the bodies and feet together, in order to pass on good qualities.

After the ngampaltjunkunytjaku 'giving good qualities' embrace, with the body and the feet, the baby's hair is looked at, and if, just say the baby's grandmother has white hair, some is cut and some is woven into the baby's hair. The mother's breasts are wetted. Later, the hair falls off. This happened to me. I had Wally Dunn's hair put onto my head, because we were born at more or less the same time and because his mother said we are ngaḻungku, or twins. So his hair was cut and given to me. He is my nephew.

If they are right-handed, then a string band, a puṯuru is wound around the right hand, and if they are left-handed, then

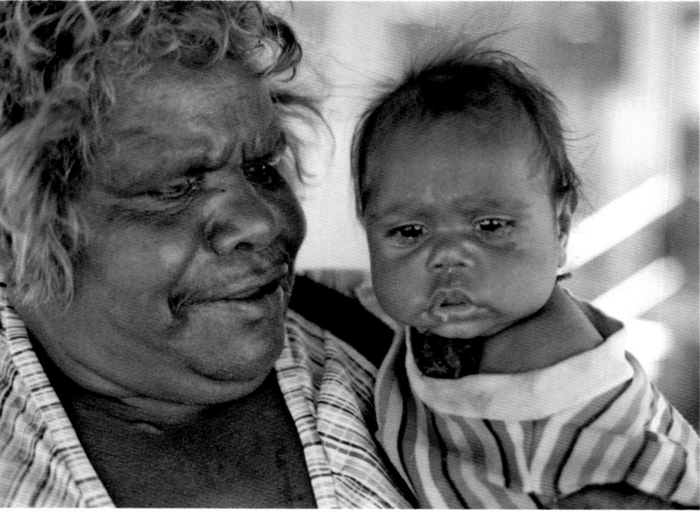

Nura holds baby Paula Young, who wears a traditional pacifier around her neck, Ernabella, c. 1996. (Photo: Suzanne Bryce / Aṟa Irititja 124040)

a puṯuru is wound around the left hand. So a right-handed grandfather will do that to his right-handed grandson, and a left-handed grandfather will do that to his left-handed grandson, so the child will grow up to be like them. The child can grow up to be as good as their grandfather, and the grandfather can also cause the child to be left- or right-handed by this method. Then people will say, 'Look, he is tjamuku aṟa kanyini!' 'He is carrying his grandfather's qualities!' This is from the loving, giving embrace, because it is given to the baby at that time. What a beautiful tradition that is! We have so many beautiful traditions like that, which we can pass on. This is the knowledge that I carry, that I wish to pass down. The old people all know about these wonderful traditions.

The grandparent's name is given, and when the child gets bigger the name is spoken out loud, and everyone else will then know the child's name. Later, when the grandparent passes away, everyone knows that the child still carries their grandparent's name and good qualities, so if they see the child speeding along, they'll say, 'Ah look at that! The child is speedy like his grandfather!' The child will be just like their grandparents, speedy, or right-handed, or left-handed, or a great hunter of kangaroo, perentie, euro and rabbit.

Mothers in the past used to always make a special string loop to put around their baby girls' necks. A manguṟi. A manguṟi would be made for a baby girl, and the baby would hold onto it, and drift off to sleep. When they woke up again, they'd look at the manguṟi and would soon drift back to sleep again. Wiṟu way. This was useful for a mother if the water was a long way away. If the mother had to climb to the top of a mountain or a hill to collect the water and have to climb all the way back down again to bring the water back to camp, it was good if the baby slept the whole time she was away. But if the baby woke up and it had a manguṟi to hold, she wouldn't cry and would just lay there happy and contented until she came back. The boys have a different story, but I can't really talk about it because it is watiku way, or men's way. Watiku. Men's. The grandfathers can tell their grandsons about it. But we give our baby girls a little manguṟi to play with.

Infants are only ever fed breastmilk – this is the nguli-nguli stage. Only when the child is starting to crawl around during the maṟa-maṟa stage are they given meat or kuka. They are given soft meats to carry around and to suck on. They are not given mai or food just yet. They are only given kuka at that stage. They are given meat on a bone to gnaw on and this is good for their teeth and bones, and the little bit of meat on the bone is sucked and eaten off. This is a good way to bring up children and it is proven to work. We never give too much, just a little bit. Mothers know what to do because they have been taught properly. They know when to give the baby their first pieces of meat because the baby will start crying for it. They see the meat and they want it and they start crying for it, and so they are given a bone with some meat on it to gnaw and carry around. White people give hard biscuits to their babies when they are ready for it. The children suck on the hard biscuits and it is good for their teeth and gums, and then when their teeth come up properly they are given a little bit of meat to eat. Their teeth don't come up all at once; they come up slowly, one or two at a time.

A child that cries all the time has dropped its bone and meat or is crying for it, and if it is offered breastmilk and refuses, then the child is picked up and carried around and is taught and shown what is around it, to teach it about its surroundings, until it is distracted and stops crying. A mother who has great love for her child will do this. Some mothers don't care though, and they go, 'Why is this child crying all the time? Why are you crying for goodness sake? I'm going to get up and walk away from you in a minute, if you don't stop crying'. If they say things like that to the child, that is not good – wiru wiya. It is a bad thing to do to a child, to speak to it in an aggressive and intimidating way.

When a child is unwell and cranky because he is starving, he will become an angry child, angry at his mother for not feeding him or giving him anything to drink. I was never brought up like this. I was brought up beautifully in a very strong way. Talking like this makes me really nostalgic for the good old days, and so does looking at pictures on Ara Irititja.

Kunma Piti is my family's country, my homeland, here at Kunma Piti. It is on Yankunytjatjara country. Frank Panma, another of my husband's older brothers, taught us all about the area. I was taught all about this country a long time ago by my father and my grandmother. My mother did not teach me about this place, it was my grandmother; not my mother's mother but another grandmother – this one was Nyinguta's, Rama's and Purki Edwards's mother. She was a brilliant teacher to us all.

After my husband learnt all about this area, he decided to make his homeland right here at Black Hill One. He came and had a good look around, and he was shown the big old itara tree, the bloodwood, nearby and he was told it was old Wati Kunma, who stopped here after going hunting. My husband and I got our home built at Kunma Piti and we moved in. We got that house from Wali Kanyilpai from the South Australian government, because we are close to the South Australian border here at Black Hill. We got the other places set up afterwards. We are not allowed to cut any of these trees as they are all associated with Wati Kunma, and so when we built our house here, fairly close to the sacred site, we made sure it was still within a safe boundary, because my husband knew the details.

Kunma Piti is also known as the Black Hill area, where there are four bores. The four Kunma bores are referred to collectively as the Kunma Piti area. We look after them all, south-east of Ernabella. There is Black Hill One, where my house is. This house is in good condition and there is the itara tree nearby, which is Wati Kunma himself. Black Hill One is Kunma Piti, because Wati Kunma is here. Black Hill Two is my brother Punch Kawaki's house. It stands empty now.

Black Hill Three is my niece's house. This house is for the children. We made Number Three for the children and we

Deanne Ward in a t-shirt featuring Nura's design of Wati Kunma, the totemic ancestor of Black Hill. (Photo: Suzanne Bryce)

incorporated all of them, so we could become official traditional owners. I live here now in order to hand the place on to my children, who are the true traditional owners. They all want to live here.

Black Hill Four is also empty. It used to be Punch Kawaki's house, but he put horses and donkeys in there. So only horses and donkeys use it now. There is a water tank on a very tall stand here, with an excellent water supply. The younger generation want to put an orchard in here, similar to the orchard at Kenmore Park, which is very productive. Black Hill Four is a very good place to grow oranges, grapes and mandarins.

My old husband always said, 'I'm living here in order to protect this place for my descendents. When I depart this mortal earth, I want all you children to take over and continue to look after it'. And I am the same, I wanted to live there and look after it too. But I have been in hospital so much lately; the children have been taking their turn at living here and looking after the place.

Not far from the Black Hill bores is Kelvin's Well. Kelvin's Well was dug by my husband Bully's older brother Kelvin Ward a long time ago. Kelvin's Well is fairly close to Black Hill One.

You know, there are many other important sacred sites near where we live at Black Hill and the whole Kunma Piti area. We forbid the children to go there. We say, 'Children! Do not climb up on those hills. Stay away. Just stay down below and play happily there, close up to camp. If you want to go hunting tjirilya, just stay down below. Tjirilya (echidnas) will hear you playing happily and they'll come up to see you. It is okay for you to play around those lower hills but stay away from those sacred places. Tjirilya comes out when it is going to rain. They love the wet weather and they come up during the damp wet weather. So if you want to see tjirilya, stay close to camp and play happily, and you will'.

Kunma Piti itself is a men's sacred site, sacred to men. My grandfather's generation used to go along that way. They would stop there on their way for hunting, and they'd pay their respects, and then they'd go back the way they came and roast their kangaroo meat over near that hill there, which is Wati Kunma's place.

We used to see that Wati Kunma tree when I was just a young lady. I remember taking Maggie Mumu on horseback to see it. That time, we were travelling along a creekbed, when we saw a kanyala. We ran and grabbed it by the tail and Maggie Mumu and I got it. It was a big river bank, which made it difficult, and the horse tried to run away. I was too scared to grab the kanyala by the tail but Maggie wasn't. She was not scared at all! We young people were always trying to catch animals by the tail, such as ngintaka and so on, but it can be risky.

Kunma would get angry sometimes if there was a drought and no meat to be had. So if there is a drought, we go and speak to Kunma and tell him our problems. Kunma would solve the problem and help to provide meat to the hungry. Wati Kunma himself looks like an enormous fly.

Kunma flies are big bloodsucking flies that bite people, horses, cattle and kangaroos. They can bite kangaroos on the eyes and make them go blind. Back in the early days when I was a little girl we protected ourselves from kunma flies by building a solid wiltja. Adults would warn us when kunma flies were coming, and we'd hear the sound they made when they arrived. They'd be seeking out fresh blood and they'd make people blind.

Frank Panma always warned us to stay away from Kunma hill. 'If you climb that hill and touch those rocks, Wati Kunma will come out, and he'll get to you very quickly. He can detect fresh meat and living things, and he bites.'

Despite these scary stories, my old husband decided this was still where he wanted to build our homeland, because his older brother had dug Kelvin's Well nearby. We would come here and work often. Gordon Ingkatji's son lived here too, and he always loved it here. Mumu was born here, so this is Mumu's area too. Everyone was very happy for us to be living here. This is my place.

6. My working life

I've been a worker all my life. I've told you about the skills I learnt as a kungkawara. I worked on lots of different stations with my father and with my husband. I worked in the craft room at Ernabella. I've been a hard worker all my life. Now I want to tell you about other work I did as a minyma, an older woman with children.

When I started being a health worker I had just the one daughter, Karatjari. I wanted to become a health worker because there was no other work I was interested in, and anyway I was already helping Purki Edwards. Karatjari and Purki (Nancy Purki Thompson) went to pre-school while I was working as a health worker. This was in the days before Nganampa Health Council. We didn't change over to the Nganampa Health Council until a long while after.

Purki Edwards taught me a lot, along with sisters Julie and Anne. They were all nurses and sisters and they taught me everything. Anne was the first nurse in Ernabella that I worked with and then she left to get married. She had a wedding in the church. She was my teacher. She was brilliant, a wonderful woman. She taught me about medicine and I understood everything and took it all on board. She taught me all about tablets and their names.

Nurse Nura reassures a patient about to receive treatment in the old Ernabella hospital in 1975. (Photo: Hancock family, Ara Irititja 76151)

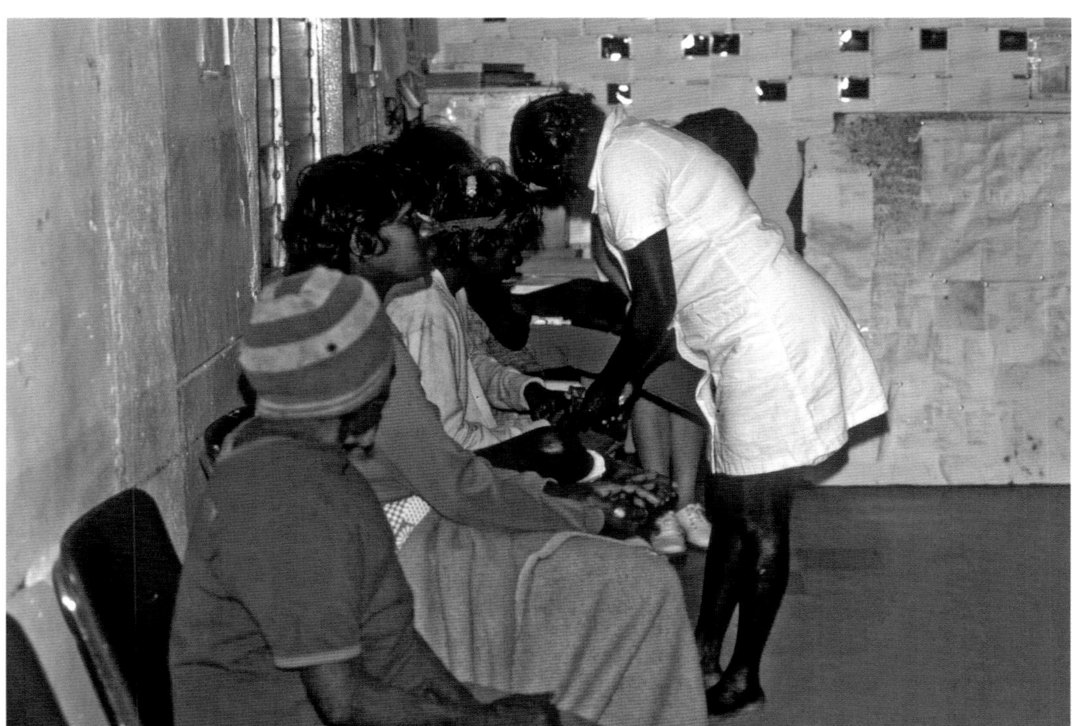

I kept working after I had my second daughter, Ampintangu. I still worked as a health worker because I loved it so much. I had an insatiable thirst for learning and knowledge. I didn't think about including bush medicine until a lot later. It wasn't until my youngest brother died, and two of his little small children – Patrick and Nancy Wawiriya Thompson – came along, that I thought about bush medicine.

I loved my work and I couldn't get enough of it. I'd start work at 8.00 am and I'd work right through until 5.30 knock-off time when I'd go home. At 8.00 am in the morning I'd go back to the clinic to start work again. We'd go together, the sister and I, working together in the clinic. I'd take my uniform off in the hospital and wash it there. Health workers these days do not wear a uniform in their work. No. They don't. I didn't have a house at Pukatja. I asked for a house but I never got one. I camped out. Then we only had wiltjas, or shade shelters. A lot of us were living in the open, outside Kawaki's house. Kawaki's house used to be next door to the policeman's house.

I worked all my life, the same as a sister or a doctor works. Our doctor was a woman, Doctor Matilda. We also had doctor Baker who looked after all the sick Anangu. Paul Torzillo is working in that capacity now. He's with Nganampa Health now. Sister Anne, Sister Julie and Sister Andrew, they were all really great sisters who taught me a great deal. Nganampa Health was encouraging me and pushing me to learn more and more.

When I was a health worker, I would go and pick up sick patients and the young children, as well as pregnant women for their checkups. I would make healthy lifestyle plans with diabetics, looking at their diet and exercise. I worked very hard with the diabetics, teaching them how to live in a good way.

After that, I started working with young mothers in Pukatja clinic to teach them about traditional women's healing techniques so they could be a bit more independent. I used to help with childbirth and the smoking of babies and working with the pregnant girls. I worked in a really good way, slowly and gently. The first thing we did with the young mothers was to teach them about putting their babies through the smoke. Newborn babies and their mothers' abdomens and breasts are put through the smoke. The babies are put through and the mothers are put through, and this makes them both stronger. I am a smoked baby and all my children are smoked. My older sister taught me about smoking babies. When I saw it the first time I thought she would give the baby bronchitis, but of course it didn't! The whole point of it is to prevent illness and to make the baby stronger. I have told you this before. That is the work I did, and I helped with. I helped with many birthings. My mother helped me to help them. We worked together. We worked all day. The hours were long.

I can heal by using the healing breath and blowing on a sore. Blowing on the injury, wrapping and blowing. It is a different way altogether to the work that our traditional healers, ngangkari, do. Ngangkari also do a blowing treatment. Blowing breath on is a quick way to heal.

I taught a lot of people the Pitjantjatjara language. I taught the people that flew the planes, the pilots. They would tell me how much they enjoyed their lessons and how much they'd learnt. I'd remind them that if a senior man, a tjilpi, wanted to talk to them that they must listen very closely. Listen closely to what he has to say. I was a Pitjantjatjara teacher for a very long time. I taught with Cliff Goddard, too. It was really good. They'd listen and learn, so when they'd go and pick up a sick person, or go some place to see a sick person, they'd be able to understand a lot more of what the sick person had to say. It worked well.

Nura and fellow health workers display posters at an AIDS awareness workshop, Ernabella, 1987. (Photo: Nganampa Health, Ara Irititja 53519)

Ernabella hospital workers, 1975. Nura (third from right) is with daughter Anne Karatjari. (Photo: Hancock family / Ara Irititja 76136)

I used to teach bush medicine as well. I would teach what to do about snake bite and everyone would listen and learn. They'd all remark on how much I knew and the reason for that is the elder women who have been my teachers over the years. I also worked as an HIV AIDS educator. I did a course in Indulkana about AIDS. We also did a painting about AIDS. We made a t-shirt with a depiction of the disease on it. The disease has germs, which look like snakes or worms, but really they are called germs. We would call those germs liru or poisonous snakes, as a way of telling the story. Either way they are germs, which live in the blood and they look a bit like snakes. After the course we went back to work in the clinic. We made the painting to illustrate the disease AIDS and HIV.

I remember when Pitjantjatjara Council got started and when the big Land Rights movement started. All the meetings were being held in all the different communities and all that, but I couldn't get very involved because I was a full-time worker at the clinic, and simply too busy with nursing.

In 1980, my brother Kawaki organised us all to go down to Adelaide together for Land Rights meetings, and we all camped together down there, the focus being Pitjantjatjara and Yankunytjatjara Land Rights. We were down there, giving speeches and talking about Land Rights, and many marvellous stories were being told, and many wonderful speeches were made. We all had a lot to think about and consider. After that Nganyinytja went right to the centre of the meeting. She had so much confidence. We were saying, 'Hang on, you are just one lady, going in to the centre of that meeting!' But she replied, 'No! I'm going in because I want to hear everything that is being said!' So in she went, all alone, while the rest of us stayed in our group. But away she went, full of confidence and she listened and gave her strong support to the government representatives who were supporting us. They, too, were impressed with her,

Nganyinytja addresses an early Pitjantjatjatjara Council meeting; her influence and mentoring led to the formation of the Ngaanyatjarra Pitjantjatjara Yankunytjatjara Women's Council. (Photo: Phillip Toyne, Pitjantjatjara Council / Ara Irititja 55805)

and remarked on her, 'This woman has strong ideas!' Everyone was impressed with her. We were all there, absolutely everybody, men, women and children, because we all wanted to make the point that we all wanted our land. It was really important for us to be down there.

I did get to go to Itjinpiri, in 1980, when we won the Land Rights. I did go and I stayed a while, and then I had to return. I did get to see the government people though. My younger brother was heavily involved, so of course I knew everything that was going on even though I was very busy. Kawaki received the Land Rights Act, which was a very large bound document, like a large certificate, bound in brown leather with gold lettering. David Tonkin, the South Australian Premier gave it to him at that ceremony at Itjinpiri.

Because of all that hard work that the main team did, they were later awarded a Member of the Order of Australia in 1994: Kawaki, Donald Fraser, my younger sister Tjikalyi Colin and Ivan Baker. Oh my goodness, what wonderful people! They put the years in, they did! Ivan was working for Nganampa Health long before even Nganampa Health was created. He set it up! He worked for the original health service, the Pitjantjatjara Homelands Health Service established in 1977, which then became the Pitjantjatjara Ngaanyatjarra Health Survey before Nganampa Health started in 1984. He also was busy with the Pitjantjatjara Council.

After years of strategic meetings, the Pitjantjatjara Council wins land rights. Nura's brother Kawaki Punch Thompson signs the historic Pitjantjatjara Land Rights Agreement in the South Australian Parliament House with Premier David Tonkin. (Photo: Phillip Toyne, Pitjantjatjara Council / A<u>r</u>a Irititja 55815)

When Dr Paul Torzillo came, and they started Nganampa Health with Glendle Schraeder, I started working with them around 1986 for UPK: Uwankara Palyanku Kanyinytjaku. I worked on UPK, helping them develop plans for the environmental health of houses, yards and communities. I was a co-researcher with my brother, Kawaki, and we were part of the Research and Development team. Stephan Rainow and Paul Pholeros were in our team too. We worked as a team of four, travelling together. I was teaching and showing everyone where the roads were and the houses and all the different places. When those first houses went in, they were lovely houses. I worked with Glendle, Mesfin Alazar and Kaisu Vartto as part of the UPK team, too. My niece Melissa was always travelling with our team, because she was still only a little girl then. She was always with us, she never missed a trip. Melissa learnt a great deal on those trips, she really did, and she's not forgotten it either. She's intelligent and very switched-on because of those early experiences. I'm pleased about that. It was good having her along, because she has picked up so much knowledge. The UPK work was brilliant work. UPK still exists, as it is ongoing. It is still a good working model. Paul Pholeros and Stephi are still working with it.

Later on, in 1988, my older and younger sister started up Mai Wi<u>r</u>u, promoting good diet and exercise to prevent the spread of diabetes. I began working with Mai Wi<u>r</u>u and soon became an Executive Member. The two sisters started up Mai Wi<u>r</u>u while I was still working in the clinic. They were doing a fantastic job. They specialised in baking healthy muffins with vegetables and bush seed, and they would hand out the muffins to the children and to the grown-ups. The muffins were good for you. That should have been the start of a good health regime. From that, we should all be good and healthy! They were intended to promote healthy eating but sadly, we'd been eating poor quality food from poor quality stores for far too long and we continued to do so. We worked together on their project, and we took it in turns to speak about it and give talks. Many of my ideas were developed during those days. Another person who was involved in Mai Wiṟu was Colin Endean, the dentist, who really supported the movement.

Mai Wiṟu came about because we continued to not have access to good food. Our sub-standard stores only ever sold sub-standard foodstuffs, and all we have ever had was rubbish. And so together, our health has collectively declined. The store management never taught us! Aṉangu had never been taught or offered advice on products. The old women and the old men simply took their money into the store and purchased whatever

Key Nganampa Health council directors and staff at a Uwankara Palyanku Kanyinytjaku (UPK) meeting, Adelaide, 1986. UPK is the environmental health program of Nganampa Health. Nura is in red at right in front row. (Photo: Nganampa Health / Aṟa Irititja 51730)

they liked, under the impression everything was nutritious. Yet everything is loaded with too much sugar and salt, and we just ate what was for sale, without any comprehension of what it was doing to us, while all the time we were becoming diabetic. Everything we ate was loaded with sugar, like those cool drinks, and yet the store managers never educated us about what was essential for a healthy life, that educational level of care for us was never implemented. Nothing. We were badly neglected.

Many years ago, I went into Fregon store and I said to the store manager, 'Come on, teach me! Explain all this to me! Which ones are the good foods? Which ones are edible?' I spoke out directly to that store manager, because we were not being taught and suggestions were never made about healthy shopping choices. The stores are stocked with jumbo-sized ice creams and cool drinks, Coke comes in huge bottles, and everything is made of sugar. Fanta, everything is sweet. And this is what we have been innocently drinking, not realizing the truth, not realising that everyone was slowly becoming sick from it. Because of that, our blood has become saturated with sugar. We've all become poisoned and diabetic, and we are all renal patients now because nobody knew, nobody had any idea and not one of our stores bothered to warn us. Nothing. We just purchased whatever was there, and all the stores ever did was take our money, and we paid very high prices for sugar-loaded products, which is wrong.

I remember when people started getting diabetes. Around the early 1980s I remember checking women's blood sugar levels. I would look at the results and I would advise them, 'You are diabetic,' or, 'You are well,' or, 'You have high blood pressure'. That sort of thing. They would wonder, 'Now why did my blood pressure become so high?' This is because nobody understood it was from what came from the store. Nobody had any idea then. It is only recently that we are seeing differences in the stores, but it is only very recently indeed.

UPK was responsible for the change. They are the ones who told us, 'These here, these are the foods that you should be eating.' But only when it was too late! Too late because we are now all diabetic. We are sick already. Another idea UPK had was to work with Anangu to write songs with health promotional messages and warnings. You can hear these on the UPK albums. But again, too late, as our bloodstreams had already been contaminated with sickness. Already. Kidney disease was already rife.

People who were told, 'You've got diabetes. You've got sugar trouble.' They gave up sugar and they started drinking tea with no sugar and they were trying to give up eating the fat on the meat, and they were trying to get more exercise. It was okay for a while, but that ended. There is an epidemic now. I worry about everything all of the time. I worry about the children now, what their future holds for them, after a history such as this.

Young mothers have to work, kids are always sick and going to hospital. The mums would sometimes leave them and walk around. They need to learn how to feed and look after them properly. I used to look after all the kids when they were little but now they are big and are going to school. Young mothers sometimes forget about healthy food and only give their kids junk food. Good food gets the kids strong. We need to put good food into the kids.

We went to an important UPK meeting and we put forward our recommendations, which we laid out in our report. We had been working for a long time on the UPK reports or going around from community to community, looking at environmental health in the communities. Stephi Rainow, Paul Pholeros, Paul Torzillo and I had been travelling around holding meetings and planning. We held many meetings. Kawaki was the chairperson and we were the main health workers for Nganampa Health. Robert Stevens was with us. We were working for Nganampa Health, and we were bringing our knowledge from the bush down to meetings in Adelaide. We were really happy with the meeting and it was a success. UPK is still going strong. Paul Pholeros looks at all the houses and makes sure they are up to standard. Paul Torzillo makes sure the children that live in the houses are as well as they can be. He wants to make sure all children live healthy lives and do not fall between the cracks. The two of them work together on this, and they are a strong team.

Dancers from NPY Women's Council and Bangarra Dance Theatre, Sydney, 2000. Nura, in black, and Stephen Page, were friends and collaborators for many years. (Photo: NPY Women's Council / Ara Irititja 21828)

Petrol sniffing was a big worry. That is so true. It was a big, big worry. Some people have died. Died and finished. And every community cemetery is filled. The community cemeteries are full of dead people – dead from wine and petrol sniffing. The surviving petrol sniffers' brains are all damaged from lead in the brain. They all have acquired brain injury. This is a great tragedy for our people. What a terrible outcome. I have been helping with those victims, where I can, and also with the young women, to ensure that young women manage their health status a bit better. Our younger women are having babies young, but we want those new babies to be strong and healthy. We want those new young mothers to be good parents.

After I finished that UPK work, after I left, something terrible happened in Mimili. A baby was born but the mother passed away. Wrong way. The baby lived, and is now a big child. What a tragedy for that family. It was after that episode that I decided to make the bush medicine video at EVTV in 1986. I made it because of that. Another older sister helped me as she was teaching me too. I'm referring to Fairy's mother Anmanari Alice Nyanitiya. She was teaching me what she knew and I was teaching her what I knew. I was using the video as a teaching tool. You can see it on A<u>r</u>a Irititja today.

I have also taught dance. I have taught the girls and also around Australia. I have had a number of dance students from all over the country, from the AIDT (Aboriginal Islander Dance Theatre) in Sydney. They came up here and were all learning about traditional Aboriginal culture, and I was teaching them different aspects of our culture. I was teaching them dances and dance steps and they were all dancing brilliantly. I was teaching them about our stories and our language, and I remember them watching me as I danced and spoke to them. After Stephen Page saw me dancing, he said, 'Hey, doesn't that woman dance beautifully! She is a beautiful dancer to that inma. Wonderful!'

Stephen said to me, 'Hey, you are an amazing dancer! Do you both dance and teach this dance?' And I said, 'Yes, I teach this dance.'

They decided to ask me, 'Hey Nura, we'd like to ask you something. Can we put a proposal to you?' I said, 'Yes, of course'. 'Would you be interested in coming to Sydney?' This was 1983 I think when they asked me. I replied, 'Really?' 'Yes. There are lots of dancers coming down from Millingimbi and Elcho Island to teach dance workshops to our Aboriginal dance students.' I said, 'Yes, of course I will go. You set it up and I'll come down'. So they returned to Sydney, Stephen Page and the staff, and they organised plane tickets and accommodation, and off we went. We went early in the morning to the AIDT in the Glebe Theatre. We went to Glebe Theatre, and I taught many of our dance steps. They'd said that they wanted to learn my dance steps to my own inma, and I'd agreed to that. I was very happy to do that, and also perfectly confident I could do it too. I wrote things down and I taught some separate girls' and boys' sessions. I taught many of the women for a good long three-hour session. Nobody had done our kind of steps before and they didn't know our inma either.

Nganampa Health UPK team members Paul Pholeros and Nura Ward consult on inclusion of better designed wet areas for community housing, Ernabella, c. 1993. (Photo: Suzanne Bryce / A<u>r</u>a Irititja 124112)

Stephen Page was a great dancer himself. He was a beautiful dancer. I remember thinking to myself, 'Hmm, he is dancing like a wati. He dances like a fully initiated man. His dancing is beautiful to see'. He showed me how he held his body, how he moved his thighs, his feet and his shoulders. I was very impressed by the focused expression on his face, and how he looked ahead and looked behind. And I loved the way he placed the weight upon his feet as he made the different steps. I told him, 'The way you place your feet is perfect when you dance, now just keep going like that.' He was dancing the Emu Dance with the others, who were dancing the steps of the young emus, and he was stepping out like a proper emu. I instructed them to step correctly. 'Place your feet like this, step along the ground the way an emu does. Be an emu. Move your head like an emu. Don't move your head like this, only move it in small movements like an emu does. Look around stiffly. Move your eyes like an emu. Keep your bodies facing forward. Stand still sometimes. You can't see what is sneaking up on you. All you can see are the other emus. Emus can't see what's coming up behind them. Just look at the other emus!'

I was the only teacher at that stage, and so later, when I was back home, a letter came for me at Ernabella. The letter asked me if I could come back again, because they'd loved my work so much, they wanted more. So I went back again.

This time I taught a dance about arriving at a waterhole. This is a bit more of a spectacular dance, a bit more special, and it is about my father's own place, where Wati Ngintaka Tjukurpa lies. I taught them the story and the dances of how Wati Ngintaka stole the Tjiwa, which is a grinding stone, and I watched the men perform the steps. The men danced it beautifully, just like a real wati. There are many special places associated with this story. There are special rocks that look just like ngintaka skin and there are rocks that are really all the different foods that he ejected from his stomach. Tourists visiting that place have all heard about that story. And so anyway, I was asked if I could teach Bangarra Dance Theatre, and so that's exactly what I did. I was teaching them the songs and the dances, and afterwards they asked me questions.

What else did I teach? Oh, yes, Tjala or Honey Ants, Ninu, the Bandicoot. Ngintaka, the Perentie Lizard and Ngantja, the Mistletoe. I taught Ngantja as well. They were very impressed in these true old stories, because these are our true history. They looked at pictures in books-- of bandicoots and perentie lizards, and they learnt about how the songs moved along the land. I have been teaching those songs and dances to Bangarra Dance Theatre. Ngintaka, Tjala, Ili, which are figs and Kuniya, the Carpet Snake. I sang for them and they recorded and were listening to my music. They were listening to my own singing and they were dancing to it. They were dancing amazingly well to my Water Snake dance, Carpet Snake dance and Emu dance and many others. Emu dance and also Walputi (Banded Anteater). They also danced Inma Walputi. They danced beautifully to all of the dances.

On those trips I met the dancers from AIDT and students from NAISDA (National Aboriginal Islander Student Dance Association) with my friend Beth Mitchell in Sydney. In 1984 the NAISDA students came to Ernabella for teaching and you can see that in the EVTV movie on Ara Irititja. In 1984 and 1985 we went back to teach at AIDT and NAISDA in Sydney and also performed Kungkarangkalpa or the Seven Sisters inma at the South Sydney Festival Sydney 1985. Katy Malyungka and Topsy Walter were the singers, and Nyinguta Edwards, Anmanari Alice Nyanitiya, Muwitja Jimmy, Nura Rupert, Inawinytji Williamson and I were the dancers. At the Festival we also showed all our skills from the craft room like hand spinning of sheep's wool and human hair, gumnut and seed jewellery, hook rugs and crochet. I kept teaching dance and we had lots of visits here and there. We kept going back and lots of different women came with me over the years to Sydney, Adelaide and other places including Inpiti Winton. In 1992 I went to Sydney with Imuna Fraser, Mulykiya Ken, Yakuyi Yakiti and Bernard Tjalkurin to teach NAISDA students lots of inma and they featured it in their end of year performance, *Dreaming*. In 1993 AIDT performed a program called *Colours* for the Sydney Festival and I danced with them.

I teach the stories because nobody else can ever own our stories for themselves. Only Anangu can teach and own these stories. So I taught them because I can. I taught the story of Ngintaka and how Ngintaka collected different kinds of foods like wangunu, parka-parka, ngantja and how he ejected them forth, from his mouth. I was asked why: 'Did he have a headache, or what?' I replied, 'No, I expect he had a feeling in his stomach. Perhaps he had an unusual feeling in his stomach which made him express the foods forth from his mouth'. We teach dance because we want to see future generations dance them too. We dance them so they could be witnessed and learnt. My daughter Jeannie knows these dances, but Ann is too shy! Jeannie and Vivian both know how to dance, and my hope is that they will teach the new generation of our relatives coming up. Melissa too, they all know. They are great dancers! They can dance Inma Irati, and Kungka Kutjara, Iyukuta and love songs. They know all them. My mother's Tjukurpa was Kuniya. Kuniya Tjukurpa. My mother wasn't a big singer, though she held her Tjukurpa strongly. My mother and the old ladies are the ones who taught me, so I now follow their line. Her Tjukurpa, her culture and their culture will never die. It is eternal and it is beautiful.

In November 1999 I took a group of singers and dancers to Sydney to perform in Bangarra Dance Theatre's Dance Clan II. I appeared with Aku Kadogo, Ruth Anangka and Nellie Paterson in Ochre and Dust at the Adelaide Festival, 2000. We were sitting on a sandhill on the stage. Together we were talking about Maralinga Tjarutja and the atomic bomb tests, and what happened there. We didn't dance that time. It was different work, talking about Maralinga Tjarutja. I was explaining how the ulpuru and the puyu – or dust and smoke, came up from there, bringing illness. Measles arrived also, bringing measles and illness. But the dust and smoke brought a different illness, different to measles. The dust and smoke was radioactive fallout.

Now I am talking about my work with women's health. In 1993 Suzanne Bryce and I worked for Nganampa Health on this women's health story. Our program was a new one, it was the first time to work like that, separate from the men (and the clinic). We took women and girls out bush for separate sacred women's lessons. We would also take the nurses and the midwives to help them understand. My teachers were the old women. There were some wonderful old ladies at Amata who were my teachers and I am carrying their sacred knowledge. They told it to me. We were able to sit together so that I could think and learn and take it in. This is how I worked. A woman's body is sacred, I can't say too much about that here but our work was based on that understanding and the old women were my teachers.

I teach the young women and young mothers in every community about the sicknesses that they are at risk of like VD, syphilis and gonorrhea. I teach about these sexually transmitted diseases. I warn young women about them. I deliberately frighten young women by telling them the facts. They get frightened and consequently they all take great care of themselves. Those same young women today are all well and healthy. We were teaching girls of the dangers because before, a lot of young

Three friends and loving relatives, Nura Ward, Inpiti Winton and Nyinguta Edwards, take a break between workshops at Bangarra Dance Theatre, Sydney, 2000. (Photo: NPY Women's Council / Ara Irititja 21821)

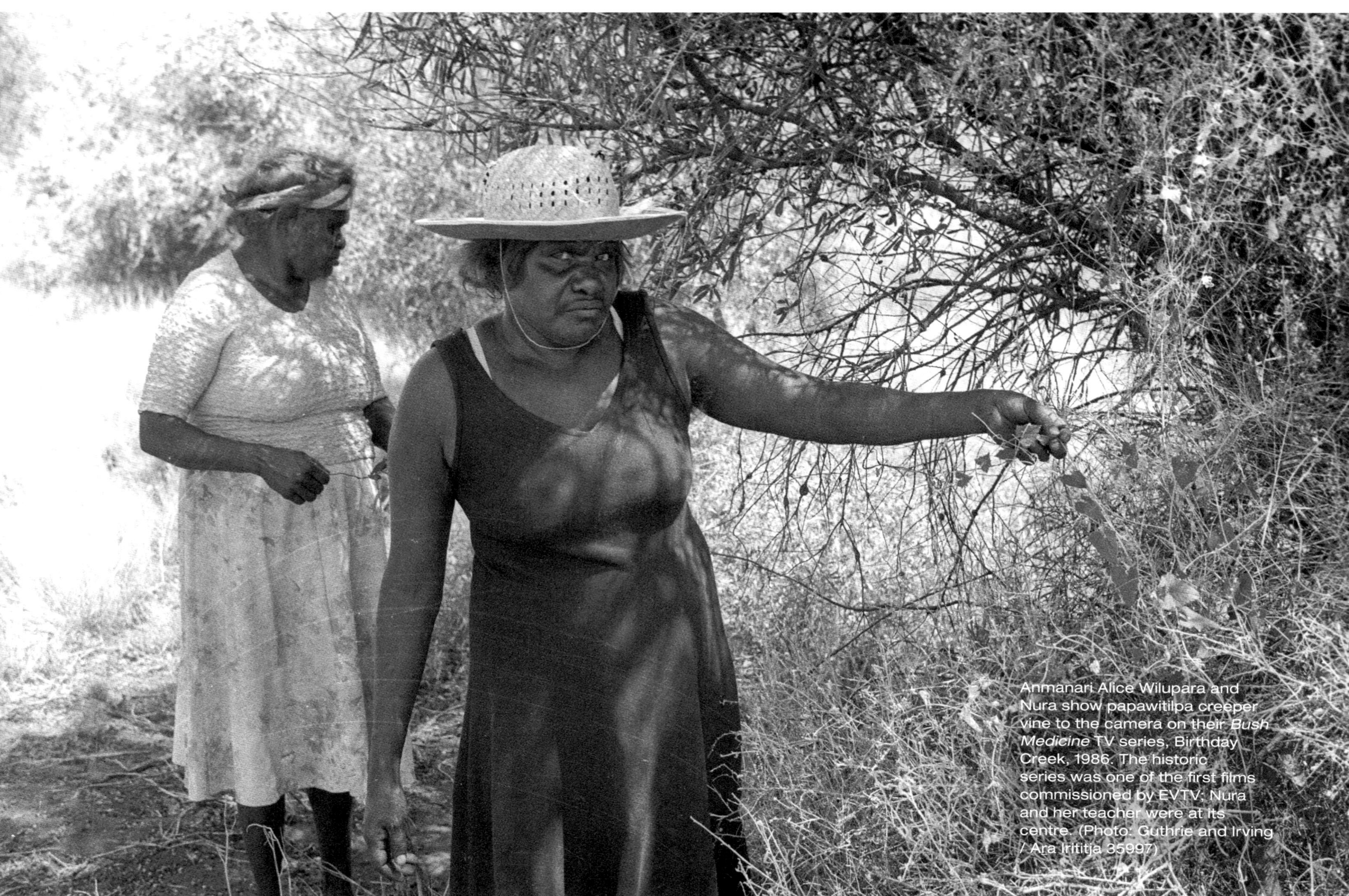

Anmanari Alice Wilupara and Nura show papawitilpa creeper vine to the camera on their *Bush Medicine* TV series, Birthday Creek, 1986. The historic series was one of the first films commissioned by EVTV: Nura and her teacher were at its centre. (Photo: Guthrie and Irving / Ara Irititja 35997)

girls were getting diseases, which was a big worry. They have all been cured since then and have remained clean ever since.

Our sons have the same information also. I do not want to stop doing this work, and I want to continue going to schools teaching young people these important facts. School children need to know. They are at the right age to know.

I have been teaching these important subjects for a very long time. I also teach women about birthing and how babies come into the world. I teach women how to smoke their babies and how to make the smoke and how to use the smoke to strengthen their newborn babies. This makes babies strong. All babies that have been birthed and smoked in the traditional way are immensely strong and healthy. It is a great way to make babies strong.

My daughter Jeannie was with us a lot of the time. I have encouraged her to take on some of the responsibilities like putting babies through the smoke, pointing out particular babies like Jamie Nganingu's granddaughter. She will have more commitment to it as she gets older. I've spoken to my older daughter also and she knows a lot. Some time ago we put Angapiya's baby through the smoke. That child developed really fast and he's never sick.

I have also been working with the Central Australian Aboriginal Congress Alukura in Alice Springs for many years, since 1991. That's where Aboriginal women can go for health checkups and birthing their babies. I was involved in starting up Alukura and what was needed. I have been on the Alukura executive for a very long time and I still am. They always come and get me to bring me to meetings and I go to every meeting. We meet the pregnant women and we talk about women's business. Us older women talk about women's health business. We talk about Arrernte, Alyawarr and other northern groups'

Nura with one of her significant teachers of women's law, Judy Everard on the right, at a women's health workshop outside Mimili. (Photo: Suzanne Bryce / A<u>r</u>a Irititja 100828)

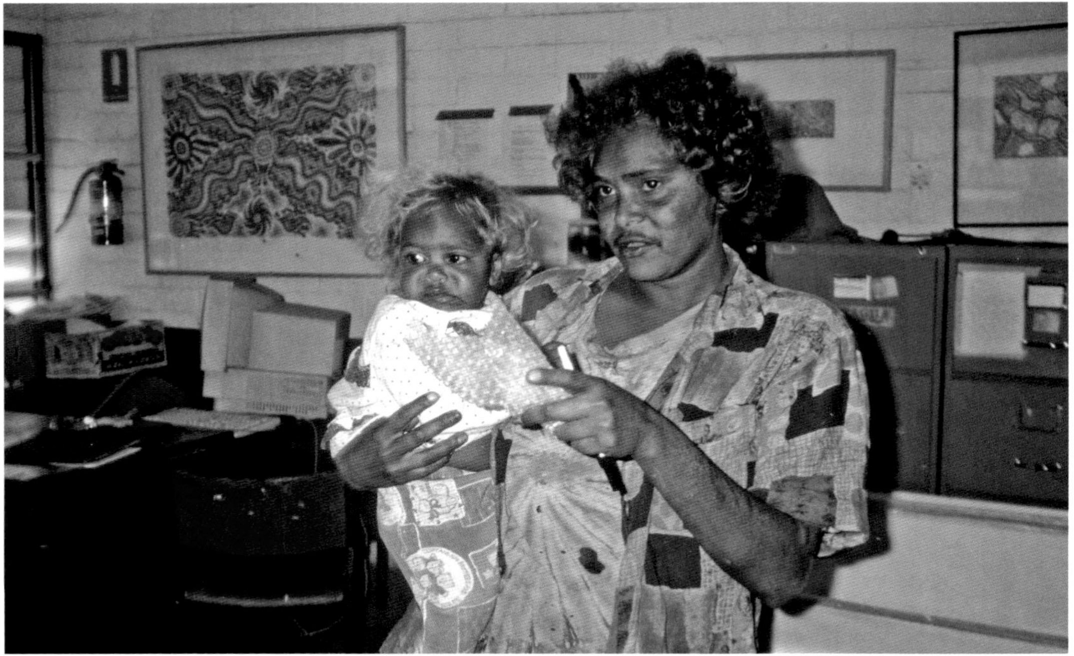

Jeannie Ampintangu with her daughter Jasmine Ward at a teaching day on home birthing at the Ernabella clinic, 1999. (Photo: Suzanne Bryce / A<u>r</u>a Irititja 124065)

Nura brings her health message to the first ever NPY Women's Council Kungka (young women's) Career Conference held at the Uluru – Kata Tjuta Cultural Centre in 1997. (Photo: NPY Women's Council / Ara Iritija 21026)

women's business. I am the only Pitjantjatjara woman that goes to represent my group. I am confident though. I know what I am talking about, that's why. I am not shy in talking up. I always take the lead in talking about it, because it is my work. They always ask me to attend all meetings because they know I speak up. I know everything about women's health. It is serious business. I have been speaking about it and teaching the subject for a very long time, for twenty-five years or more. Alukura recently held its twenty-five years' celebration and I was there. They were very happy that I was able to attend.

Now I want to talk about the Ngaanyatjarra Pitjantjatjara Yankunytjatjara Women's Council, which we also call the NPY Women's Council. It started in 1980 when all the women gathered at Kanpi. The Kanpi meeting was the first time all the women had gathered together to form and launch the Women's Council. After that, everybody came to understand the strength of the women and their Law. Women have their own Law, culture and knowledge. The Women's Council grew up from that meeting, and awareness of the women grew amongst the white women. We Aboriginal women taught everyone else about who we are and what our situation is. At our meetings everybody gets a chance to speak, and when we speak we tell the story straight, and we speak the truth. We speak a true story. We make good appropriate plans. Women's Council has been set up with clear goals to take care of women and families. Our Women's Council now has many teams within the organisation, and its job is to advocate for us in a very strong and appropriate way.

Sadly, many mothers are witnessing their sons bypass the life they would prefer for them, and watch them choose alcohol, marijuana and petrol. When mothers see their sons taking this wrong path in life, they now have someone to report it to. So they put in a report to the NPY Women's Council, who listens to this big worry about the woman's son going off drinking and smoking. Women's Council works straight and true to help sort this problem out.

I was on the NPYWC Executive from 1994 until 1996. In 1994 a large group of us went to Germany to showcase women's Law and culture and dancing.

I became a staff member of the Women's Council in 1996 as Aged Advocacy Project Officer. It was great work and I loved it, working with Tjikalyi Colin and Louise Atherton. I worked with the Tjungu Team on the Aged and Disability Advocacy Project. We used to travel everywhere, collecting information about people with disabilities and the aged. We would collect facts and details and we reported them back to the office, reporting on how people were living and how they were faring. We would report what these people needed. NPY Women's Council's Disability and Aged Advocacy Service is doing a fantastic job of looking after the needs of elderly men and women. I would hear stories and pass on messages to the Women's Council. Some people don't get enough support. People would ring me up for help. I would say, 'Ask me for help too – don't just ask the whitefellas. I can speak English well. Ring us up for help. We want to help.'

This is how we work: white people and black people working together. It is a good way and it is our tjukurpa. Women's Council's way is the proper way; it's the best way. I think there was a really good choice of staff working for the NPYWC, and the staff worked well alongside their Anangu colleagues. I devoted myself to my work at the Women's Council and the Aged Advocacy team, and I helped to formulate the idea of the Tjungu Team. Tjungu means working together, and in this case it meant 'combined services working together co-operatively'. We shared knowledge and the workload. I would share my perspective, knowledge and assistance, and then my offsider would share her perspective, knowledge and assistance. My offsider would follow the proper path as laid out by us Aboriginal women, in other words they are working the way we want them to. And we want them to work together with us, to work alongside of us and to work equally with us. After I got my job in the team, I got myself a malpa colleague. I worked at different times with Jay Nelson, my good friend Kerrie Miller, Nurse Anne, and Muyuru Burton, and in 1997 Maringka Burton joined the team.

It was a great way to work, and I've always been pleased at the way we operated. I have been thinking I might have to raise what I have just said, at the next meeting. Everyone needs to be reminded of how good the Tjungu Team was, and what it was that made it so good. It was truly together, really tjungu. Piranpa, maru; non-Anangu and Anangu working together.

Nura (centre) with fellow members and directors of the NPY Women's Council ready themselves for a long flight to Germany where they showcased their law, culture and art. (Photo: NPY Women's Council / Ara Irititja 22075)

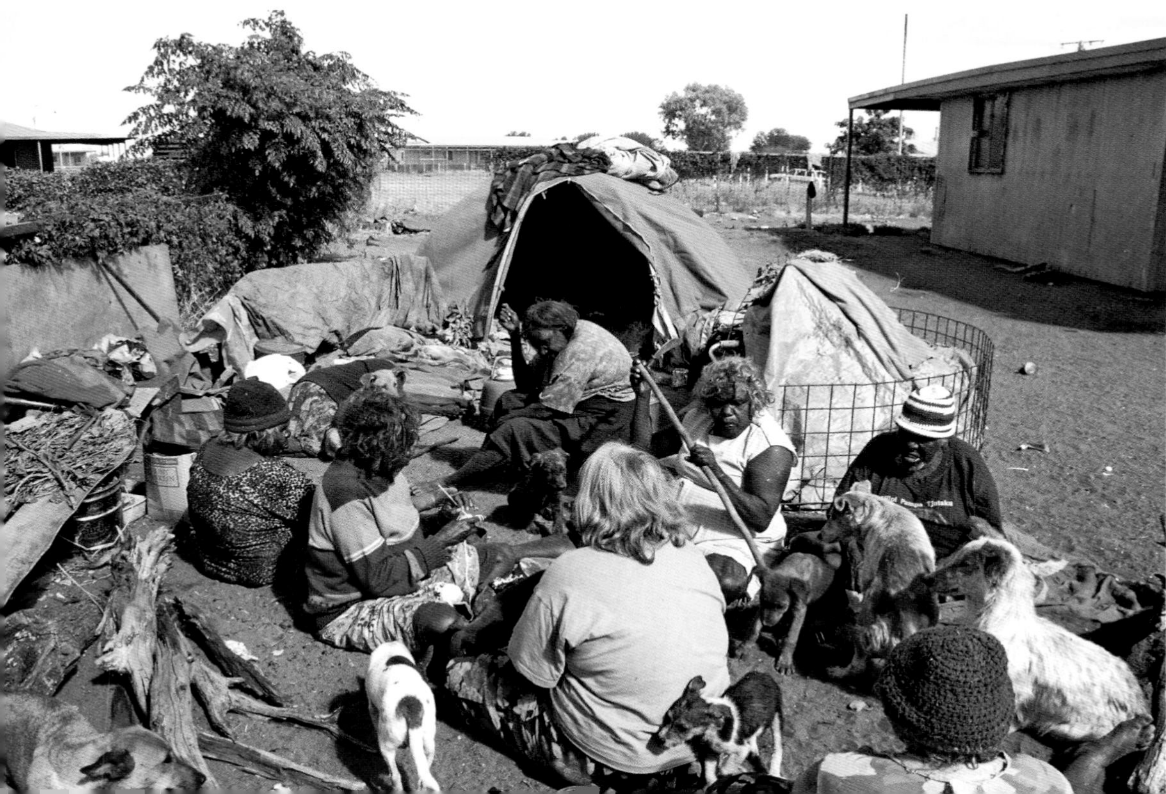

We worked together and shared our knowledge and perspectives, so as to be as effective as we could possibly be. I felt that the team worked really well together, with the team members travelling together and working together, going to meetings together, and going to Law and culture gatherings together. It was great, wiṟu mulapa.

That was a good job, working with the Disability and Aged Advocacy teams, working with the Tjungu Team across the borders in three states, South Australia, Western Australia and Northern Territory. We would go and see all the old and disabled people, we would arrive at their homes and we would say to them, 'I want to sit down with you and talk to you and all your family together. Can we all sit down together and have a discussion? Your family can support you'. We worked as a team of four. We got the oldies blankets and food, and made sure they had a good wiltja and firewood to keep warm. We helped with washing blankets. When they had too much rubbish or no food we spoke to the family about sorting it out. Swags are really expensive, and blankets. Lots of people ask for food. Families should help, that's what a carer's pension is for.

Today, too many disabled people are eating rubbish food. Too many stores sell the wrong food. Diabetics are getting their legs amputated, and then they become disabled. Some people still eat rubbish food and get poisoned from this food, such as getting high blood pressure. Alcohol is a problem, especially for grandmothers looking after the grandchildren while the middle generation is drinking.

That was my work. We worked across the borders, looking at the issues. The families would be really happy to be involved. It was great work. Our idea was to get the families to look after

Nura at the annual Treasures Week, Amuroona, 2000. The week celebrates senior A<u>n</u>angu Pitjantjatjara Yankunytjatjara people. (Photo: Aṟa Irititja 25453)

Nura, in pink, with her mother in striped hat, cuts spearvine for making spindles at a craft workshop, Fregon, 1999. The workshop was part of Nura's aged-care advocacy work with NPY Women Council's Tjungu Team. (Photo: NPY Women's Council / Aṟa Irititja 21747)

the person with the disabilities themselves, and for the person to have occasional respite in Alice Springs. Our policy was for the person to live at home for as long as possible, and as well as possible, until they perhaps needed to go into an aged-care facility. We used to have big meetings about this all the time. We had a big meeting about this in Wingellina once, in order to set up the program and develop the policies. It was great work.

We looked at lots of issues to help, like houses, stores, blankets, swags, food and tents. Remember, in cities, people have houses and accommodation. On the APY Lands there is very little accommodation and people are poor. Life is harder for people on the Lands than in the cities. I've been to places in Adelaide and Sydney where disabled people live. They are looked after well because there are more facilities and social workers. On the Lands there is not much support for wheelchairs. Some family members have been sent away to institutions, and it is hard for families to visit because it costs money for travel and accommodation. This is a big problem. It is very difficult for families to visit their loved ones in institutions. NPY Women's Council disability and carer respite projects have done a good job helping these people, but it still is not enough. Women's Council helps with food and other support.

I would teach my malpa everything. I would train her, and we always worked together well. Whitefellas can get lost and have to be shown the right road. I would always make sure they drove safely and didn't zoom too quickly between communities. I would tell them, 'We have got plenty of time. We will go to each community in its turn and when we arrive, I will go in first to each old lady's or old man's home. Then you will come in and we will work with the family together. We will try to speak with the person's daughter or son first. The first thing we need to do is to listen to what they have to say. What they have to say is very important. Perhaps the old person cannot speak for themselves. Perhaps the daughter needs to speak for her. They will probably speak only to me, so I will get the story first and then I will tell you what they said. Maybe the old lady doesn't talk in English. So I have to help you to understand the issues that are being talked about.'

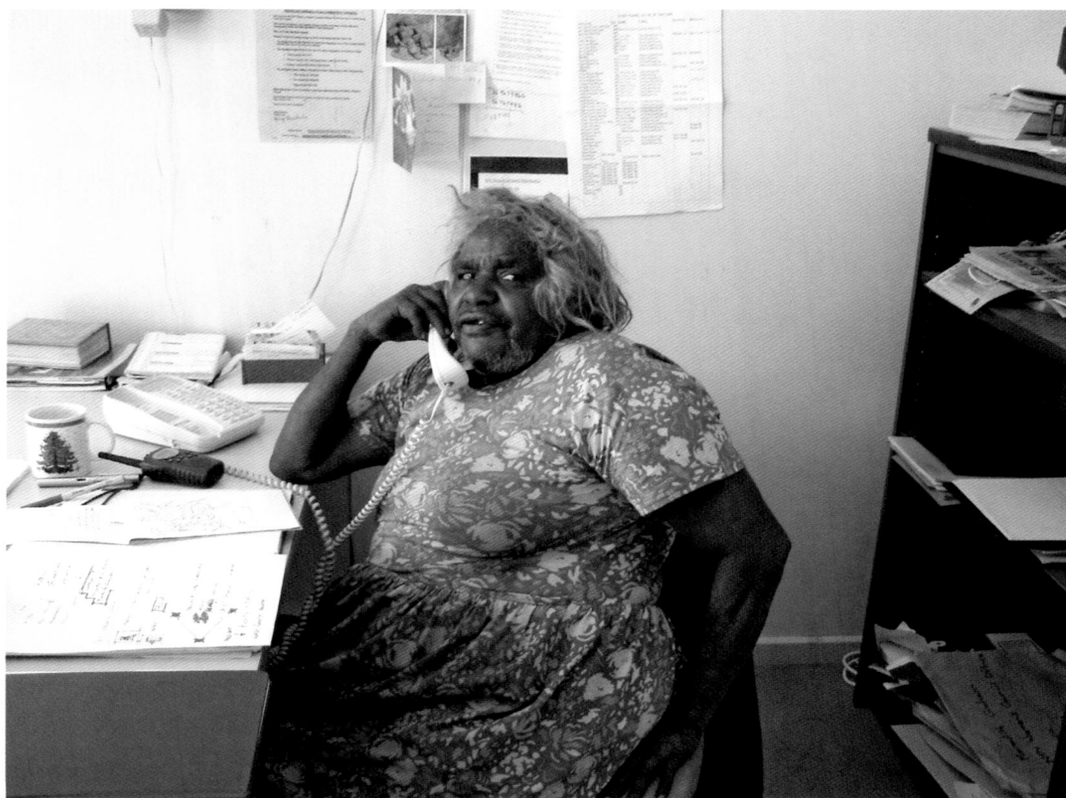

Nura organises respite for clients from the NPY Women's Council office, Umuwa, 1995. (Photo: NPY Women's Council)

We would ask people if they wanted to have a short break in a respite facility, to give the carers a rest. The daughter may be in need of respite herself, and it would do everyone some good. The daughter would talk it over with the parent, and make sure the older person is happy with the arrangements. We tried to not have people go too far away. We didn't want to send people to Coober Pedy or to Port Augusta if we could help it. They are too far away. We only wanted to send people for respite as close to home as possible. Nganampa Health has been speaking up for a large aged-care facility for a long time on the Lands. We have always told them that we need somewhere as close as possible to the people's homes. People want to be close to their families. So now we have our Pukatja Aged Care Centre and it is really good, where daughters and sons and grandsons and granddaughters

Nura and her longstanding colleague, Maggie Kavanagh, cheer on and congratulate members and directors of the NPY Women's Council at a meeting in Kanpi in 2000, for 20 years of successful governance and achievement. (Photo: NPY Women's Council / A<u>r</u>a Irititja 21673)

Stephen Page of Bangarra Dance Theatre, and Nura co-ordinate logistics to get 300 women from across three states to perform at the Sydney 2000 Olympic Games Opening Ceremony. (Photo: NPY Women's Council / A<u>r</u>a Irititja 21720)

can come to visit. They can visit and this makes the older person really happy. If we send people into Alice Springs, it is too far and people begin to forget each other. If we send people a long way away, it is just no good for anybody. We can't send people past Indulkana. That's why Ernabella is such a good location for everyone all around. People from Indulkana go there, people from Fregon go there, people from Amata go across to there, and people from Kalka come across from there, to Ernabella. It is a really lovely place, the Pukutja Aged Care Centre. There are lovely paintings everywhere, and people all talk and tell stories. Family members can come and visit anytime because it is not too far. Family members can bring in mingku<u>l</u>pa too, because the old people crave it.

So that was my work, from 1996 until the year 2000, and it was really good work. We had great team members and we all had good ma<u>l</u>pa, good colleagues and good working relationships. We worked together all the time because that was the policy. It was policy to work together to make sure that there was a proper understanding all around. Working as a team ensured good communication and proper understanding. One person may miss a vital point. It is too much to handle. Not everyone can understand everything. We need to speak clearly and be understood.

I was an Executive Member for the NPY Women's Council again from 2000 until 2005, which is the year Opal unsniffable petrol was launched. For my work with Women's Council, as an Executive Member, I went to Sydney to meet Tony Abbott who was then Federal Minister for Health. He was there and I went to meet him. I told him of the great tragedy that is killing our people. I sang my own petrol sniffing song to him, that my brother Kawaki and I wrote. He understood the words, and I cried as I sang the song, and I told him, 'I have lost everybody in my family, from petrol sniffing. They are all dead. None of the others are in school. They are just wandering around sniffing petrol, defiant of their parents. He listened to me, and then he agreed to give me funding to put Opal in all our communities. But Erldunda won't supply Opal, and Kulgera won't supply Opal. Marla Bore has not put any in. Nowhere on the highway has bothered to put Opal petrol. Curtin Springs has put Opal on.

I must tell you about some of the groundbreaking work of the NPY Women's Council. Since 1988, for many, many years us women had talked at meetings with great sadness about our young people going off drinking at Curtin Springs. So many of our family members were dying on the roads. In 1990 Women's Council marched on Curtin Springs in an anti-grog demonstration. Then we went to Imanpa for a big Women's Council meeting to discuss petrol sniffing and alcohol. Everyone was outraged. We demanded that the place stop selling alcohol.

We finally got the selling of alcohol stopped in 1997, which was a fantastic outcome. My old friend from Curtin Springs, Peter Severin, didn't recognise me. He didn't remember who I was. Peter came to the meeting, and he came up to me and he thanked me. He said, 'Thank you, ladies. We are very happy that you were able to stop the selling of takeaway alcohol because I just want to concentrate on my bullocks and looking after tourists'. He spoke in a good way. Wiṟu way. There were lots of hugs and handshakes. He was perfectly happy and there was no animosity between us. We told him all about how tragic it has been for us, suffering all those car accidents. We told him how every cemetery in every community is filled and overflowing with our young people. We told him we wanted him to stop selling to our people and to just concentrate on the whitefellas. You can see that march at Curtin Springs on Aṟa Irititja that Unkari Pantjiti McKenzie made for EVTV.

In the fight against petrol sniffing, the NPY Women's Council turned for help with lobbying for unleaded petrol to police and other groups, including the Central Australian Youth Link Up Service. Nura and leading NPY consultants workshop the issues at a conference in Alice Springs, 1998, which lead to the formation of the Opal Alliance. (Photo: NPY Women's Council / Aṟa Irititja 21312)

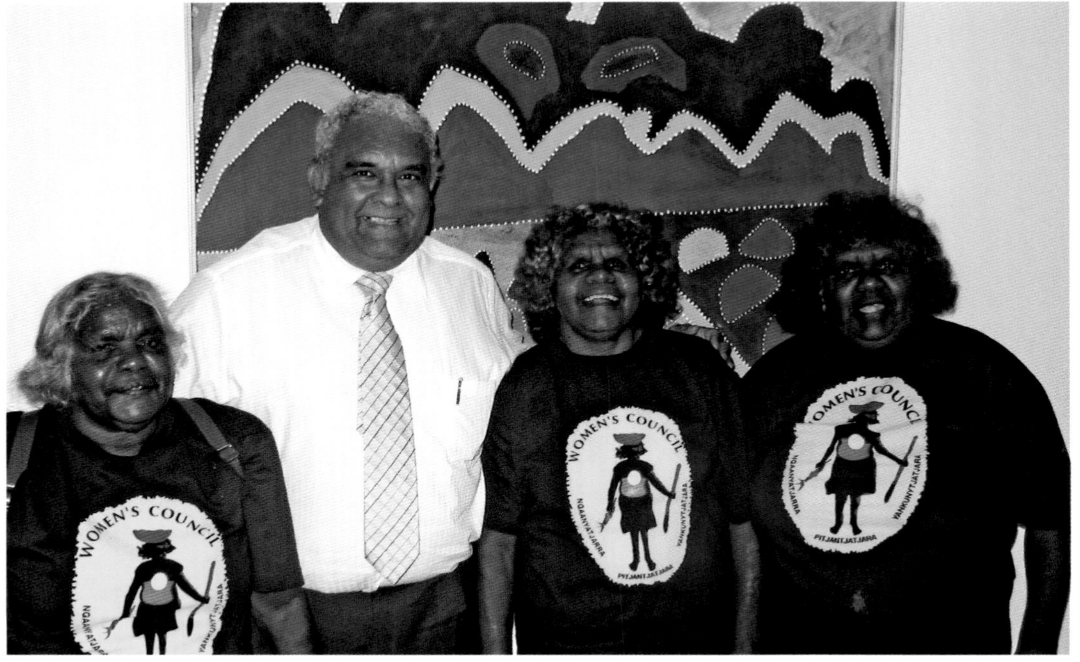

Nura Ward, Janet Inyika and Yanyi Bandicha, representing the Opal Alliance, meet with Aboriginal and Social Justice Commissioner Tom Calma at the Australian Human Rights Commission headquarters in Sydney. (Photo: NPY Women's Council)

A big group of the Pukatja school children came to see me today in Pukatja Aged Care. I had told them to go and collect aratja and irmangka-irmangka and they did so, and brought the herbs to me. I taught them how to make tea with the irmangka-irmangka leaf, and how to drink it for colds. I pounded the aratja leaf on stones, and added a little bit of water to make a paste, and then I showed the children how to rub it on the head for headaches. I wanted to do this because I think children of today take too many Panadols and pills for headaches and everything else, whereas they could be using bush medicines instead. I told them that pills are damaging in the long run and affect the blood and the kidneys. The teachers are very supportive of my teaching, and they organised for the children to come up to see me because they know I am a bush medicine teacher. Everyone got to ask questions and I answered the questions. It was really good, everyone was very happy. I might be old but I am still teaching!

I have been going down to the school when they do health checks with the children. We have been looking at ears and eardrums, talking about blowing the nose, washing the hands, going to the toilet, avoiding constipation, eyes and teeth. I am still a health educator and the teachers pick me up and take me to the school for health education. While I am there I tell stories of the old ways and the old laws, because things are so different now. I go to the school often to tell stories. I want the children to know how the families stuck together so strongly, living together in strong family groups, and drank from rockholes.

This is just some of my work.

Nura, Nyinku Adamson and other senior women discuss midwifery at a women's health meeting in the Ernabella creekbed. (Photo: Suzanne Bryce / Ar̲a Irititja 124211)

The Ernabella Video and Television (EVTV) crew, Joseph Minutjukur, Simon Tjiyangu and Pantjiti McKenzie, shoot footage for the Bush Medicine series which starred Nura Ward, Anmanari Alice Wilupara and Nura Rupert, Birthday Creek, 1986. (Photo: Guthrie and Irving / Ar̲a Irititja 53874)

7. Grandmothers' Law

I dedicated myself to following Women's Law and consequently my health as a female has been excellent. Grandmothers and older sisters, that's their job to talk about these things. Aunties and mothers do not broach these subjects – because they are inyurpa – they are from the wrong group. The wrong group is referred to as the inyurpa group. Grandmothers and sisters are in the right group, the nganalungku group. I'm talking Tjukurpa now. This is our Law.

My grandmother was the one who told me straight out about women's business and women's health issues. My older sister was the same. She told me a great deal – and more. My mother and my auntie, on the other hand, did not speak to me about these things – and neither did my daughter. This is how women's business is passed down, this is tjaka, the way it is done. It has to be discussed by the right women, amongst the appropriate women. Kamiku tjaka, this is grandmothers' Law. So it was my grandmother who taught me about life, in order for me to hand on what I know to the future generation and for the Law to continue. Nyinguta taught me a great deal about Kungkawara Tjukurpa, the young Women's Law and Kamiku Tjukurpa, the Grandmothers' Law and also about pregnancy and childbirth, and all about getting married and other important subjects. She taught me a lot. She also taught me many songs and law, and Women's Law. I have followed faithfully my Grandmothers' Law, and she taught me beautifully and clearly. She was a great teacher and she promised me I would never be alone, and I would always be a treasured and beloved child. She told me I had been taught very ancient laws and ways and I was to follow them always. She told me that I had learnt well and to always remember that what I had been taught was part of my own special heritage, the stories and the songs.

Cousins Tjikalyi Colin and Nura Ward in full body-paint dance at an inma festival at Angatja. (Photo: Suzanne Bryce / Ara Irititja 124116)

I still hold onto all that Law very strongly. I'll never let it go, as it is our special knowledge, knowledge that is handed down, passed down to us through the ages. I have not been able to teach the young girls those sacred old women's inma; it hasn't been possible, but I still want to teach them. Perhaps it will happen later on; I want them all to learn, but they have to be old enough. We are not allowed to teach this Law to girls that are too young. We have been teaching the young girls how to dig for tjala, and we have been digging honey ants a lot around here, because tjala are so plentiful. I'd like to teach more, but I've become a bit of a sorry old thing due to my age and illness and reduced mobility.

We have a lot of children now. There are lots of young girls in school and there are a lot of young boys. But those boys and girls are not educated in proper behaviour. Some are doing wrong things. But nobody is instructing them in the right way to behave. They only find out when it is too late. When everyone is devastated by what happened, the young people realise they have made a mistake. Then of course, sickness is spread. And then there are the unwanted pregnancies and the babies that come from that. It makes bad blood, both literally and metaphorically. All people must take care of their blood. Especially women. But this subject is not spoken about now. It is not spoken about enough. This is my work and I worry about it and I still

Nura dancing in Mimili.
(Photo: Suzanne Bryce / Ara Irititja 124111)

want to keep educating young people about this. I keep saying that I want to teach this in schools but I keep getting told, 'Later, later, another time.' But I am a pensioner now and I can hardly get around. It is hard for me to do this but I am scared something terrible is going to happen and girls are going to do something terribly wrong in front of the men and then there will be terrible trouble. But I can't prevent this if I can't get my words across to the young people. I can't do what I want to do anymore. And some people even say, 'These girls are not your family. Stay out of their business. These girls are my family. They are school girls. They are not your family. Worry about your own kids.' So it is a worry.

I am worried about all the girls who live in Ernabella. There are supposed to be people working in this field but it isn't good enough in my opinion. I am confident in talking to young people and I feel I should be the one who educates them. Those children coming out of school in the afternoons should be just playing, not getting up to no good. Who knows what the children get up to? The only thing the kids are learning is what the teacher is teaching them. Our grandmothers used to say to us, 'I will teach you everything. Remember, if you like a man, and you are still a little girl, you must look after yourself. Remember, you girls, that you have a uterus, and from that uterus blood will come out every month. The uterus is where babies come from.' This is what I was taught when I was little. But this is not taught in school. My granddaughter is growing up now and I want to teach them about these important facts. They say to me, 'I haven't got a boyfriend!' but I say to them, 'No, I am telling you this anyway so you can know in the future!' 'But I'm not going to run off with any man!' 'No, but you need to know these facts! You are only young now but you need to know these facts before it is too late! You are a person, and things can happen to people!' It is their body and it must be looked after. I warn them off getting themselves into dangerous situations. I teach them about sex. One time one of them asked me, 'Is it like what the donkeys do?' I told them, 'Well, yes, it is a little bit like what the donkeys do!' She was asking me that question! So I had to say, 'Well, yes, it is a bit like what the donkeys do!'

Nura passes on grandmothers' law and knowledge to a younger generation at an inma festival, Amata, 1985. (Photo: Cynthia Shannon / Ara Irititja 76239)

Anangu have teaching skills and knowledge, which should be taught. Anangu knowledge and culture must be taught. We all have knowledge and culture. We used to teach children in the evenings when everyone sat around the fire. Grandmothers would use that time to teach the grandchildren Law and culture. Grandmothers' Law is about the proper protocols for a good life. Today I think that alpiri, and by that I mean communication, may be the key here. You know what alpiri is, I have told you already. Alpiri is for advising the younger people. 'What will you do when you are older? What kind of partner will you choose? Will you speak your grandmothers' tongue?'

This is how I was brought up. This is what I was told. We women were brought up in this way, by the telling of the Laws and the singing of the inma. We were taught sacred inma also, and it was explained to us to never sing such songs in the wrong company. We were always to be very careful where we sang songs of this kind and make sure nobody else was around, to be strictly careful to never allow it to be overheard. Love songs are

Using stalked puffball fungus as a paintbrush, Nura teaches writing to her grandchildren. (Photo: Phillip Toyne, Pitjantjatjara Council / Ara Irititja 55865)

the same. We were warned that if ever a man heard the songs, we could suffer for it, and he could cause us harm because of it, as well as cause him to become obsessed with you and want to sleep with you. I was told all these strict laws. I want my granddaughters to live like that, to know Women's Law and to be able to hunt for themselves. We who know the Law know what and what not to do, or else risk being killed for breaking the Law. Some of the Laws are extremely serious. My grandmother explained a lot to me. It is the role of the grandmother to explain the rules of life to their granddaughters.

It is now 2013 and I am getting on in years. I am not well enough to be living on my homeland at Kunma Piti. I have other troubles, because I have become a diabetic as well, and I have kidney problems and my own heart is weak. I can't walk. Both my younger brother and I had strokes, and sadly he passed away on 5 May 2013. In 2007 I was living in Pukatja in a wiltja made of branches. Now I am living at Pukatja Aged Care. The time will come when I may have to go into palliative care. I've not had any experience with palliative care; I've heard of it of course, but I've not been involved. I've only worked in disability and aged care. It is the doctors who put people into palliative care; they will die soon after. They rest in a bed near relatives, and soon fall into their eternal sleep. That is what happens to them. I wish it to be known that when I die I want to be buried in Ernabella with my father and my two brothers. I don't want to be buried in Mimili with my mother. I want to be buried in

Ernabella. My family is here at Ernabella Cemetery; my father, my grandfather, Barney's father, Ada's father, my brother, another brother, my nephew, my older sister Tinimai, Barney's two daughters and three sons. But I don't like to think about it really. You see, I have new grandsons coming up. I do want to see my new grandsons and granddaughters. They are always delighted to see me too.

I grew up living such a very happy life that sometimes I grieve for those days again. I get sad inside when I remember those days, when those memories come flooding back. I have got a big history, with big stories, a big true history. Tjukurpa mulapa, true history; knowledge mulapa, true knowledge. I have learnt so many things in so many ways in my lifetime, in ways that are equivalent from pre-school to school to university. I have been taught the Law and way of life from all my relatives: from my mother and father, my grandmother and grandfather, my older sister and older brother and all in between.

I have been thinking about the life I have lived. I have been a hard worker all my life, and I want to write more and still have more stories to tell. I want to write a midwife book. I have been thinking about all the good lessons I have learnt and all the good things I have held on to. So we listen and learn from these important life lessons, if we want to live a long and healthy life. Which I do; I want to live a long life. I want to live. I still think about the old ways. I can never forget.

Ali Beale and Beth Mitchell, friends from Ernabella hospital days, visit Nura and family; front: (left to right) Nura Ward and Beth Mitchell; back: (left to right) Melissa Thompson, Ali Beale, Jeannie Ampintangu Ward and Rebecca Ward. (Photo: Beth Mitchell / Ara Irititja 123419)

After Nura's death on 14 November 2013, the family gather at Kenmore to make funeral plans; front: (left to right) Murika Ward, Jeannie Ampintangu Ward, Mary Fraser and Hazel Fraser (nursing Dakota McIntyre); back: (left to right) Jasmine Ward, Imuna Fraser, Marrianne Fraser, Anne Karatjari Ward and Lois Fraser. (Photo: Suzanne Bryce / Ara Irititja 157855)

Afterword

Black Hill is a beautiful quiet bush place and being here we think of Mum and Dad and our grandparents and all the things they taught us. It all makes sense. We come out here to our place and make a dinner camp and go off into the bush where we can easily find honey ants or dig for witchetty grubs. We eat them with real pleasure and appreciation knowing that all the people who came before us ate these foods and many more besides. We use our skills to find our ancestor's foods and as we eat them we feel our stomachs full and deeply satisfied and we think this is the way to live, out here with all this wonderful food.

ANNE KARATJARI WARD

Jeannie Ampintangu and Anne Karatjari, with Jeannie's two daughters Murika and Jasmine, visit Bully Ward's grave at Black Hill following Nura's death, 2013. (Photo: Suzanne Bryce / Ara Irititja 157869)

Afterword from the compilers

I am at my desk in the Aṟa Irititja office in Alice Springs, watching Nura's bush medicine television series. The Ernabella Television and Video (EVTV) crew has the camera trained on Nura Ward, standing beside the red boulders of her father's country in the Musgrave Ranges. It is 1984. Nura has my full attention. She speaks directly to the camera. She knows the camera position, the setting, the subject matter, and the big picture. She is fully aware that her film will never date, will always be pertinent. She is vivacious and pretty in her Ayers Rock t-shirt. She is what they call in the film industry '*talent*'.

Nura knew intimately both aspects of medicine and healing – her own traditional Pitjantjatjara practices as well as western medicine. She had been trained in both, and she used and promoted both. Though she was a trained nursing practitioner in Ernabella hospital, Nura effectively utilised bush medicines. She gave bush medicine the status it deserves. She knows the active parts of the natural medicines – the rhizomatous outer roots, the fruit, the leaf, the bark, and how they are used. She knew the value of the life-giving power of fresh, juicily cooked bush meat and blood. She was a great proponent of mingkulpa, the life-saving bush tobacco.

Today, the NPY people have created a large cottage industry around bush plant medicines made of beeswax, olive oil and the active ingredient, but it was Nura – along with her beloved teacher, Anmanari Alice Wilupara – who popularised the medicines. Her favourites were irmangka-irmangka, aratja, and the lesser-known papawitilpa. Her specialist knowledge and repertoire of bush medicines knows no equal.

The camera follows Nura as she takes a group of younger women through the shrubland, pointing out the plant they are headed for. She is authoritative, instructive, demonstrative, illustrative, a natural teacher and a good actor. She nimbly climbs trees to reach her target, and her voice reaches the microphone. She describes the presenting complaint, the symptoms, preparation and application and expected result of the medicine, all in a way that is memorable to the student.

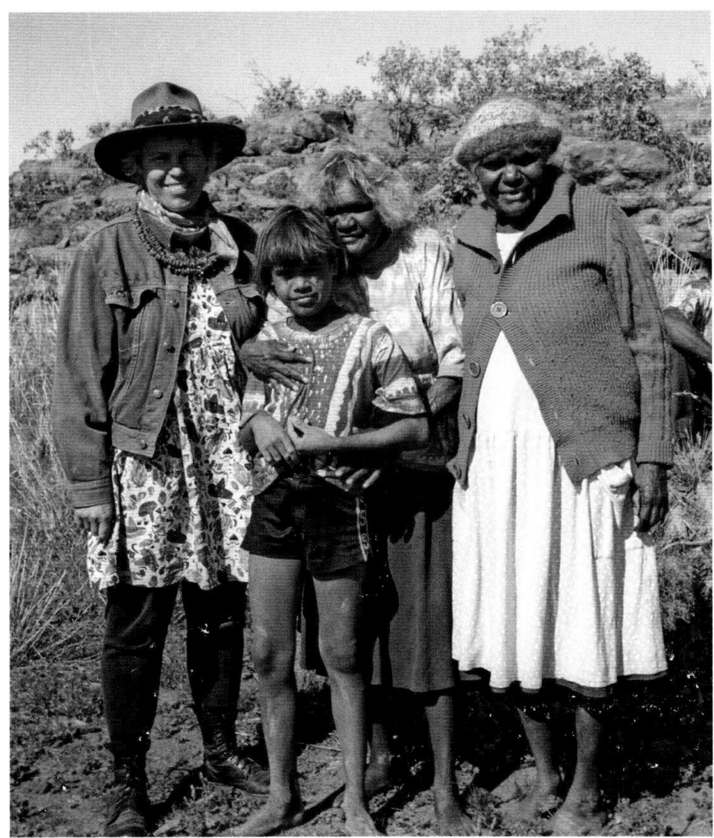

Linda Rive with Pirpantji Nelson, Anmanari Alice Wilupara and Nganyinytja in the Mann Ranges. (Photo: Linda Rive / Aṟa Irititja 126931)

This is the Nura I knew – self-assured, confident, robust, charming, intelligent, thought-provoking, an understated leader. We would bask in her authority. Her authority paved the way to get things done. She was a pleasure to be around, and she always said 'wiṟu way' – meaning, she liked things to be done properly. She exemplified the word 'malpar̲ara' — meaning, she liked working in a team. She and her colleagues worked together across cultures. She got things done. She was a 'doer'. Nura was the only Pitjantjatjara person I knew who could use the words 'membranes' or 'penicillin' and 'Tjukurpa' in the same sentence.

Nura was well aware of nutrition, and she always prided herself on the knowledge that she had been loved and treasured as a child, and had been raised healthily and with plenty of good nutritious food. She always self-assessed her own nutrition over her own life, and says she was thin and bony only once, during her family's long journey to the west, during a drought so serious that it killed many people. Nura loved good food, good bush meats, garlic, cabbage and pumpkin. I will never forget Nura in the 1980s shouting at a storekeeper for not ordering enough pumpkin for the people in Fregon. She demanded to see inside the cool room and demanded that he bring out all the fresh fruit and vegetables he had, so she and the women could purchase it. At the time I was shocked at her audacity, but I realise now that she had a far greater understanding of her people's lack of food security and nutrition than anyone else. She spearheaded the movement towards better nutrition.

Some people might have called her bossy, but Nura was self-assured. She had absolute integrity. She underestimated how important she was. Nura had no idea how special she was, how unique and how treasured. I will never know why Nura did not receive a medal for her work.

LINDA RIVE

Suzanne Bryce with Nura Ward at an NPY Women's Council meeting. (Photo: Suzanne Bryce / Ar̲a Irititja 157711)

For a long time my favourite picture of Nura was her standing with the stroller, where her exhausted little granddaughter Ruby slept. We were at a festival of Inma, traditional song and dance. Nura had danced and was back in her dress, but still covered in the painted design of the Ngintaka, white and yellow dots liberally spread across her arms and chest. She was, as always, able to manage her worlds and move easily between them.

She showed me grandmothering long before I was to become one. Now as I push the stroller myself I fully appreciate Nura's steady love, her patience and care for her children's children.

Nura was an older sister for me and showed me other life lessons that women learn from each other. We worked together on a women's health project. She had a passion for teaching women that our bodies are a physical manifestation of the sacred, and she strove to build a bridge that women and midwives and nurses could meet on.

When I first met Nura in about 1986 she was part of Nganampa Health Council's UPK, a public health project doing groundbreaking work on housing and hygiene. I saw her vitality and engagement, her ownership of the principles. She brought the same vitality to everything she did and NPY Women's Council was lucky to have her as a staff member and ambassador to important causes in the 1990s.

I have many memories and images gained over a long time. But to share Nura as fully as I want to, my mind turns towards the end of her life.

In 2012, living at the Aged Care, she could still weight-bear, get herself into her battery-powered chair and take off. She would visit the school — still teaching on occasion — and the arts centre and if she was having a visitor, she would wait on the road. Sometimes she and her friend Dora were out together, their chairs sporting tall flags for visibility. I loved being her visitor and walking around beside her, calling at her favourite hangouts. We recorded our conversations and laughed that Nura's 'office' was the concrete picnic table under the athel pines.

One day we got to touch on the dying process. This was rare as Nura was intent on being alive. She said so emphatically,

'I know about palliative care, I understand it from when I was doing disability work. A doctor will say a patient is going into palliative care and the end comes fast after that. The family comes and the patient lies down to sleep and dies. I'm not interested in that. I've got a number of grandsons and a new one coming up and I want to see them all, my grandsons and granddaughters.'

Later we were talking about Jasmine, the granddaughter away at school. Nura said that Jasmine called every day at four o'clock. She added, 'then she calls again at bedtime to say goodnight'.

Nura might have been physically reduced but she still had her days to fill. And like many active people who are forced to accept immobility and ill health, she channelled her energy into art. She painted to continue the internal conversation between herself and her world, her spirit dancing across a canvas where her body had once so eloquently evoked the Dreaming.

We came to cherish her painting and had a large canvas on display at her memorial service, arranging to buy it for the Ngaanyatjarra Pitjantjatjara Yankunytjatjara Women's Council collection.

Of her book, Nura said, 'People will listen and cry and listen and cry.'

She is right. How else to experience the enormity of her heart?

SUZANNE BRYCE

I met Nura Ward early in 1995 during my first visit to the APY lands. As a volunteer, I'd driven the five hours to Ernabella to transport NPY Women's Council members to their executive meeting in Alice Springs. Not far out of Ernabella, Nura's sister Tjikalyi, who was driving, suddenly stopped. She said, 'Nura Ward is over there hunting rabbits. She must come to this meeting.' So she drove over towards Nura and then wedged the car stuck in a rabbit hole. Nura jumped into the driver's seat, passed her shotgun to me, and effortlessly reversed the car out of the rabbit hole. From there to the Stuart Highway, she shot at 'roos and rabbits out of the passengers' window. I was in awe.

Nura was a committed advocate for the needs of old people. When we worked together in the later 1990s with Women's Council's tjungu team — the aged and disability services — she was always on call. Her work realities extended far beyond the nine to five. A weekend at the football meant an opportunity not just to catch up with extended family but also to find out who needed support. Cross-border interagency workshops were opened with Nura dancing. Still painted with the dotted design of the ninu dance, Nura would move seamlessly from dancer to keynote speaker.

Nura was brave. As a woman she was not afraid to speak up. She spoke out to regional Aṉangu organisations, state governments and to Canberra about what she saw that her people needed. She admired deeply the strong women who had taught her — cultural law, grandmothers' law, bush medicine and advocacy — and she wanted to live up to their expectations and follow their example. She worried that her daughters and grandchildren had not had the same opportunities as she had, yet she was proud of their achievements.

Nura respected and followed Aṉangu Law. She took her responsibilities seriously. She wanted her grandchildren and their children to feel that Aṉangu Law and culture was strong, straight and true. And it would guide them to happiness. She wanted to gift her stories to her descendents. She knew that in this modern world one way to do that was to make a book. And so at least a decade before she passed away, she began recording stories at every opportunity — in my backyard, in her hospital bed, in the office, and at home on Yankunytjatjara and Pitjantjatjara country.

Nura was curious about other cultures and generously shared aspects of her own culture. I recall her teaching Kalahari Bushmen a traditional dance when they visited Women's Council. She had national and international networks and relationships that transcended culture. Her bush camps were enviable with skilfully made shade shelters, a camp stove and tuckerbox containing bush tucker, fresh fruit, vegetables and condiments.

She was kind to me as I tried to navigate my way alongside another's culture. I was fortunate to be swept along with her energy. Her love extended to my children, who are her children and, as she would tease me, to 'our' husband . . . both of us, two little minyma (women). When my daughter was born premature, Nura was dismayed that we couldn't take her out of her humidicrib to smoke her. So she bossed me into running away from the hospital, collecting bush medicine plants from along the roadside, and in my backyard she built a fire and smoked me to make infant and mother strong.

Towards the end, I spent the night with her at Ernabella Aged Care. She did not have much energy for conversation. Instead we listened to the birds outside. She spoke their names in Pitjantjatjara and mimicked their calls, teaching me as she always had. We listened together to the sounds of her country.

JULIA BURKE

Nura and Julia at Prayers for Change, a special ecumenical service for renal sufferers held at Alice Springs Lutheran Church in 2010. The service prayed for governments to make wise decisions that will give renal clients in remote Central Australia choice in where they receive renal dialysis. (Photo courtesy Julia Burke)

Glossary

A

ailuru	drought, extremely dry times
ailuru kuka	meat animals that persist through severe drought
alkarka	meat ant, large black ant, *Iridomyrmex purpureus*
alpiri	early morning or late evening speeches and instructions
alputati	pussytails, *Ptilotus* spp.
alu	liver
alukura	separate women's camp
Anangu	Western Desert Language–speaking Aboriginal person
anumara	a type of witchetty grub
apara	river red gum, *Eucalyptus camaldulensis*
Ara Irititja	digital archive of the Ngaanyatjarra, Pitjantjatjara and Yankunytjatjara people
aratja	hill fuchsia, *Eremophila freelingii*
aralapalpalpa	crested pigeon, *Ocyphaps lophotes*
arnguli	wild plum, *Santalum lanceolatum*
Arrernte	an Aboriginal language of Central Australia

B

billycan	metal can with handle for boiling water
bludging	begging
buffel grass	*Cenchrus ciliaris*

I

ikarka	spotted bowerbird, *Chlamydera maculata*
ili	wild fig, *Ficus platypoda*
ilytji	bush or scrub
inma	ceremonial singing and dancing
Inma Minyma Ninu	the songs and ceremony of the Ninu Woman
inunytji	blossoms
inyurpa	wrong skin group, wrong marriage partner
ipi	breast, breastmilk
ipiri	curly-wire grass, bunched kerosene grass, *Aristida contorta*
ipuru	spinifex pigeon, *Petrophassa plumifera*
irmangka-irmangka	native fuchsia, *Eremophila alternifolia*
itara	desert bloodwood tree, *Corymbia opaca*
itjanu	lush green growth
iwara kutjupa	a different path
iwiri	root

K

kaanka	crow, *Corvus bennetti*, *C. orru*
kalaya	emu, *Dromaius novaehollandiae*
kaltu-kaltu	native millet, *Panicum decompositum*
kami	grandmother
kamiku tjaka	grandmothers' way
kamiku tjukurpa	laws and behaviours associated with grandmothers
kampurarpa	desert raisin, *Solanum centrale*
kangkuru	senior sister, one's own older sister
kanpi	emu fat
kanturangu	desert poplar, *Codonocarpus cotinifolia*
kanyala	euro, hills kangaroo, *Macropus robustus*
kaputu	ball, wad
Kaputuni!	Give me a wad! [of tobacco]
karu	watercourse, creek
kiily-kiilykari	budgerigar, *Melopsittacus undulatus*
kipara	bush turkey, bustard, *Ardeotis australis*
kuka	meat
kukaputju	skilled and prolific hunter
kuka walkalitja	meat that has been poisoned by *Duboisia hopwoodii*
kuka wiru	delicious meat
kulata	spear vine, *Pandorea doratoxylon*
kulypurpa	wild gooseberry, *Solanum ellipticum*
kumpu	urine
kuna	faeces
kunakanti	summer grass, armgrass millet, *Urochloa piligera*
Kungkarangkalpa	the Seven Sisters, also the Pleiades star cluster
Kungka Kutjara	the ancestral Two Women
kungkawara	tall girl, teenage girl
kungkawara tjukutjuku	younger teenage girl
kungkawara tjukurpa	laws and behaviour associated with teenage girls

kuniya	woma python, *Aspidites ramsayi*
Kuniya Tjukurpa	ancestral Woma Python Tjukurpa
kunma	a large, biting fly
kuntili	a person's father's sister, 'auntie'
kupikupi	dusty whirlwind (unpalara in Yankunytjatjara)
kura	bad
kura-kura	rubbishy, poor quality, not good
kuri pikatja	promised or potential wife
kurku	mulga, *Acacia aneura*
kurku inunytji	acacia blossoms
kurukuku malanypa	Kuruku's younger sibling
kurupiilyurukatipai	dizzy
kurunpa	spirit, life force
kuta	older brother
kutaku tjukurpa	older brother's stories
kutitjakantja	associated with the word 'to run'
kutunpa	eagle chick, nestling, fledgeling
Kuwaripa!	Not yet!
kuwirkura	cocky, cockatiel, *Nymphicus hollandicus*

L

langka	Centralian blue-tongue lizard, *Tiliqua multifasciata*, also the eastern blue-tongue, *T. occipitalis*
lolly, lollies	confectionary, sweets
likara	bark
liru	snake, poisonous snake

M

mai	food, non-meat food, vegetable food
mai ratjina	ration foods, flour, tea and sugar
maku	witchetty grub
maku ilykuwara	witchetty grub from the ilykuwara bush, *Acacia kempeana*
maku lunki	large maku, edible grub like a fully developed cossid moth grub found in witchetty bushes
malpa	companion, colleague, pairing Aboriginal and non-Aboriginal staff at NPYWC
malu	red kangaroo, *Macropus rufus*
malu milkali	blood of red kangaroo
Malu Tjukurpa	Kangaroo Tjukurpa
mama tjilpi	grey-haired father
mamu	malignant and dangerous spirit force
mamu kunpu putingka nyinantja	There was an unseen malevolent poisonous force right throughout the bush.
manguri	circular head-ring
mara	hand
mara-mara	child at crawling stage, and eating meat, crawling on hands and knees
marutju	man's brother-in-law
mayatja	boss, supervisor, in charge
mayatja-mayatja	second-in-charge
miilmiilpa	sacred
mina	water
mingkayi	woman's mother-in-law or daughter-in-law
mingkiri	mice, various small rodents such as *Pseudomys hermannsburgensis*
mingkulpa	native tobacco
mininy-mininypa	yellow rumped thornbill, *Acanthiza chrysorrhoa*
Minyma Kaanka	Crow Woman, *Corvus bennetti*, *C. orru*
Minyma Kakalyalya	Pink Cockatoo Woman, *Cacatua leadbeateri*
Minyma Kutjara	Two Women Tjukurpa
Minyma Ninu	Ancestral Bilby Rabbit-eared Bandicoot Woman, *Macrotis lagotis*
minyma pampa	elderly woman
miri tjutaku mai	ancestors' food
miru	spear-thrower
mulapa	true, genuine
mungartji-mungartji	late afternoon
muturka	prized fat found in the innards and tail of a kangaroo

N

ninu	bilby, or rabbit-eared bandicoot, *Macrotis lagotis*
ngaltatjiti	kurrajong seeds, *Brachychiton gregorii*
ngalta	kurrajong tree, *Brachychiton gregorii*
ngalypa-ngalypa	pretend
ngalungku	twins, born at the same time, age mates
ngampaltjunkunytjaku	grandparent's hug bestowing good qualities on baby
nganalungku group	right marriage partner from our group, i.e. from the Ngananantarka (lit. we-bone) or Ngananamiri group (lit. we-skin)
ngananamiru	a training spear-thrower made from *Sida* spp. stalks
ngangkari	traditional healer
ngantja	mistletoe, *Lysiana exocarpi*
ngapartji-ngapartji	reciprocal, turn in turn
ngaya	feral cat, *Felis catus*
ngintaka	perentie lizard, *Varanus giganteus*
nguli-nguli	very young infant
ngunytju malatja	younger mother
ngura miilmiilpa	sacred site
nyaaku?	what for?
nyampa	tasting bad, horrid
nyarilpa	cooling-off hole
nyarumpa	a person's sisters, brothers and cousins of the opposite sex
nyii-nyii	zebra finch, *Taeniopygia guttata*

nyii-nyii kuna	droppings of zebra finch
nyii-nyii ngampu	zebra finch egg
nyiinka	pre-initiated boy
nyiti	lizard fat
nyurka-nyurka	thin and bony
nyurka-nyurka tjuta katingu	really thin people brought in

P

paku	tired, euphemism for pregnant
palkunpa	scar tissue
palya	good
pampa tjuta	elderly women
pannikin	enamel mug
Panya nyangangka Maralingala bomb waninyi.	The effects from the atomic bomb at Maralinga will reach this far.
papa miri	skin of dingo, dingo scalp
papa patjina	poisoned dog meat, dingo poison
papawitilpa	medicinal creeper vine, *Mukia maderaspatana*
patilpa	Port Lincoln parrot, *Barnardius zonarius*
patjina	from English 'poison'
Pertame	a dialect of the Southern Arrernte language
Pertame Arrernte	the Pertame dialect of the Arrernte group of languages
piil-piilpa	yellow throated miner, *Manorina flavigula*
piilyuru	dry, papery bark on trunk or root of tree
pika lirutja	infection of the skin and joints, possibly yaws
pikati	aggressive
pikatja	promised or potential wife
pilpira	ghost gum, *Corymbia papuana*
piranpa	white person
piriya	hot, dusty westerly winds
piriyakutu	the start of the westerly winds bringing hot weather
piti	wooden dish or bowl
Pitjantjatjara	a large dialect group of the Western Desert Language
pulyi	umbilical cord, belly button
pulyi punkanu	where the umbilical cord falls off
punti	bushes, *Senna* spp.
punti inunytji	cassia blossoms, senna blossoms
Pupakati!	Bow your head down!
purtju	scabs, scabies
puturu	headband
putu	hard, flat top of underground termite nest
puturu	headband
puyu	smoke from fire, atomic bomb dust and fallout
pulka	big, large

R

rapita kumpu	rabbit urine
ratjina	from English word 'ration'
rikina way!	good looking way!

T

taa	explosion, something burst open
tangka	properly cooked
tawaltawalpa	wild tomato, *Solanum ellipticum*
tawaritja	pre-initiate seclusion camp
tinka	Gould's sand goanna, *Varanus gouldii*
tiiringanyi	drying out
tipinypa	sharpened stick
Tjaa Wirtjantjatjara and Kutitjakantja	small dialect groups of the Western Desert Language, similar to Pitjantjatjara
tjaka	typical, usual
tjala	honey ant, *Camponotus inflatus* and *C.* spp.
tjalpu-tjalpu	black-faced woodswallow, *Artamus cinereus*
tjamuku ara kanyini	keeping grandfathers' law or ways
tjamu	grandfather
tjangara	ogre, man-eating ogre
tjanpi	spinifex grasses, *Triodia* spp.
tjanpi awilyura	porcupine grass, *Triodia irritans*
tjanpi maliki	strange grass or weed
tjanpi tjiri	porcupine grass, *Triodia irritans*
tjanmata	bush onion, *Cyperus bulbosus*
tjilkala	roly-poly bush, *Salsola kali*
tjilpi	grey hair, grey-haired man
tjitji karangki	cranky kid, naughty child
tjitji nyiinka	pre-initiate boy-child
tjirilya	echidna, *Tachyglossus aculeatus*
tjukurpa	creation times, traditional law and stories
tjukuritja	associated with the ancient times
tjukurpa mulapa	true tjukurpa
tjukula	rockhole, waterhole
tjulpun-tjulpunpa	wildflowers, e.g. daisies, pussytails and everlastings
tjungu	together, combined. The NPYWC Tjungu Team provides advocacy and services for NPY people with disabilities, aged people and their carers.
tululu	bark disk rolled along the ground for spear practice

U

ukari	nephew or niece
ukiri	green grass, green growth, green wild tobacco leaves
ulpuru pulka	a massive cloud of dust or atomic cloud
unmuta	native cress, *Lepidium muelleri-ferdinandi, L. phlebopetalum*
unpalara	whirlwind
upa	weak

urtjanpa	spear vine, *Pandorea doratoxylon*
uwa	yes

W

wakalpuka wata	trunk or large branch of wakalpuka, *Acacia tetragonophylla*
wakalpuka iwiri	root of wakalpuka, *Acacia tetragonophylla*
wakati	inland pigweed, *Portulaca* aff. *oleracea*
walawuru	eagle, *Aquila audax*
walputi	banded anteater, *Myrmecobius fasciatus*
walytja	relations, kin
walkalitja	poisoned by *Duboisia hopwoodii*
walkalpa	emu poison bush, *Duboisia hopwoodii*
walkuni	addressing someone respectfully by their kinship term
walu	shallow basin in flat rock
Wanampi	Rainbow Serpent
Wanampi Tjukurpa	ancestral Rainbow Serpent Tjukurpa
wanka	raw, alive
wanka	processionary caterpillar, spider
wankaku manngu	nest of processionary caterpillar
wanngilpai	to court with intent to marry
wangunu	naked woollybutt grass, *Eragrostis eriopoda*
wangunu alta	charcoaled naked woollybutt outer root, *Eragrostis eriopoda*
waputju	man's father-in-law
warika	long stick used as a shovel
warku	rock hollow, rockhole
Warpungkula!	Hurry up!
waru	black-footed rock wallaby, *Petrogale lateralis*
warutja	hot from being cooked in the fire
wata	trunk, large branch, log
wati	initiated adult male
watiku	men only
Wati Kunma	Fly Man
Wati Ngintaka	the Perentie Lizard Man
Wati Tjangara	an Ogre Man who eats people
wati tjilpi	grey-haired man
wati wara	tall man
Wati Wirtjantjatjara	a man who speaks the Wirtjantjatjara dialect of the Western Desert Language
wati wiru	a good man
wayanu	quandong, native peach, *Santalum acuminatum*
wayuta	common brush-tail possum, *Trichosurus vulpecula*
whitefellas	non-Anangu people, white-skinned people
wili	poking or pointing stick
wiltja	shade, shade shelter
wilu	bush stone-curlew, bush thick-knee, *Burhinus magnirostris*
wintalyka	seed from the mulga tree, *Acacia aneura*
wipiya	emu feathers
wirkanu	arrived
wiru	beautiful, lovely, delicious, very good
Wiru alatjitu!	Absolutely beautiful!
wiru mulapa	very beautiful
wiru wiya	no good, not good
wiriny-wirinypa	bush tomato, *Solanum cleistogamum*
wirtjan-wirtjantja	associated with the word wirtjantja, 'to run'
wita	spit, saliva
witaku	to make saliva in the mouth
witapi	spine, backbone
witjinti	corkwood, *Hakea divaricata*, *H. suberea*
witjitji	baby common brush-tail possum, *Trichosurus vulpecula*

Y

Yankunytjatjara	a dialect of the Western Desert Language
yakutja	bag
youngfella	young man, teenage man

A note about language

Nura Nungalka Ward was a speaker of the Pitjantjatjara dialect of the Western Desert Language of north-west South Australia. The Pitjantjatjara text in this book follows the spelling system in the *Pitjantjatjara/Yankunytjatjara to English Dictionary* (1996) published by IAD Press, Alice Springs. Nura's stories were recorded in her own language by Suzanne Bryce, Linda Rive and Julia Burke, and then translated into English by Linda Rive.

A message from Ara Irititja

Ara Irititja is an award-winning project. It is a multimedia digital archive, repatriating both historic and contemporary cultural and language material back to Ngaanyatjarra, Pitjantjatjara and Yankunytjatjara people, in remote Central Australia. It is now the custodian to over 170,000 records that are accessed daily by Anangu. The software, which was designed according to Anangu cultural protocols and sensitivities, is interactive. Anangu add stories by way of text, audio or movies in real time.

Nura recorded her life story primarily for her own descendants. She worked with Ara Irititja to make her book. Nura Ward passed away on 14 November 2013.

John Dallwitz of Ara Irititja with Nura Ward, 2000. (Photo: John Dallwitz / Ara Irititja 25454)

Acknowledgements

PROJECT MANAGEMENT TEAM:
Julia Burke (project co-ordinator)
Suzanne Bryce
Linda Rive

ARA IRITITJA:
John Dallwitz
Dora Dallwitz

OTHERS WHO HELPED:
Anne Karatjari Ward
Melissa Thompson
Inpiti Winton
Rachel Bin Salleh (Magabala Books)
Mark MacLean (editing)
Sylvia Lawson (editing)
Noah Pleshet (mapping assistance)
Fiona Walsh (botanical editing)
Anangu Pitjantjatjara Yankunytjatjara anthropology unit
Tjilpiku Pampaku Ngura Aged Care Service, Pukatja
Mark Weaver
Beth Mitchell
Lianne Bronzo
Adam Greenberg
Tony Messenger
Ngaanyatjarra Pitjantjatjara Yankunytjatjara Women's Council Aboriginal Corporation supported and shared the vision for Nura's book.

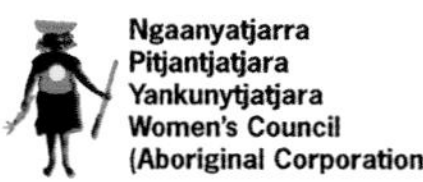

Ara Irititja Project

This book was supported through funding from the Australian Government's Your Community Heritage Program.

First published 2018
Magabala Books Aboriginal Corporation, Broome, Western Australia
Website: www.magabala.com Email: sales@magabala.com

Magabala Books receives financial assistance from the Commonwealth Government through the Australia Council, its arts advisory body. The State of Western Australia has made an investment in this project through the Department of Local Government, Sport and Cultural Industries. Magabala Books would like to acknowledge the generous support of the Shire of Broome, Western Australia.

Magabala Books acknowledges the support of private donors through the Magabala Books Literary Fund, including the J & C Stewart Family Foundation and the Spinifex Trust.

Cover image: Nura Ward, 1999 (Photo: Heidrun Lohr, Ara Irititja / 0182708)
Design: Christine Bruderlin Map: Brenda Thornley
Printed by Toppan Leefung Printing Limited, China

ISBN: 978 1 925360 54 7

A catalogue record for this book is available from the National Library Australia.